To my dear friend Jean. I hope you feel 30 … I hope … had a wonderf… I hope to visit you … Enjoy the trip. From your … Fijian friend Bogi … xox.

Our Love

BEYOND THE SKIES

A story of life, laughter, love & leukaemia

GALUOKO BOGIDRAU SECIVO

Facebook blog: Galuoko Secivo

ISBN: 9789829816511 (paperback)

Cataloguing-in-Publication information for this title is listed with the National Library of Australia.

Published by Galuoko Bogidrau Secivo and InHouse Publishing
www.inhousepublishing.com.au

IN HOUSE PTY LTD PUBLISHING

I dedicate this book to my late husband Tevita Secivo, the love of my life, who taught me how to live fully, how to love unconditionally and selflessly, like there is no tomorrow. You will always be alive in my heart, wajiqu.

To my children Nau, Ipa, and Yaca, I love you three so very much. You all have been strong. Your father would have been so proud. Stay strong, stay wise, and always stay humble. May your children and their children continue your father's legacy. Love Na.

To my parents, I hope I've done you proud.

I also dedicate this book to the two inspirational women who I've lost, my late sister Luseane Annie Laliqavoka and my mother-in-law Melaia Secivo.

Contents

Acknowledgements

Writing this book has greatly helped me in this journey of coping with loss, healing and moving forward in life. For that, I would like to sincerely thank the following for making this memoir possible.

First and foremost, I thank God, the author of my life, for writing my story so far. Thank you for the special gift I called my husband Tevita, who prepared me well to carry on this life without him. For teaching him to love me selflessly and unconditionally, and for him always believing in me no matter what. Through him I was taught how to love, how to be strong and how to remain calm amid a storm. Through God, all the wonderful people I needed were right there at the right place and time in this journey.

To the three greatest gifts, my children: Nau, Ipa and Yaca. You have been my strength since the day I lost your father. Thank you for putting up with Mummy's crazy moods and for understanding me when I had to lock myself in my room in quiet to write. For the times I had to go out with my friends to have some fun. For letting me hold your little hands whenever I missed holding Ta's. For wiping my tears and for loving me dearly still. I love you all to infinity and some more.

To my parents, I owe a generous heap of gratitude to you both for raising me right and always being supportive, loving and caring to me, my late husband and our children. Thank you for sharing the load when it seemed unbearable. We love you both.

To Tevita's family, especially his father, I thank you all for raising the smart man I grew to love and shared this journey of life with. Thank you sincerely to Nei Tarovi and Momo Kelevi for always leaving your door and heart wide open for me and my children. Nei, you remind me of my mother-in-law Nei Mela whom we dearly miss. Thank you for always treating me like a spoilt princess.

I take this time to thank my family and relatives both from Ono-i-Lau and Cicia. Your support through the whole funeral process has been beyond measure. I would never have been able to bear this brunt alone. I am proud to call you family. To my dear sister Atelaite Maraia, thank you for your tremendous loving heart. You are a blessing that my children and I treasure.

To all my devoted followers, friends and family on Facebook, my sincere thanks to you all for your loving comments, messages, support and suggestions, which inspired me to write this book. I now have a book that my grandchildren will get to read. I hope it will give them a chance to get to know more about their grandfather, who they will never have the privilege to meet.

To Melaia Katonivualiku, I want to thank you for helping me write this book. I had zero clue about writing a book, let alone how or where to start. You did an astounding job with the magazine article and skilfully steered me into writing this book.

To the elegant, eloquent and intelligent Doreen Datta, how can I ever thank you enough? I've only known you for several months, though it seems I've known you a lifetime. You never cease to amaze me with your big kind heart, your immense support and efforts at making sure I got the best publisher the book deserved. Those back-and-forth emails, your honest ideas and you going out of your way to provide the lovely gifts for the guests at the book launch. I am always boasting to friends that you were an angel sent from God to make this book a reality. You're beyond amazing, dear!

To my sister from another mother, Michelle Motokana Mefeae, aka Shelly. My strong shoulder to cry on and greatest encourager, my personal editor who added sugar and spice and all things nice to this book. Thank you so much for your words of wisdom. I greatly appreciate all of it, especially when it was honest and brutal. Thank you for all the counselling coffee sessions that wiped away tears and replaced my fears with laughter. Thank you for pouring your time and heart into this book. I can't say I did it alone because *we* finally did it!

To my other strong shoulder, my twin sister from another mother, my Twinny, Tali Mefeae Piokole. Oh my, where do I start! I've got a million things to thank you for! I'm fighting back tears right now while trying to find the right words. Twinny, I would definitely be utterly lost right now if it weren't for you. You've always been there when I needed you, even though your husband and six kids needed you too. For that I thank my brother Clark Piokole for lending me your wife when I needed someone. Thank you, Twinny, for always knowing the right words to say to comfort me, to make me smile a little more and laugh a little louder. Thank you for your constant love and support. Also, if it weren't for you, I would not have met the wonderful inspiring ladies from our Commit To Be Fit (CTBF) group, whom I now call family.

To my gorgeous fitness sisters, I cannot thank you enough for your tremendous support in making life in PNG as beautiful as it is. To Nicole Lopa, Jessie Cruikshank Pitil, Jeanne Augerea, Marilyn Espolong aka Lynn Cheah, Vani K. Nades, Vani Naduva, Jacqueline Pinda Kandiu, Judy Suave, Caroline Casupang, Sarah Kiniafa, Belinda Koivi, Celestine C. K. Ricky, Lois Pala, Mirriam Ablett, Apeame More, Belinda Grant, Daea Acott, Evelyn Mano, Helen King Dai, Melisande Boletu and her sister Ruth Pisi, and many others. You all know who you are. Thank you for sharing this fitness journey, the social activities, karaoke sessions, the family get-togethers and for being with Tevita and I through our storm, up until his funeral. Thank you all for your great leadership and initiative in the fundraising drive for the book launch. I would not have come this far if it weren't for the bond we have shared. You all rock and I love you all!

To Maizel Koroi and Lilly Lasei, thank you for always having my back in Fiji and for our fun times in Nadi from way back. Thank you for the friendship we continue to share. Without you, I would not have burnt my fingers but I would have missed my flight that morning.

To the Fijian community in PNG, *vinaka vakalevu* for your *veiqaravi* through the funeral arrangements from PNG to Fiji. We were able to grieve through this painful time as you were there by our side supporting us throughout.

To former colleagues and good friends of Tevita and I from the Pacific Flying School, Pacific Sun, Air Fiji, Hevilift Ltd. and PNG Air: Thank you for being on this journey. In one way or another, you all supported Tevita to live his dream of flying. Thank you also to the supportive management of PNG Air for allowing me time off to heal before returning to work. This prepared me to fly the skies I used to with my dear late husband Tevita.

A special thank you to the uncles Fred Puni, Ben Baleikanacea, Ben Latu, Esira Donu, Fotu To'ofoe, and Oliver Aquino for dropping by and checking on us and organising BBQ specials. Thank you for your handy hands with the car, gas and lights that needed changing. We appreciate you in our lives and for being a one-minute drive away from home.

To Iyata Tavinke, thank you, my brother, for easing me through this difficult time. Your experience of struggle and loss has made mine bearable. Your support has been immense.

To our dear house-meri Auntie Benny, thank you for always being there for me and the kids. Life was easier to juggle knowing you were there. We have a place called home because you make it possible.

To Izar Tunabuna, thank you, darling, for sharing your mummy and daddy, Tiza and Naibuka Tunabuna with my kids. I have been afforded my much-needed 'me' time during all your weekend cinema and outing time.

Last, but certainly not least, to my husband's other half, before his better half came along. Thank you, Seru Saukuru, for that special brotherly bond you shared with Tevita right from childhood. This bond has enabled my children to have a special uncle they see a bit of their father in. Thank you for making it possible to have Tevita resting in a place he called home. We know you will always be there for us. You are treasured and we thank you.

To all of you, I am truly grateful. You are all God-sent!

You can find **Bogi's personal blog** on Facebook

Search for **Galuoko Secivo**

1

Goodbye, My Love

In the end we only regret the chances we did not take.

LEWIS CARROLL

I lay my head on his chest, begging for his heart to beat back and assure me that this was all a terrible mistake and just a fragment of my imagination. Seconds rapidly turned into minutes, yet all I could hear was an eerie silence foreign to my ears. The very chest I lay endless nights cradled against in safety and comfort, in the still of night with our hearts beating as one, was now a vacuum of emptiness devoid of life and stripped of all meaning and sense.

I stared down at my Tevita's body, still in great shock. My thoughts flashed before me, memories of all our years of marriage, refusing to accept that death had abruptly interrupted, and split us apart. I never thought or dreamt that I was never going to grow old and grey with him. With this realisation, a painful spasm surged into my heart. I realised I was going to someday hold our grandchildren without him beside me. I could picture a framed photo of a happy family with no Tevita in it. I refused to believe or accept this and in agony tugged at his shoulder, trying to wake him up – my ear pressed against his chest and tears streaming uncontrollably down my cheeks.

They say people go through different phases during the loss of a loved one, beginning with shock, then grieving and acceptance, and eventually, recovery. I was still in my first raw state of shock, and completely unaware of how long I was there, although the nurses kept coming to tell me that he would need to be transferred to the morgue. I hated life and how unfair and dark everything had now become. Time stood still as I held on to my husband's body, now losing warmth, half hoping I could alter this decision and bargain back his breath of life.

Taking him to the morgue was something I refused to accept, as I blinked back the tears from my eyes. In my mind that place was only for the dead and my husband was still very much alive to me. I kept refusing to leave his side, not fully convinced that he was gone, although the nurses comforted me otherwise. Finally, still refusing to accept all that was unfolding, I managed to go through the motions of doing what needed to be done.

I made the first call to my mother. She immediately answered the phone, and heard the pain in my sobs echoing on the other end as I tried to empty my heart of all this suffering that it had never felt before. Several minutes passed and I managed a few words between the wailing.

'Na, Te is gone,' I whispered through the sobs. I must have been holding my breath too when I said that, as I let out a sigh of relief after managing the first call. The state of shock was slowly replaced by grief as I came to terms with the fact that my husband was no longer suffering and was now at peace.

The second call was to a Tongan friend of ours, Ben Latu, whom we'd known for years. He was a close friend who lived closer than three minutes away from home. It was still very early in the morning, about 4 a.m. The fact that Tevita was gone was yet to sink in and I found myself struggling again over the phone. After a few rings, he answered.

'Hello? … Hello? Bogi?'

I could barely hear him over my crying.

'No no no no no please don't tell me no … no … no.' Ben could tell something was wrong.

'Te is gone, Te is gone, please can you go and pick my mum up and come,' I cried.

The third call was to another very close friend of ours from work, Iyata Tavinke, a pilot as well. He was one of the many workmates whom we had grown close to and had been more like a brother to us. Not only was he a dear friend but one I reached out to as he had unfortunately suffered two great losses. I knew he would know exactly how I was feeling so I reached for Tevita's phone. I had used Tevita's phone to call Iyata earlier that morning and was surprised that he picked it up after just a few rings.

'Tevita?' he answered.

I froze for a few seconds while that name echoed through my ears. How I wanted Tevita to have responded himself. I stared down at his peaceful face with his thick eyelashes now resting shut as though he was only sleeping. My tears were now uncontrollably flowing down my cheeks and with a deep pain in my heart, I struggled to tell Iyata, in words, what my mind could not make sense of yet.

'Bogi?' Iyata asked.

He obviously heard my sniffing and sobbing over the phone and knew that it was not Tevita.

Slowly he called out again for me. 'Bogi … Bogi?'

More sniffing and sobbing followed before I was finally able to gather some words together. 'It's Tevita,' I cried. I couldn't bring myself to tell him that he was gone.

'Where are you? I'm coming,' he said.

'Pom Gen, Ward 7,' I managed to reply.

Alone, standing next to Tevita, my mind wandered back to how I had heard a loud wail bursting out from one of the rooms next to ours when Tevita was first admitted. A cry filling up the passageway, up to where we sat. We looked at each other and knew from the sound of that agonising cry that a family had lost a dear one and their time was up. Now it was my turn to yell, scream, and cry out loud but I couldn't. I was still deep in shock, sitting beside my husband, waiting for help to come. My mind, my heart, and my body were still fighting reality and refusing to let it sink in. With our home only five minutes from the Port Moresby General Hospital, my mum quickly arrived with Ben. All the other patients in that ICU were asleep and the ward was almost peacefully quiet except for the footsteps of nurses walking around. I rushed into my mother's open arms, finally able to cry some pain out.

'Na, na wajiqu na wajiqu sa qai sega na wajiqu.' Mum, my husband, my husband, I am without a husband now. I wailed as pain stabbed the core of my heart. It was raw, and painful, and at that point it was all I wanted to do.

Oh, how my heart was hurting, and burning inside of me, now crying as a widow in my mother's embrace. I gathered myself together after some minutes of heartfelt crying. I glanced over to check my husband, who looked as if he was in a sweet, blissful sleep. I held his hand, and thought of all those times when I would reach out to hold it, and how he would always squeeze mine back. I held on now, one last time waiting, and waiting for him to squeeze mine back but all I could feel was cold creeping in.

My mum turned to me, snapping me back to reality and said, 'You will need to pick some good clothes for him to wear.' It was strange and sad knowing that it was going to be the last clothes I'd ever select for him to wear. As much as I loathed this, I knew it had to be done.

I wondered, What clothes am I going to pick for him to wear? Instantly I remembered the date was December 17th. Hours earlier as the clock struck midnight, I had tried to cheer him up and wish him a happy eleventh wedding anniversary. I hoped this would trigger some positive vibe as his body fought against the cancer with renewed strength and hope. That exact date, the previous year, was when we had renewed our wedding vows, and shared beautiful memories together with our family and friends.

A day that we could have happily enjoyed and celebrated together, to mark our union in marriage, was ironically turning out to be the worst day of my life. We had planned to renew our wedding vows every ten years and to wear the same outfits. It was at that moment that I knew what clothes I was going to pick for him to wear; the same handsome purple shirt and charcoal vest he wore on our tenth anniversary and at the renewal of our vows.

Iyata finally arrived, and I turned around to see him standing still, staring at Tevita in shock. He rushed over, after my call, expecting that Tevita's condition had worsened, but not that he was gone. At the sight of Iyata, I broke down into tears again. Crying out my devastation and loss on the shoulder of a close friend who understood my pain gave me solace. I felt a little bit better having them there with me to support and strengthen me enough to go through the formalities in the ward.

Moments later I found myself again packing up all our stuff that I had just unpacked when we were moved down from Ward 8. How wrong was I to have thought that I was going to be spending months in the ICU with him, when we first arrived there that morning. I had reassured myself that he had only gone into a coma and I was certain that he would eventually wake up, feel better, and everything would be back to normal. I had anticipated sleeping on the floor for months while waiting for him to wake up just like they did in the movies with happy endings. How terribly mistaken I had been.

Iyata had arrived with his partner Valyne and they kindly offered to drive me home to pick up Tevita's change of clothes. As we moved closer to the house, there was something else weighing heavily on my heart. How was I going to relay this heartbreaking news to our kids with their fragile young hearts?

We arrived home and our house-meri, Auntie Benny, as we called her, opened the door without a clue that we had just lost Tevita. Without mentioning anything to her, I wanted to quickly rush upstairs to our room when I noticed my father sitting quietly on the couch.

I went past without a word from him. Upstairs I opened the door to our room quietly and found that the kids had left the light set to dim, and all three of them were fast asleep on the mattress on the floor. My heart ached even more when I saw them, realising their tomorrows would be forever changed once they woke up. I tiptoed past them making sure not to wake any of them and quietly packed Tevita's purple long-sleeved shirt, black pants, vest, and his purple-and-pink tie. I held the shirt to my face and inhaled the familiar scent that was uniquely him. I took one more look at the kids sleeping peacefully, before I closed the door just in time to hear my house-meri's loud cry. While I was busy upstairs, she had found out from Iyata that Tevita was no more. I rushed downstairs to comfort her, begging her to keep her voice down and not wake the children. I wasn't ready to tell them yet, nor to leave them with the news and head back to the hospital without them.

We arrived back at the ward and helped dress him up for the last time. I wanted to be as close to him as possible through it all. All the while my thoughts were racing. I was struggling to find the right time and the words to send my close friend Tali in Fiji to tell her the news.

She had been my pillar of strength ever since he was admitted, always encouraging me to think and stay positive no matter what. I finally managed to send her three words as they wheeled Tevita's body out of the ICU. *Te is gone,* I typed.

It was difficult to leave his side, so I got into the ambulance going to the morgue to be next to him. I sat as close as I could, to watch over him, and Iyata's partner got in to keep me company on the short ride. I didn't want to take my eyes off of him. I stared at him just as I did when he'd slept next to me. This time, he strangely looked too peaceful, like he was smiling in his sleep. This gave me a little comfort as if to remind me again that he was finally free from all the pain and suffering. I slowly ran my hand over his face and whispered to him, 'You will always be alive in my heart, Ta.'

I knew he was not able to hear me, but that was ample for me then – that though death had taken him, it could never take him away from my heart. I thought that for as long as this heart of mine was still beating, it would beat for us, and he would be alive, living in it. It wasn't easy having to leave him at the morgue, and return home without him. The most difficult task, though, was yet to come: telling the children that their father had died.

I got home and was surprised to see my father still sitting in the same spot where I last saw him, three hours earlier. From the look on his face I knew he was worried about me, his last-born daughter. I on the other hand just wanted to escape all this confirmation of reality and flee. I wanted to run upstairs to our room, lock myself away from the world, and cry for the rest of the day, or better still, for the rest of my life. I tried to sneak past again, as I had earlier, but his deep, stern yet loving voice called out to me just as I landed my first step on the stairs.

'Galuoko, come back, let me talk to you,' came his voice.

I stopped, slowly returned and sat myself on the couch opposite him. At that point, my father gave me some very encouraging words that I least expected from him, and hadn't known I desperately needed to hear at the time. Words, I think, he must have thought long and hard about while he was sitting there waiting for me for hours. I had just lost the closest man to my heart and the remaining one, my father, was stepping in to give all he could, to lift my dying spirit. From a father to his now-widowed daughter. I sat and listened, wiping the tears away from my puffy red eyes.

'Galuoko, I want to thank you for all the efforts that you have put into looking after Tevita these past few weeks. You have not slept or eaten well, going back and forth to the hospital. For that I thank you. You have done all that you can and know that the doctors have also done all that they could. *Ia sa mai yaco na veikacivi ni kalou medatou na ciqoma, sa mai yali na tamadratou na gone. Ia mo na vakaukauwa tiko baleta na nona soqo o Te sa vakarau mena vakayacori qo, mena vakayacori vakacavari vakavinaka. Mo kaukauwa tiko. Keirau talega kei Na sana tu vakarau tu me Keirau na vukei iko ena nodratou qaravi na gone. Kaukauwa jiko.'* My father told me to accept that the father of my children had been called by his maker, and for me to remain strong till all the formalities and funeral arrangements were completed successfully. He assured me that as my parents they were there by my side through the ordeal until their son-in-law was laid to rest. 'Remain strong,' he concluded.

As I wiped away the tears, I heard a vehicle coming through our gate. As I looked out through the door I saw a big maroon Nissan Patrol stopping in our driveway. I got distracted for a few seconds trying to figure out why it stopped. Then I watched as the door opened and recognised all the ladies that were getting out. They were my sisters from our Commit To Be Fit (CTBF) fitness group. I was so overwhelmed with emotion that I got up and ran towards them just like a little girl running towards her mother for comfort.

From the looks in their eyes I knew they had received word that my Te was gone. We hugged and I felt some slight relief, as though they felt my pain and my despair as we all cried together. We cried so loudly that we woke the neighbours on that Saturday morning. I turned and saw my elderly landlady in tears, standing beside me.

We'd only gotten to know each other during the last year and I learnt that she was also a widow. At that point, she knew exactly how deep I was hurting. I hugged her as she cried with me. My mum ushered us into the house and we all sat down on the mat. I was so relieved to see my fitness sisters, their presence was like a blanket of comfort, and the house gave warmth to my broken heart. More of my fitness sisters arrived later that day devastated and in tears, and filled up the living room.

Now, the hardest part was telling our children who at this point were still deep in sleep despite all my loud cries with the ladies. They finally woke up about an hour later when I had exhausted all my tears and lay there weak and fatigued. My mum went to bring them down while I waited with the rest of the ladies in the sitting room. One by one they appeared with their sleepy eyes, descending the stairs with my mum behind them. Oh, how my heart weighed heavily at the sight of my sweet innocent children, ignorant to the fact that they had just woken up fatherless.

They joined us downstairs half-awake and puzzled, wondering why there were so many ladies in the house. I caught a glimpse of my daughters' faces changing from curious to sad. I later found out from them that they had figured out something was wrong with their father when they saw me distraught with all my friends, but they desperately hoped that it was not that he had died.

I asked them to sit down next to me, as I struggled with all my might not to break down while I told them, 'I want you to understand that *Ta* (Dad) is now sleeping, but remember that he will always be in our hearts.' My two daughters instantly knew and they broke down and started to cry. My youngest son, on the other hand, was still a bit confused and I was not sure if he was even fully wide awake.

He looked up at me and asked, 'Wait, did Ta die?'

I hugged him and sadly answered, 'Yes, *luvequ* my child, he is now living in our hearts.'

My children continued to cry their tender hearts out in agony, except for my son. At that point, he was in obvious shock and disbelief, just looking around at everyone, confused. Not accepting what was happening, he innocently asked, '*Na* (Mum), is this a prank?'

Oh, how I wish it was my son, I thought to myself. I composed myself and answered, 'No son, it's not a prank. Ta is now resting with Jesus.'

I was mindful, and also grateful and thankful, that a few of my close friends in the fitness group had lost a parent when they were in the same age range as my kids. One of the ladies in particular had been through the same ordeal of losing her father when she was very young. She shared her story with my two girls and son as we sat around in our circle of comfort. This dear sister and friend encouraged them to stay strong for each other and for me, their mother. My son took her words to heart and with all his effort tried to be strong for his sisters and me throughout. It was as if he forbade himself to cry for fear that it would be his acknowledgement of the truth that his father was no longer with us. Looking back, he was never seen to shed a tear all throughout the funeral process. He stepped up as the man of the house in his father's absence, just as we had joked about on numerous occasions whenever Tevita was staying away overnight as a pilot.

The day started very slowly as time crept by, and soon enough with mobile technology and social media, word quickly got around. Our driveway became busy as more friends started arriving in shock, to share our loss, and comfort us as we all mourned the loss of my husband and their dear friend. Some, to my relief and without invitation, got themselves busy in the kitchen to help prepare breakfast for everyone. My last meal had been with my husband the evening before, and without sleep, food or drink my body lacked the appetite and interest in eating at all. Gradually with all my crying, my tears seemed to dry and my head spun in a haze with a million unanswered questions. My body, on the other hand, grew weary with exhaustion, and I forced myself to lie down.

Amidst all this I noticed that our second daughter Ipa was nowhere to be found in the living room or kitchen. She was the one that I was most worried about, particularly how she was going to handle the loss of her father. In a panic, I quickly rushed upstairs but could not find her in any of the kids' rooms. I then heard a sob coming from our room. I reached for the doorknob to open it but realised it was locked. I became alarmed, wondering what she could be doing inside, given the circumstances.

'Ipa, darling, please open the door,' I begged and continued knocking in desperation. Her sobbing only got louder and louder. I pleaded in a commanding tone, 'Ipa, please let your mother in.'

She finally opened the door and I found her sitting in her father's seat, crouched down, hugging her knees with her head buried in between. I could not see her sweet little face but could only hear her bawling uncontrollably.

'Ipa, darling, come and give Na a hug.' I reached for her and recalled, with some guilt, how I had assured her that her father was not going to die. I felt like the biggest liar ever. How would I comfort her now, seeing how hurt she was? I was at a loss. I managed to soothe her sobbing after giving her one of her father's singlets to keep hold of and wipe her tears with. It still had her father's scent and she held it in comfort.

The children all took the news differently. My son did not cry, but instead asked to watch all the videos of him and his father from when he was a baby. He spent the following hour watching all their videos. While Ipa had gone and locked herself in our room crying, our firstborn Mela, after mourning, went into cleaning mode as if to keep herself busy. She cleaned our room, and placed all the photos of her father and me nicely on our shelf. She arranged all his shoes neatly and his work bag and overnight carry-on case along his side of the room.

Friends slowly left us to tend to their own families as the sun set that day. By 10 o'clock they had all gone except one of our closest family friends and fellow pilot, Naibuka Tunabuna. By 11 o'clock the kids were fast asleep next to me in the living room. They had dragged down their blankets and pillows for us to sleep in the living room instead of our room. I was completely worn out and exhausted by then. I had not eaten anything, yet strangely I wasn't hungry at all. My body desperately needed rest, but my mind just wouldn't allow it. I begged Naibuka to keep me company and tell me stories until I fell asleep. I finally dozed off at around 1 o'clock and Naibuka stayed, making sure I went to sleep before he too eventually left.

My Tevita had passed away at 3:40 a.m. the previous morning, December 17th. Despite falling asleep around 1 o'clock, for some strange reason, I suddenly woke up and glanced at my phone. The time was 3:44 a.m., December 18th. Strangely I kept waking up around the same time for the following few days, right up until two days after his burial. That morning I woke up with this overwhelming and extreme sense of loneliness, so powerful that I felt empty and hollow inside. All hope and joy of living was gone. It was my first experience of waking up to a world without my darling husband Tevita in it. Oh, what a painful first morning it was. I turned and saw our three children still fast asleep. 'They no longer have a father,' I cried openly.

The pain instantly multiplied and I despised the emotions I was feeling. It was all too painful, with nothing I could do except cry and cry. It was another sunny Sunday morning with the chirping of birds outside as the kids woke up. Sleeping seemed to numb the pain of our loss, yet as we stirred and woke each morning, we again felt the pain, and our heavy hearts confirmed that this was not a bad dream, but our reality.

When our son Yaca woke up he asked, 'Na, now that we don't have a father, who is going to be our father?' A question asked so innocently but one that pierced my heart. It was the first of many questions my children would ask. 'But we prayed so hard Na, why did Ta still die?' Some questions I managed to reply to, yet others were so difficult, even I had no answers.

I was at a point in my life when I needed Tevita the most to comfort me, yet he was not there. I reached for the closest thing that would allow me to watch him full of life and to hear his loving voice – my phone. I desperately needed him to say something to me, to tell me anything that would comfort me at that very moment.

I stumbled across one of the videos on my phone that I had watched many times, but it never spoke to me like it did that morning. It's a thirty-nine-second video that I had recorded of us singing karaoke at a friend's house. In all the lyrics he sang, there was this particular line where he slowly turned, looked straight at me as I held the phone, and in his sweet angelic voice sang the words I desperately needed to hear: 'Baby, don't you cry for me, it's an illusion, just an illusion.' An intense pain instantly pierced my heart, as it felt as if he was reminding me that although he was really gone, he was telling me not to cry for him.

'How can I not cry for you my love?' I cried out loud in agonising pain with my phone in my hand. It was at that point that I just totally lost it. The pain, the heartache was just too much to bear. I cried out a loud wail, unaware of those around me. My daughter Ipa was seated right beside me.

My mother was trying to calm me down and remain composed and strong for the kids, but I was hysterical and yelled back, 'Just let me mourn and grieve for my husband.' I was even kicking my feet on the floor like a child throwing a tantrum. It was all too painful and too much to take in. I leapt off the couch and ran upstairs. In the privacy of our bedroom I cried even more, now pouring my heart out to the Lord.

'God, you have taken my husband. What is the point of me living now? You might as well take me too.' I felt like there was absolutely nothing and no other purpose to live for, my world was gone. I wanted to go too, if that was what it would take to end this unbearable pain. I cried and wept as though something had died within me that day.

My sobbing was interrupted when I heard Ipa crying uncontrollably and screaming downstairs. 'I want my ta, I want my ta, I just want my ta back.' I quickly composed myself, wiped off my own tears and ran downstairs to comfort my child. Both my parents had struggled to calm and comfort her, but to no avail. I had known this was going to happen as Ipa was closest to her father. She continued crying as I gathered her to my chest, and clasped my arms tightly around her. Through her weeping and sniffing she repeated, 'I just want Ta back, I just want him to come back and read a story to me, I want my ta back.'

I had to think hard and fast of how I was going to comfort my daughter. I knew that the children were also desperate to see their father. After assuring Ipa that I was going to take all of them to see him, I handed her one of her father's singlets to wear. 'Put this on. This will keep Ta close to you and will be like Ta giving you a hug.' Thank God the singlet managed to console her and put an end to her crying.

Lynn, a dear friend and sister of mine from the CTBF group, used her connections with the funeral home owners, and made possible our first visit to where Tevita's body was. It was as if God had gradually introduced the right people into my life who He foresaw I would be needing during this particular phase, and now they were taking the lead in making all the arrangements. There was the cooking, travel tickets, funeral home arrangements, banner design, funeral notice, the casket, church service, police escort for the convoy and numerous other responsibilities that needed to be attended to. With this supportive and caring web of friends, I was afforded some time to grieve for my dear husband and comfort our precious children.

On the way to the funeral home I sat in silence as I listened to their conversations. The two younger ones seemed to still believe that their father was not dead but only asleep. Yaca kept telling Ipa this, in the hope that she would be the one to wake their father up from this deep sleep, as if she held some power to break this spell. We walked quietly into the small chapel prepared for viewing his body, and I saw him lying on a bed wheeled out into the middle of the room. It was as if he was only sleeping. Yaca seemed to be a bit reluctant to go to the viewing and kept clinging on to me like he did not want to see his father in that state. He slowly realised, on seeing the various coffins on display in the salesroom next door, that we were not in a place where people sleep.

My two girls walked straight ahead to be closer to their dad, standing over his head and staring down at his pale, cold body, before crying their hearts out. Looking on as a mother, the pain multiplied and was absolutely heart-wrenching.

Battered and broken in spirit, Ipa called out to her father, 'Ta … wake up, wake up Ta.' With no response from him she continued adamantly, refusing to give up. 'Why won't he wake up, why won't he wake up?' She reached out to feel his forehead and felt he was ice-cold. 'Why is he cold?' She continued crying. More questions were to come later, some that I could explain and others even I did not have answers to.

After some time, they finally understood that their father was not going to wake up. We must have spent an hour with him there but it only felt like a few minutes. It was very difficult having to leave him behind, to be separated from him again and not to be going home together like we always did before. The kids and I held his hand and gave him a kiss each before finally leaving.

We arrived back home and I went straight to take a shower. Our bathroom became my little go-to space to cry on my own, hoping the water would wash my pain away as it did my tears. I had millions of questions that I wanted to ask God, but only one question kept coming to mind: Why did he have to go, Lord? Why him? I could not find it in my heart to be angry at God, but instead I cried and said a little prayer. 'Lord, I hope and pray that one day you will allow me to understand why my Tevita had to go, I miss him too much.'

Bit by bit, my heart began to settle in peace, knowing my future, though bleak and painful, was hopeful, in days to come.

2

The Pacific Flying School

Believe you can and you're already halfway there.

THEODORE ROOSEVELT

I had a simple, strict, and typical Fijian upbringing back in the village, where both my parents also worked at the time. Tarukua, where my dad is from, is one of the five villages in Cicia Island located towards the eastern part of Fiji. My dad was a very strict, straightforward man – a yes was a yes, and a no was a no. I wouldn't even dream of asking anything twice let alone nagging. Growing up as the youngest of five, with three sisters and a brother, gave me a chance to learn from my older siblings' mistakes and mischief. It saved me from some of Dad's beltings – or as he would call them, corrections.

I had great admiration for my dad growing up as I would follow him around and do almost everything he did. I spent quite a lot of time with him when my mum had to travel for work that sometimes took her all over Fiji and the Pacific. I missed her every time she would go. The loneliest time for me followed when all my older siblings had to move to the city for higher education. On the other hand, that gave me more time with my father. He ended up practically teaching me everything a father would teach a son. He would take me to his yaqona or kava plantation and taught me how to plant it. I would help him with harvesting, cleaning, cutting, sun drying, pounding, and even selling it.

After school, my home activities with him mostly involved getting my hands dirty in digging and weeding our garden next to our house, helping him fix our truck and changing the tyres. This also included pushing the grass cutter around our compound, collecting coconuts, and even feeding the cows and pigs. Though there were many chores, the one that stands out in my mind the most was going to our piggery farm, which was about fifteen minutes' drive from home. It was my favourite chore because Dad would let me drive our two-and-a-half-tonne truck all the way there.

Dad had bought his blue Mitsubishi truck from Suva and by now it was heavy and unsuited to village life and the hard labour it endured. Out of my father's three daughters, I was the privileged one who got driving lessons from him. He taught me how to drive when I was only eleven years old. It was a great feeling when he first let me drive by myself to our deserted farm. I would definitely not have been allowed to do this if it had been elsewhere! I was excited even if it meant that I would have to collect about thirty coconuts by myself, and cut them in half to feed the pigs. To gain that much trust from him, that I would not crash his truck, was quite an achievement for me. I made sure I didn't (crash) because that, to me, would have meant letting him down.

Needless to say, I found all these activities more exciting than cooking and sewing in the house like my peers were doing. Other after-school activities would mostly be by the beach or the sea with my string and hook, catching fish for my cat Peggy. The beach was my favourite place to go for relaxation, to think, and to dream about where I wanted to be in the future. Our house was conveniently located just a few metres away.

At the beach, I later gained a bit more confidence and ventured further into the sea trying to catch bigger fish. Sometimes I got lucky and caught enough for dinner and for Peggy. With my fishing line in hand I would sometimes gaze up into the sky as a plane flew by and I remember thinking, isn't that the most amazing thing man has ever created! A heavy machine that can fly. We only had the plane service on our island once a week, with the airport situated closest to our village. I remember one day being at the airport with my hand clutching the diamond-wired fence, and staring at this fascinating machine that just landed. I was probably only seven years old, yet I vividly remember having my first crush that day. I fell in love with the pilot as soon as he stepped out of that plane, not for the man he was, but for passion over the uniform he was wearing and the profession it represented. From that day onwards, I knew what I wanted to become – a pilot. Though the journey was tough and challenging, the first seeds of my dream had been sown in my heart all those years ago on the sands of Cicia.

One challenge, as I vividly recall, was that disappointed feeling when I saw the look on my father's face after relaying to him my Form 6 examination results. The crease in his brow revealed that I had let him down, but he encouraged me to repeat Form 6 and try to do better.

I knew he was going to suggest that I repeat Form 6, so I had already gone ahead and looked for another school to repeat in. I did not want to repeat in the same school where everyone would know that I was repeating. In trying to avoid being branded as a repeater, and save myself some embarrassment, I had found a school far away from my previous school and almost in the heart of Suva city. This was Dudley High School and they wore my favourite colour purple, and I would finally get a break from the orange-coloured uniform of Vunimono High School I had been wearing for the previous four years. Only the girls there would relate to why I detested the colour so much after the numerous remarks and ridicule we would get from other schools calling us 'curry'.

I could not wait and for the first time I was actually choosing my own school. I filled in the forms and all my father had to do was agree and pay the school fees. He, however, was not happy with my choice of school and there was not much discussion about which school I was going to attend next until one January afternoon. It was the second day into the first week of school, in 2002 – a quiet Wednesday afternoon at home with my father on the couch watching TV. The only conversation that could be heard in the living room was from the TV program he was watching. In the background could be heard the distinct sound of the bus engine changing its gear, abruptly echoing into the house. It was probably the bus that could have been dropping me off, had I gone to school that day. The reality of having failed my main Form 6 exam, known as the Fiji School Leaving Certificate exam, had only just sunk in – although I was not surprised.

I had also been avoiding any conversation on that topic with my father. I knew that I had not worked hard enough and that I had not put in all the effort that I could have. I was therefore not surprised at all when my eyes scrolled down and stopped at the number that was just two marks shy of the passing mark. The previous years of high school had become a little bit boring for me and school slowly became just an obligation I had to fulfil.

Being a shy girl, it was quite a big adjustment from a typical village life to a busy town life. From a small number of students in class to a big number, from Fijian-speaking classes to English ones. Understandably my biggest fear in school was being laughed at in class if I asked a 'silly' question that everybody else knew the answer to. That was one hurdle that for years I could not overcome and it was the very thing that was holding me back from being all I could be. I knew that for me to thrive in school I needed to ask questions when I did not understand the teacher. But at that age with no one telling me otherwise, I had chosen to keep my inquisitive mind from actually asking questions. I decided that I'd rather not be laughed at, let alone be humiliated in class. I had let my fear come between me and my dream of being a pilot. This eventually led to my lack of interest in school.

However, I had found interest in certain subjects of the sciences and had chosen to take up chemistry, biology, physics, mathematics and English in Form 4. I also knew that they were the necessary subjects required to get into pilot school. However, before that, I was graded a C student when I completed Form 4. Not so smart for a pilot, eh? I thought to myself. But deep down I still wanted to be a pilot. I don't recall telling anyone else about my dreams at the time except my high school best friend Mele Laqekoro. It was to her I could tell my crazy dream because I knew she would not laugh at me. Looking back now, I wouldn't blame anyone for laughing at me at that time, because I was so far off the mark from anything even close to making it into pilot school. I once told a friend when I was still in primary school that I also wanted to be a scientist and she laughed at me. From then on, I kept the pilot dream to myself. Going to the lab for experiments was pretty much the only thing in school that I looked forward to; the rest was just boring classes that I would be sitting in, pretending to be listening.

Mathematics was my least liked subject out of the five – I found it too confusing and complicated with many formulas that did not make sense. For mathematics to become my strongest subject that year was in itself perfect proof, that any student can be good in any subject, if all efforts are put into it by both the student and the teacher. You wouldn't believe that by the end of that year, I had fallen in love with my very least liked subject – mathematics.

Out of all the school exams I could remember having sat for, my first fail was for the Form 6 main exam. For the first time, I felt like an immense failure, embarrassed and ashamed. I hated it. There was no way I was going to make it into pilot school if I continued like this. I then remembered my dream from all those years ago, on the beach in my village, and the pilot in that uniform I watched get off the plane, and I reminded myself of what I knew I was destined to be – a pilot. After serious thought that year, my failure became the driving force behind determination and hard work to accomplish my dreams. I told myself, I am going to do whatever it takes to pass and get a very good mark this second time around.

One afternoon in January, I had one of my friends Lina, who had also attended Vunimono, my old school, stop by the house. She lived just a couple of houses from ours and would come by every now and then. She entered the house still in her short-sleeved orange dress uniform with a white shirt underneath. I reintroduced my father to her since I could not remember the last time they had met or if they ever had.

'So, you're still in Vunimono High School?' my father asked.

'No,' she politely replied.

'Then which school are you attending now?'

'Nakasi High School, just down the road.'

Uh-oh, I thought to myself. I knew straightaway what was coming next. Why did she choose to come home that day? And why was she still in that orange uniform? I silently asked myself. At that point, I noticed that my father was getting too interested in this school.

'So, they have the same exact uniform?' he asked curiously.

'Yes, I just had to change the badge,' she answered.

'Galuoko, you hear that?' Dad asked, amazed.

'Yessssss,' I replied in a slur.

'Galuoko, do you still have your uniform?' he asked again.

'Yesssssssssss,' I slowly replied.

'Alright, that's done. Tomorrow you will go to that school – get me an application form and ask them how much the school fees cost,' he commanded. There went my Dudley High School, out the window.

I now realise the importance of being obedient and trusting our parents' decisions, even though most times they seem totally opposite to what we want. On reflection, I know God had better plans, and a path marked out for me already.

After all, my father did know what was best for me. I doubt that I would be where I am today if I had not listened or been obedient to him. I would not have made it to the Pacific Flying School and would not have met my husband and the father of my children – Tevita.

The following Monday I found myself again in my old white shirt and orange dress that I wished I had thrown away. But out of respect I dutifully followed what I was instructed to do. It was in this school that I made a big turnaround with my studies.

Surprisingly after a few weeks, I felt that Nakasi High School was just the right school for me. I liked the school atmosphere, and I loved the close relationships I had with the teachers. They were more approachable, friendlier, and encouraging. This was perhaps because it was a smaller school and there were only a few of us taking pure science subjects. It made it easier for me, a shy student, to come out of my shell and be able to ask questions when I needed to and be more interactive in class. I had only three teachers – one for English, one for biology and chemistry, and one for mathematics and physics. I adored them all equally. They made each subject much more fun and interesting in their own unique way. Mr Dutt, my mathematics and physics teacher really impressed me with both the subjects that I had found great difficulty with at my previous school.

Both my parents had to leave Suva and return to the island for work not long after I started school. My older sisters had moved out and gotten married, so I was left with my older brother, Epeli Jnr, to look after me. He was attending a tertiary school at the time. I think he did well as a big brother since I felt well cared for. He would give me twenty dollars, from the money being sent to him by our parents, and that was my fortnightly bus fare plus some weekly food money, and that was it. I would budget and make sure we would always have food on the table for dinner. He was easy and friendly with my friends and got along well with all of them.

His after-school weekly routine would either be playing touch rugby or volleyball, except some Fridays when he would come home very late or not at all. I remember being woken early one morning with a loud bang on the wall. My room was the closest to the main door and the sitting room. I heard some sort of commotion coming from the sitting room, and curiosity sent me out of my room to check what was happening. I got the shock of my life when I saw two of my brother's friends, drunk and beating up another guy. With my brother passed out in the other room, I quickly ran back to my room and locked myself in.

These were big guys and either of them could bust my door down easily, I thought to myself. I looked around my room, and the chest of drawers caught my attention; I quickly pushed it against the door to secure it. No, they could still push the door and the chest away easily.

The next item in the room that caught my eye was the iron. I plugged it into a power outlet, sat it on the chest and turned the switch on. I slowly returned to my bed, lay down and pulled my blanket over me. From there I watched the door in silence and looked at the small red light on the iron as it rested on the chest. I even pictured the hot iron plate landing on someone's head – whoever dared to open that door. Luckily no one had any iron markings on their faces the next day.

In Form 6, my after-school routine was simple. I would arrive home, wash my lunchbox and uniform, prepare dinner, shower, and then it was onto homework time. We did not have a television so there was little distraction at home. I would make sure I completed all my homework before I dozed off to sleep, and left my studying for when I woke up fresh in the mornings. That was my little secret; complete the homework, read the notes I wrote that day, then study in the morning. It seemed to work as my own marks started impressing even me and I was becoming more motivated. I was doing well in school and I could see my dream of being a pilot slowly becoming a reality. I would go to bed each night dreaming of this – I would fall asleep seeing myself in a pilot's uniform, flying a plane and would wake up again to the same vision. I was finally focused and working hard towards my dream.

Years later, I found out from Tevita that he had actually seen me from a distance that year (2002). He was in his final year in Fulton College completing his primary education studies. A relative of his, Naioba had just given birth, and just moved into the house next to ours with her family. Her younger brother Seru Saukuru, who was very close to Tevita, was also attending Fulton College, and they were both paying her a visit. They saw me standing outside our house in my orange dress and white shirt uniform, washing clothes. However, I didn't get to meet Tevita that day, only Seru. I can only recall the funny talkative guy who came around the fence to ask me for a lighter. It was Seru. I wonder what would have happened if I had met Tevita that day.

School went like a breeze for me that year. Before I knew it, we were already getting ready for the annual exam and the Fiji School

Leaving Certificate exam. Teachers were also distributing tertiary school and university application forms – all the forms except the form I wanted. All my efforts at studies throughout that year paid off. Unlike previously, I wasn't panicking and doing last-minute studies but instead could hardly wait to see the exam papers. The prize-giving day came and with my parents still on the island, they asked one of my aunties to attend on their behalf.

To my humble surprise, my name was called out to receive the dux award for the school. I realised something, while walking up to receive that award – we are all capable of achieving whatever we set our minds to, and if we fully commit ourselves to it, only the sky and beyond is the limit.

By then, despite receiving the dux award, I still had not told my parents what I really wanted to do. I recall early on, how fighter jets would fascinate me and I would cut out pictures of them from newspapers for my collection. I even imagined myself becoming one and told my mother about it. It wasn't a surprise when she threw me a big 'No!' so I settled on just becoming a normal airline pilot. I finally managed to tell them what I wanted to do. Mum made a few calls and I finally got my hands on an application form to do my pilot training at the Pacific Flying School in Nadi.

They were impressed with my choice of career, but not when they found out how much it would cost them. I had managed to pass with flying colours, with well above the minimum required mark to get into the Pacific Flying School – just another step to achieving my dream. I remember how my father asked me one day if I could hang around for another year doing Form 7, to give them time to gather funds for my school fees. For the first time, I dared to disagree with my father. I could not see myself wasting another year and not getting my hands on a plane to fly. My parents managed to pay the deposit of $10,000 just in time before the closing date.

January 2003, I found myself sitting in a small office in front of the chief flying instructor of the school at the time. He introduced himself as Sakaraia Bolanavatu, who happened to be from the same province as myself, Lau. He was friendly during the interview and confirmed that I was to start the following month.

The school was still undergoing renovations, with some boarding quarters rented from Airport Fiji Limited known as SSQ, short for Single Staff Quarters. SSQ was intended to accommodate students coming from other parts of Fiji and the Pacific. While the renovations lasted for almost two months, my parents arranged for me to stay at one of our relatives' houses not far from the airport. From there I would catch a bus or sometimes walk to the main road through cane farms, to catch a minibus to the flying school.

To say the first day was exciting is an understatement. I was excited, thrilled beyond measure and fired up. I got to meet the rest of the students starting with me that month. There were twenty-one male students and four female students including myself. We introduced ourselves on day one, as our flying instructor took the class, and we shared why we wanted to become pilots. It was interesting listening to other students and their reasons for wanting to become pilots. One particular response that stood out for me that still echoes to this day was that of Richard Yuen. I could tell straightaway that he was very intelligent. He was of average build for a Chinese lad, and always wore a big smile. He pushed his chair out and stood up to introduce himself, before going on to share what inspired him to become a pilot. He quoted a few words and confidently said, 'Like they say, shoot for the moon because if you fall short you will land on a star.' He added a few more words afterwards but his last words, boldly said, were, 'The sky is the limit.' With his firm, confident tone, he immediately caught my attention. I knew that he was a determined, driven, and wise individual who I would need to hang around with in school if I was going to learn from and be as intelligent as him.

I grew up in the village on Cicia Island living in the Public Works Department compound where my father was employed as the leading hand. The compound consisted of six houses including the one we lived in and an office. Ours was the biggest house in the compound. Towards the north were three vacant houses used to accommodate relief workers from the Public Works who were called in to assist during natural disasters that mostly affected small islands in that part of Fiji.

It was the middle house where about twenty to thirty men would gather for their regular kava sessions hosted by my dad. Opposite these three houses was the south fence separating the office and another house from the main road and the white sandy beach. On the east fence lay the village graveyard. Because I refused to be home alone, I would drag my blanket and pillow in the dark from two houses away and lay beside my father, who sat at the very top. This was my normal routine whenever my mother was away. I would listen to all their discussions, funny stories and some interesting ones too, before I would finally fall asleep. Those seated at the top, during a kava session, signify their status in society, thus women are seldom allowed. With this in mind, I was taught to show respect, with my head bent and back slightly arched whenever I stood up to go outside, and I was reminded to say '*jilou*' or 'excuse me'. Sometimes I was not loud enough, and I clearly remember my father telling me to discreetly walk all the way back and repeat myself, louder, before exiting. This instilled respect in me to this day and I treasure my cultural upbringing in shaping the woman I am today.

Looking back now, such gems I picked up always registered and echoed in my mind. It was at one of his kava sessions with my older brother and cousins that I overheard him giving a piece of wise advice. He said, 'You will become like whomever you hang around with. If you hang around with law-breakers you will become one. If you hang around more with people who love to read, you will eventually come to love books too. So, choose your crowd wisely.'

I had always felt like I was well below that intelligence level and knew I had to work extra hard to fulfil my dreams.

From my father's words, I figured if I hung around more with intelligent people, I would become one. I eventually became very good friends with Richard. He was renting a two-bedroom house with a fellow Vanuatu student about seven minutes' walk from the school. After I was given a room in the single quarters, we would meet with a few other students and study together at night in school.

Sometimes though we would turn our two-metre classroom tables into beds. Each student got comfortable on one of the eight tables and dozed off to sleep at 2 a.m., sleeping till the sun came up. Richard was a good companion and would invite me to come and cook some Fijian dishes at his place for dinner before we studied together. He was a very good cook and that was another reason I loved going to study with him. It was no surprise that with hard work, he became the first student to ever complete his pilot training within eleven months. I am so proud of this good friend of mine, who is now a captain of the Airbus A330 with Fiji Airways. It is true – I like to think that happiness and success attracts like. Richard is happily married to the successful pilot Mrs Hartlene Yuen who is currently a captain on the ATR72 with Pacific Link.

Richard is still a very good cook and he prepared a massive delicious feast at his residence and invited the kids and me for dinner after Tevita's funeral. I got to his place and found him again in the kitchen cooking, just like in the flying school days.

It was there in the flying school that I first saw my future husband with just a stare from a distance. Come to think of it, the previous year, Tevita was not just watching a girl in an orange uniform doing her laundry, but his wife-to-be. I remember it was a Saturday, a few months into our training and I had just been cleared to fly solo. Like any other normal day, I got dressed and headed down to the flying school for my flight, obviously clueless that I was going to meet my future husband, the love of my life and the father of my children.

Had I known, I would have bathed myself with perfume. For some reason, I wanted to go a bit early to school that morning. I walked into the school's small tearoom and noticed a new guy sitting on a stool to my left as I entered. He was sitting quietly with folded arms and a cap shielding his forehead, allowing me just a glimpse of his handsome eyes. To this day, I can still vividly recall what he was wearing – a blue t-shirt and khaki shorts. I thought, I cannot be rude to this guy and not introduce myself. I stretched out my hand, shook his, and did so. 'Bula, I'm Galuoko, but everyone around here calls me Bogi, my second name.'

'Bula vinaka, Tevita Secivo, from Viwa, Bau, Tailevu,' came his response.

We talked a bit and I recall how he seemed to be rather curious all of a sudden. He said that he had gone to the all-boys boarding school, Queen Victoria School, which explained the QVS tattoo I had noticed on his left thumb. 'My brother also attended that school,' I exclaimed.

'Is your brother Laliqavoka?' he immediately asked. Without giving me a chance to reply, he continued. 'Epeli Laliqavoka is your brother, right?' he asked charmingly with a smile.

I uttered a slow 'Yes,' tilting my head with amazement and caution.

I just met this guy and he can tell who my brother is? I wondered. Out of the thousands of students that attended QVS, how could he tell? With curiosity, I just had to ask. 'How can you tell that Epeli is my brother?'

'The resemblance and the eyes. You both have big round eyes,' he answered, still with a smile.

I admit I was impressed. I had never met someone able to tell who my brother was, out of the thousands of possibilities. Being raised to respect my older siblings, I had taught myself to show my brother's friends, or anybody that went to the same school with him, the same respect I had for my brother.

With that in mind, I fixed myself a cup of coffee and quietly took a seat opposite Tevita at the table. Having sat down I made myself busy reading the newspaper, while waiting for my slot to fly. I had caught a glimpse of his squinting eyes staring from just under his cap a couple of times. His eyes on that day were deep as they slanted at the corners. He had thick eyelashes that I, like many girls, wished to have, and the colour was shiny black, just as his hair was. His eyes rested at almost half-moons and were warm with the same smile he had when we first shook hands. I had no clue that while I was busy reading the newspaper, someone was secretly falling in love with me, as he later confessed. I only found out about it after, when we were finally dating.

He loved telling me the story, how he was silently talking to me that day and I loved hearing it each time he told it. With a slow confident tone, he spoke of what had been going on in his mind. *You sitting there, you are going to be my wife.* And he reassured himself, *This girl will be my wife.*

Meanwhile, this future wife was still busy reading the newspaper. 'How could you possibly know that I was going to be your wife?' I would ask him a few years down the line.

'After some close observation, I kind of figured out the type of person you were,' he'd say. 'Just a simple village girl who was not too fancy for my taste, yet determined to make the most out of life,' he would add.

Tevita was in his first year of teaching in Suvavou Primary School, in Suva when we first met that day. He was asked by his dad to find something to do while waiting for the funds to do his pilot training, and he ended up completing three years of primary education study at Fulton College. Being a pilot never left his mind, so he decided to take the three-hour drive from Suva to the Pacific Flying School that day for a visit. His main purpose was to come and observe what went on around the school. He had previously arranged this visit with the chief flying instructor of the school. He had no idea of the bonus, that he would end up observing his future wife too.

Going our separate ways, I went out flying that day, not knowing that I had just met the father of my children. A few more weeks passed before we ran into each other again at Pacific Flying School. It was late one evening, probably after 6 o'clock and I had just finished a flight.

Ben Baleikanacea was one of the students who started just ahead of me. He's one of the happiest and cheerful persons I've ever met, always smiling, cracking jokes, and laughing with everyone. He was always lively and could tell a story that was better to listen to than watching a movie, which is how Tevita described him. He helped a lot with theories and things about flying with new students like me. That day he had waited to walk me up to our quarters since it was getting dark. We crossed the road just in front of the school and could make out a person approaching us. We got closer and Ben recognised him. They happily greeted each other and chatted a bit while I stood to the side. I noticed the smile, and then I remembered that it was the guy from the tearoom I had met a few weeks earlier. It was Tevita or Tex as Ben had called him. I could tell that they had known each other for a while.

Listening to their conversation, I figured that he was going to start with the next batch in October that year. After a while, Ben finally realised that I was still waiting, so he excused himself, shook Tevita's hand and wished him well. Out of politeness I took a step towards Tevita to shake his hand too. I held out my right hand as he shook mine and to my astonishment, he held on a bit longer and did not let go. I felt his strong warm hand squeezing mine tighter and tighter, like it was supposed to be some kind of signal, yet one I was not catching. What is wrong with this guy? I wondered. Why is he squeezing my hand? My heart started to beat faster before he finally let go.

Several weeks passed before some students came up with the idea that we should all go for a dance night in Suva on the weekend. A bus was organised and we headed down for what was to be my first ever night out. In the weeks leading up to that night, Ben became Tevita's confidant and every time he returned from a weekend in Suva, he would look for me just to pass on Tevita's message. Sometimes with, 'I met Tevita, and he said hi,' other times with, 'Bula Bogi, Tevita sends his regards.'

Having grown up in the village with no serious boyfriend, all this puzzled me. I called my parents in the village to tell them about the dance. My mum then informed my older sister Annie in Suva to be ready to take me to my first dance. I was excited and nervous at the same time, but having my older sister there with me eased off the nervousness.

We were the first to arrive at O'Reilly's nightclub that night. I nervously followed behind my sister towards two huge guys guarding the entrance door. They pushed the door open for us, letting out the roaring music from inside the club. With the intermingled smells of smoke and beer, the loud music, and disco lights, we made our way in and took some of the seats around a table to our right. I watched as she yelled out her order of drinks to a man in a black-shirt uniform, then I asked for a glass of Coke. It wasn't long before Ben and a few other boys arrived and took the table next to us. I remember introducing him to my sister as he walked past our table, and he informed me that the rest of the students were also on their way.

After a few drinks, I could sense that my sister was getting a little bit restless, like she wanted to party but we were just not in the right club for her. So, I was not surprised when she suggested that we go and check out another club. I asked if we could wait just a little bit longer for the rest of the girls to arrive.

A moment later I found myself walking back from the ladies' room and I noticed someone familiar. All this time he had been sitting right behind me? We were almost brushing shoulders and I hadn't realised? I thought to myself.

It was Tevita, who had been sending the *hi*s and the *hello*s. I couldn't ignore him so I turned and said, 'Hi.'

The rest of the girls still had not arrived and I was unsure if they were still going to come, so I finally gave in to my sister, and we left O'Reilly's for another club. Birdland was a club just across the street, a short walk from O'Reilly's. I remember descending the stairs underground and having all the hairs on my hands standing up. Why were everyone's eyes glowing in the dark? I asked myself.

It terrified me, like they were some kind of aliens staring and ready to eat me alive. I quickly asked my sister, who explained that it was the light. Oh dear, what kind of club was this? The Fijian music, and friends she ran into, and her happy smiley face told me that my sister was having fun. It was her type of music and club; however, I was still feeling terrified and I wanted to just disappear from that place. I excused myself and told her that I wanted to go home, so she instructed me to go straight home from there.

'Galuoko, get a taxi and go straight home from here, do you hear me?' was her commanding instruction.

'Oh yes, but I will first go to O'Reilly's to say bye to the other students and also check if the girls have arrived,' I replied.

Back at O'Reilly's, I was so happy to see some girls from school there, who were just about to leave with the other students to check out another club. We slowly made our way towards Traps Bar, which was about five minutes' walk from O'Reilly's, but without Ben and Tex. In there, I had my first taste of Kahlua with milk. One of the senior students, or it might have been the instructor who accompanied us, bought me that drink. It was slightly sweet with a strong coffee flavour and a hint of vanilla – I loved it. I think I must have had only two glasses the whole time we were there, until it closed. I don't recall the exact time the bar closed but I do remember that it was very cold when I stepped outside.

It was quite a long drive home from Suva so I knew I had to find a trustworthy taxi driver to get me home safely. Waiting in front of Traps Bar I saw Tevita approaching from my right, in a red checked shirt with blue jeans. There was that familiar smile again from the tearoom becoming more and more visible as he got closer.

'Is everything okay?' he asked.

'Oh yes, I'm just trying to see if I can find a good taxi driver to take me home safely,' I replied.

'I can drop you home,' he kindly offered.

'Oh really?' I said.

And after a few seconds of judging his state, I was happy that he didn't seem to be drunk at all. I agreed and thanked him. I felt some comfort in knowing that he knew my brother and I was confident that he would not try to do anything silly.

We took a five-minute walk, arrived at where his red Toyota Tercel was parked, and saw two of the boys he came with, waiting for him. He introduced me to one, who was his cousin, and the other a friend, and said that he was dropping them off too. In my mind, I immediately thought to myself that he would be dropping me first. A few minutes into the drive I noticed that we were not heading to where I had told him I lived – he had obviously decided to get rid of the boys first.

As soon as they got out, the atmosphere in the car changed all of a sudden. It was just him and me on the other side with only the gears and handbrake separating us. I noticed that he was now driving slower than we had, before dropping the boys off. A moment later he was reaching for his radio to change the cassette. Next minute, Mariah Carey was singing one of her love songs.

Hmm, I started to wonder. Is there an intention behind the change of music? No, no, no, I can't dwell on this silly thought. He is just being nice. The drive home that night was evidently longer than normal. But he had set a sweet romantic mood that made the thirty-minute drive home seem only like fifteen minutes. We finally got home, and I asked him to just park along the road and I pointed him to the driveway up to our house. I again thanked him for his kind offer. I cannot recall how many goodbyes I bid him that morning; how many times I'd opened and had to close the car door again. For each goodbye, he would ask another question or come up with some other topic to talk about. It became obvious that he was trying to keep the conversation going. I knew that he was joining us at the flying school, so I was not surprised at all the flying questions, which I was more than happy to answer. But something was puzzling me – I had noticed that he kept changing the gears, turning the steering wheel left and right, all the time we were parked. Then he asked, 'Can I have your number?'

'Oh sorry, I don't have a phone but you can call the school and you can easily find the number in the phone directory,' I blurted out.

By now, I noticed that he was not only changing gears and turning the wheels, he was turning the car lights on and off too. Then finally came the question he had been dying to ask. 'Galuoko, can I ask you something?'

'Yes, sure,' I replied.

'Are you seeing anyone at the moment?' he blurted out.

'Ummmm, no, why do you ask?' I replied.

'Because if you are not, can we go out sometime?'

Oh, my Lord! What did he just ask? I was taken by surprise. Questions after questions were now running through my head. He seemed like a very nice kind man and I admired his bold move of asking me straight out, but it was far too soon for me. Why ask me so soon when you hardly even know me? I wondered. Maybe he was either a player who was taking advantage of the opportunity or he was a real gentleman who really liked me? After some quick thinking, I thought of asking him to give me time to consider it, but I knew so very little about him that I decided not to risk it.

With a heavy heart Tevita drove away after I firmly and bluntly turned him down. 'I am so sorry, but we can only be friends.'

3

A Change of Heart

It often happens in love that your mind 'thinks' it has had a change of heart, but in true love, no matter what you 'think', your heart will never change its mind.

Anon

It was a warm Monday morning two days later when I was back into studying, flying and settling into one of the rooms in SSQ. There were more students than there were rooms available, so some students had to share rooms while the construction people worked on the middle SSQ building. There were three quarters altogether, the upper one that was now occupied by us, the middle one that was under renovation, then the lower SSQ occupied by the Airports Fiji Limited (AFL) workers.

Venaini Ravudakua was one of the four girls who started with me. A very kind, honest, and sweet girl. From a distance, she could mistakenly be thought of as a shy, quiet girl, but upon getting to know her, I discovered she was never afraid to speak her mind, question the instructor, or tell one straight if she was not happy with you. I admired her confidence and boldness. She became my roommate for the few months before I moved to a room on my own.

I remember one time, when she had gone home for a weekend and the boys in flying school all went out for a function. They ended up going to a club afterwards with some other students who were not staying in SSQ. It was no surprise that most of them came back drunk, looking for a room to sleep in. In the early hours of the morning, I heard a knock on my door. I opened the door to see one of my colleagues who was a day-student who lived in town. Half-drunk, he begged to crash in our room. I was exasperated and immediately said no. There was no way I was going to sleep in the same room with a drunken guy – my mother would kill me! After a few minutes of desperate begging, I knew in the state he was in, he was not going anywhere and would just be a nuisance for the rest of the night until the sun came up. In the end I unwillingly let him get some sleep, on one condition; that there shouldn't be any dirt or a slight wrinkle in Vena's bed when he woke up. He happily accepted and slept with his legs on the floor, not daring to risk any dirt or wrinkles in the bed. I did not sleep a wink. He had disturbed my sleep, so I left the door ajar, just in case he tried to do something silly, and I was ready to kick him right out that half-open door!

A few weeks later we received word that they were done with renovating the middle SSQ, and had decided to move some boys over. I, on the other hand, managed to get a vacant room right next to Vena's. It wasn't long after, I had one drunken pilot student from the other flying school trying to bust my door down. From the rumours, I knew that he admired me and there he was, drunk. He had probably heard the rumour about the other student who'd had the luxury of sleeping in my room. I trusted my instincts and this time was absolutely terrified and refused to open the door. As usual, for my defence,I turned to my trusted iron, turning it on to maximum high, ready for anyone who dared intrude. Lucky for him, someone else came and dragged him out of the quarters. Had this not happened, the rumours the next day would have been of how he earned himself a burned iron mark on his face.

Life in SSQ was exciting and challenging. My fortnightly allowance was about fifty dollars – from that I had to budget for food and toiletries to last me for two weeks. There were twelve rooms in each of the quarters and together we became one big family. We would all generously put our money together to buy food and share meals among ourselves – most times it was bread and tuna. It was a phase in life when tinned corned beef and rice would be a feast whenever our contributions added up, and we could afford it. Other times I would get invited to the houses of relatives who lived close by, for lunch and sometimes dinner. That helped immensely as I could only stretch my fifty-dollar budget so far.

In the midst of all the studying and flying, I was dreading the month of October that year when Tevita was to start – yet surprisingly a part of me was also looking forward and counting down. Weeks and months seemed to have gone slower and slower as we got closer to October. I had played the scene over and over in my mind, thinking about what had happened after that dance and how I had turned Tevita down. I would recall that dim-lit dawn in his car, that faint melodious sound of insects buzzing outside, his charming approach and my final response to his question. Then within that few seconds of still silence, I saw his hopeful look dissolve, slowly transform into disappointment, ending with a slightly embarrassed look. I must confess that every time I would recall that moment, I felt a little pang of sadness in my heart.

A cousin of mine had advised me, when I was only in Form 4, that I should start praying for my future husband. I surprisingly took her advice and found myself praying for my future husband before I went to bed each night. I was very specific with what I wanted in a husband. Some of the qualities I required were that he must be a very good cook; have a good sense of humour; and be generous, kind, tall, and broad, with pink lips and straight hair. Tevita was tall, broad, and as far as I was concerned, up to that night in flying school, he seemed kind and generous, so he had ticked a few boxes. From the first day, I immediately noticed and had ticked the pink lips box.

I remember the pink lips box was very popular in high school on most of my girlfriends' lists – we believed that only non-smokers had pink lips. So, for me a non-smoker would have been an instant bonus. I was yet to find out if he could cook, and he did not have straight enough hair, which created a tiny bit of doubt, yet I was willing to make an exception.

By the time October came, he finally started in school. Oh, the awkwardness of running into him in the classroom, the tearoom, and outside. All of a sudden it was like we did not know each other at all, as I would walk into the classroom and say good morning to everyone except him, unless of course he greeted me first. I avoided going into the tearoom if he was there, and anywhere close to him was a no-go zone for me. It was quite a relief that he was not staying in the quarters with us at the time, which earned me a little bit more room to breathe and act myself without the worry of bumping into him. Judging from my reactions it felt more like I had broken up with him that night instead of turning him down. There was always an air of awkwardness between us.

Several weeks later when he finally moved into the middle SSQ, I found myself having mixed feelings about him. By now I was secretly enjoying running into him in the quarters, in school, and in town. I had slowly started to notice the generous gentleman in him. I had even assumed we could be very good buddies had he not ruined it by asking me out too early. Why couldn't he just wait? I wondered in disappointment. We could have become very close friends. I could help him out, we could probably study together, and maybe one day I would drop my pen and we would both reach to pick it up. Then our hands would touch, and everything would be in slow motion from that instant. Still in slow motion, I would look up to find him right in front of my face, staring at my lips. Then he would gently kiss me, just like in the movies. My mind raced with the endless possibilities of young love … puppy love, to me. Sadly, he had ruined it all that night in his car.

On one particular afternoon, we were all walking back to SSQ from the school when I decided to take a shortcut from the normal winding road around staff houses. I had decided to separate from the group and head for the shortcut across the mown lawn by myself, just because Tevita was also walking with us. I had started to develop some funny feelings towards him and it was confusing me. How could this be? After all, I had turned him down. Needless to say, from my reactions, it was obvious to the rest of the boys in school that he had great affection for me. Regardless I continued to avoid him. I was trying to fight off what I was beginning to feel. The boys would try to convince me that he was my perfect match, but I would just tell them not to be silly. They had even tried unsuccessfully to set us up a few times. One of the boys that started with him was Suliasi Ravunikau, a tall, fair and soft-spoken guy. He had very distinct pitch-black thick hair and eyebrows, which perfectly contrasted his fair skin tone. Suli, as everyone called him, occupied the room right next to Tevita's so they called each other 'neighbours'.

I had wondered why, out of the blue, Suli had suggested coming to study with me in my room. I didn't mind, so he joined me for a study session. I later learnt of his real intention. Barely had a few minutes passed into our studying before he started mentioning Tevita's name nonstop. His conversation ended with saying Tevita had been suffering back pain for a while and suggested that I go and massage his back. I agreed, only because I had been told that I possessed some sort of miraculous Fijian massaging touch in my hands, passed down from my father's side.

Suli disappeared for a few minutes, then returned with a slight smirk on his face to tell me that Tevita was now waiting in his room. Immediately I knew this was a set-up. I initially felt that I should refuse, but a part of me wanted to help him. Also about 0.01 per cent of me just wanted to see him. I thought maybe this might be a good time to talk about what had happened the last time we had a conversation and perhaps explain why I had been avoiding him, and just sort out the 'as far as I was concerned' bit of information we needed, to relieve the tension between us.

I got to the middle SSQ where Tevita was staying and was startled to find most of the boys in the main common room, wandering around the long passageway. It was almost as if we were the cast of some reality show, and they were waiting to see some grand finale in this love story unfold before their eyes. There was no way I was going to walk into Tevita's room without being seen or heard. They were everywhere, and I knew that it was probably going to be the talk of the school for the next few days. 'Galuoko went into Tevita's room' would be the heading for the upcoming rumour. Sweeping away that thought, I nervously made my way towards Tevita's room. A few doors on the left and further down towards the middle of the dim-lit narrow passage, I found his door, which had been left partly open. It was a welcoming sight as it instantly gave me the impression that he was expecting me. This realisation woke up that dormant little butterfly that fluttered in my tummy. After a few knocks without any response, I realised that the room was empty, he wasn't even there.

Is this some kind of a trick? I nervously thought. This is silly and humiliating! What was I thinking? I thought in disappointment.

Just as I turned to leave, I felt a heavy hand on my shoulder. It was not Tevita but one of the boys in middle SSQ now determinedly ushering me into Tevita's room. I was told that Tevita was in the men's room and the boy asked me to make myself comfortable, as if it was his own room. 'Tevita will be here soon,' he reassured me.

I slowly lowered myself to sit on Tevita's neatly covered double-bed while glancing about his room. His purple towel hung tidily just under the mirror with his shaving gear and cologne range orderly organised on his chest of drawers. Books were perfectly stacked like a mini-library in the small bookshelf next to the window. This is quite impressive, I thought to myself, and nothing like how I imagined a guy would keep their room. I got busy ticking another box off in my head without realising the number of boys who were now in the room with me had grown, eager to get a seat as this grand love story unfolded. A few boys but not Tevita. Where did they come from? I asked myself in annoyance. And what are they doing here in Tevita's room? There was no way I was going to awkwardly massage Tevita's back, however-painful it was, in front of these five boys. They knew why I was there in Tevita's room and I thought that they would be leaving after a few minutes. Instead they too had made themselves comfortable enough to cause me discomfort.

Still without any sign of Tevita, I left his room with a surprising sense of relief. Anywhere other than a room full of boys to massage his sore back in would have been a relief for me. How were we ever going to talk about that night in front of all those boys? However, fortunately, there were only a few students in the flying school who knew I had turned him down.

In those few weeks, I slowly came to notice just what kind of person Tevita really was. He always kept himself handsomely groomed and his slightly curly black hair was immaculately combed every time I saw him. He never failed to dress tastefully in bright colours or in his spotless neat pilot's uniform. I also came to see the kind, loving and outrageously generous gentleman that he was. I recall one night he had prepared dinner at the middle SSQ for the boys, when they invited us to join them. We went down and all sat around the table where we got to share a delicious, simple meal of rice with chicken flavour and fried onions. Though it was an extremely low-budget meal it was certainly cooked from the heart. And that was dinner – anything to fill our empty stomachs was considered a yummy meal during our SSQ days. He was the last one to take his seat because he was serving food for everyone, and then I noticed that everyone had a spoon except me.

'Is there an extra spoon?' I asked.

There were a few seconds of silence. I didn't know if they had meant not to offer their own spoons, to give Tevita the chance to be my knight in shining armour, and save me from eating with my fingers. That was exactly how I felt when he generously offered me his own spoon before anybody else did. My knight in shining armour just saved me. Another box ticked, and I could feel my heart slowly beating with great admiration and slight affection for him.

What is happening with me? I wondered. I now knew more about him than I had during that conversation in his car, but why did I feel like he was still some kind of mystery man? He seemed to be a determined and persistent young man who worked hard at making sure he got everything he wanted. The kind of man who would not take no for an answer, and would always want to win. That much about Tevita, I thought I knew. The mysterious and unpredictable side to him was now puzzling me, and this threw me off my normally guarded approach when it came to guys. I had expected that he would try to make another move on me, or worse, be all over me like a bad rash, trying to win me over as I saw others would. But surprisingly this did not happen, and whatever secret spell he was using to win me over was obviously working. I was getting the crazy butterfly feelings each time I saw him and they would seem to multiply and let loose inside me. He left me yearning and longing to know more about him and to be with him.

One afternoon with everyone outside, the boys were playing touch rugby while I sat and watched on with the other girls. I found my eyes secretly following him around wherever he ran and I hoped that no one would notice it. For some unknown reason, I stood up and left the rest of the girls. I walked through the passage, passing each door with their cheers and yells slowly echoing in my ears, then fading behind me. I got to the main common room and loved the quietness that surrounded me there, but what was I doing here? In my mind, I imagined Tevita following behind me. Oh, how I wanted him to follow me. But that was just my imagination.

I continued to the kitchen and filled a glass of water with Tevita still on my mind. A few seconds later my heart almost stopped when I walked back into the common room and found Tevita there on the bench. He had his head down, looking at his bleeding toe. I felt both pity for him, and happiness for me, all at the same time. So, he did follow me, I smiled with contentment. Maybe not as I had imagined it, but because he hurt his toe.

I spontaneously went into nursing mode without his consent. I quickly ran outside to collect some herbal leaves and squeezed them on his toe to stop the bleeding. A buzz of electrifying energy rushed through my body the moment my hand touched his toe, awakening the countless butterflies in my stomach. Being the gentleman he was, he let me nurse his toe, politely thanked me and went back to join the boys. His distinct qualities of being gentle, polite, humble, and kind, melted my heart. His spell of magic definitely seemed to be working. He knew what he was doing, he knew that it was only a matter of time before I had a change of heart. The feeling was overwhelming and it was also troubling me. He was the last thing on my mind before I fell asleep each night and the first face I'd picture when I woke up each morning. He was constantly in my head and I was beginning to let him into my heart.

So, this is what love feels like, I marvelled. Yet what am I supposed to do about this feeling? I'd ask myself. It would be too embarrassing, not to mention awkward, I reasoned, to ask him out now after already turning him down. Besides, it just isn't how things work. Girls don't ask boys out, I reminded myself. What do I do? Should I let him know how I feel? What is the right thing to do?

I could not contain the feeling anymore and needed to let it out, but just how to do that was my dilemma. I needed someone to tell me what to do, so I asked one of the girls at the dorm. 'What would you do if you started developing feelings for someone? Would you let that person know how you feel, or just keep it to yourself?'

Her answer was clear, but I wanted reassurance of what I needed to do. She told me she would definitely let that person know. A few days later I found a small Christian book with questions and answers that youth would ask about relationships. There I found the reassurance I needed – the book advised that it was not healthy to keep it in, so I knew I should tell Tevita how I felt.

To keep me from embarrassing myself, I needed a guy's advice. I approached my good friend David Dakuitoga. David, like Tevita, loved to sing. He would spend hours in his room that was right opposite mine, with his keyboard, singing. I remember he once told me that 'anyone can sing' and made me sing one of Shania Twain's songs with him. He was a sweet friend, always smiling and revealing his cute dimples on both cheeks. We became very close – we would share secrets, spend hours telling stories and giggle in each other's rooms. He was a good friend. It was late one evening, just after dinner, when I remember calling him into my room to tell him that there was something I wanted to ask him.

'What would you do if you started developing feelings for someone?' I asked. The same question that I had asked one of the girls. David's response, however, surprised me.

'Why? Do you have feelings for my "Name" now?' he asked with a teasing smile.

I blushingly nodded yes, while shyly hugging my pillow. 'Tevita' in English is 'David', so they would call each other 'Name', since they shared the same name.

David left me puzzled when he immediately excused himself and disappeared out the door for a minute or two. I had a quiet, still moment by myself. My heart was gradually beating faster as if attempting to escape the confines of my chest. Has he gone to tell Tevita? I thought in shock. I would not have had a clue of what to say, if Tevita had walked into my room at that moment. Then David reappeared again. Big relief washed over my pale face when I saw he was alone without his 'Name'. David walked in with his phone in his hand, busy texting, or at least that's what I assumed he was up to. He sat down at the other end of my bed, got himself comfortable and started asking me questions. 'So, you have feelings for my 'Name' now?' he asked, still looking at his phone.

'Umm, yes,' I shyly replied.

He looked up at me with a grin then back at his phone. 'Do you want me to go and call him so you two can chat a bit?'

For a moment I was discouraged, thinking David wasn't taking it seriously enough, since he was busy with his phone.

I hesitantly agreed. 'Yes.'

He quickly jumped off my bed and ran out of my room, reappearing a moment later with thumbs up. With a slight grin he said, 'Just wait here, I'll go and buy some juice first then "Name" will come.'

Half-an-hour later, there was a soft distinct drumbeat knock, almost like a rattle of fingertips, on my door. A knock so different from the countless knocks I'd heard on that same door. This unfamiliar knock eventually became my favourite, it was like a code announcing 'hey, it's me'. I took a deep breath and a last look again at the mirror, making sure I looked presentable, before opening the door. There stood Tevita with his handsome, confident look, with a two-litre bottle of Coke in his hand. He did not seem nervous like the last time we were alone together – instead I was the one who was nervous.

I welcomed him into my small cosy room. He sat on the Fijian mat on the floor, while I settled back onto the chair next to my study table. This meeting was very different – we spent a full seven hours chatting endlessly, yet it felt like only a few minutes. We talked about anything and everything so comfortably into the early hours of the morning, dreading it's end, but daylight was fast approaching. As students, we both needed to rest. I politely told him that he needed to go and rest. He agreed and I watched as he slowly lifted himself off the floor, as our first unplanned date was coming to an end. I got up from the chair and sat down on the bed next to the door to lock the door behind him as he left. I was missing him already, although he was still physically in the room, and all of me did not want him to go. He made it to the door, but then he abruptly stopped.

The doorknob was right next to the light switch. Whatever was going on in his mind, Tevita surprised me by doing the unexpected.

Instead of unlocking the door to go out, he reached to turn the light switch off. It was now pitch-black. I was physically and mentally in shock with the darkness that surrounded us, and his action. My eyes were still slowly trying to adjust when I felt his breath in the dark moving closer. I could just make out his strong arms reaching towards something behind me. Then there was light. He must have been scanning the layout of my room and where every item and poster was, when he noticed the lamp on the shelf behind me and turned it on. The lamp immediately changed the room from a bright well-lit room to a warm, cosy, and dim-lit room, creating a lovely romantic mood.

He slowly lowered himself and sat right next to me, while I sat there half-frozen both in fear and excitement. A tingle shot up my spine, then to the rest of my body as his soft, smooth lips touched mine. Before I knew it, I was slowly kissing him back. I was in my own shining universe with my eyes closed, inhaling his pleasant masculine cologne with his sugary sweet lips on mine.

Our first goodbye was difficult and he finally left twenty minutes later. That early morning I went to sleep with a smile, hugging and sniffing the cologne scent he left on my pillow.

I remember how he would later tease me mercilessly about how he won me over – how his spell worked. I would just giggle like a schoolgirl. He did not want to be overly persistent in his pursuit, but he made sure I saw what I was missing out on. 'I'm gonna show her what she's missing,' was his favourite line to tease me with, with a snap of his fingers. His spell worked.

Several weeks later I looked at him assertively and teased, 'You had the guts to kiss me on that first night, eh? You did not want to wait?'

With a smirk on his face, he firmly replied, 'You have no idea how long I had been waiting to kiss those lips.'

I smiled, blushing away my change of heart.

4

Bogi and Te

Important encounters are planned by the souls
long before the bodies see each other.

PAULO COELHO

Ever since high school, I found most people had difficulties in pronouncing my name, 'Galuoko'. On many occasions, they would ask me for my second name to address me by.

'Bogidrau is fine,' I'd usually respond.

'Do you have another name?'

'My surname is Laliqavoka.' When translated, this literally refers to the drum sound made from the banging of two skulls together. Our forefathers had passed down folklore about how we had earned our name, which was through the winning of many battles. Our great ancestor, a tough man, showcased his bravery by his fierce display of might, with the banging together of skulls in battle, thus earning his name and our surname Laliqavoka.

'Don't you have a shorter name?' I remember one teacher asking since it was also too long. I ended up using Bogi, short for Bogidrau. This translated means 'one hundred nights'. Where I come from, our name usually has a story or meaning attached to it. After the death of a loved one, a family member would name a newborn in memory of the deceased. Some are named Bogidrau after the death of someone, especially after the one hundred nights. Despite this easier option, I still found some people pronouncing it in some funny ways. And so it stuck, I was called Bogi, by my many friends.

A few weeks into our relationship, Te and I slowly discovered that we had a lot more in common. We not only were the youngest in our families but we both had the same dream of becoming pilots ever since we were very young. Also being the youngest in my family, my mother continued to call me by my baby pet name, 'Pei'. Pei means 'baby' when translated into English. As I grew older, I started to feel embarrassed about being called by that pet name, Pei. I knew I was getting a little too old for that and recall begging my mother not to call me it, especially in public. She, however, continued to call me Pei, regardless of my numerous desperate requests for her not to. To save me a bit of embarrassment, I thought it would be a good idea to mention it ahead of time, before Tevita got around to meeting my mother. To my surprise he burst out laughing when I told him about how embarrassing it was that my mother still called me Pei, because his mother too was still calling him Pei. That came as such a relief.

He pleasantly surprised me by saying, 'If it'll make you feel any better Galuoko, almost all my relatives call me Pei; even my nephews and nieces call me Momo Pei (uncle baby). I've asked my mum to stop so many times but eventually I gave up.' We both had a good belly laugh at that.

Just a little while after we started dating, Tevita had to move into a two-bedroom flat about twenty minutes' walk away. He was sharing the flat with his cousin Seru Saukuru and two other boys. Occasionally he would invite me to join them for dinner, and it was there that I learnt how good a cook he really was. I was very impressed that he finally ticked the good cook box on my list.

He would never miss the touch rugby match every afternoon at the grounds next to SSQ and I loved watching him play. One of my favourite sweet memories in SSQ was how we would sneak back into my room for a rare goodnight kiss before he returned to his flat. That became our little anticipated routine after every game. At first, he was a bit reluctant when he was all sweaty and smelly, but I didn't care; I loved it even more. Being all dirty just made him more manly and sexy – or sometimes I would wonder if I was just being young and crazy in love.

As students, I was ahead of him in doing our flight training and would occasionally take him as a passenger on some of my training flights. He later told me about how he felt when he first saw the long stretches of white sandy beaches on one of my cross-country flights to my island home of Cicia.

'Isa na nodratou vanua ni vasu na luvequ,' he would coax. 'Oh the beautiful motherland of my future kids.'

He must have immersed himself deep in thought about our future together, and his absolute certainty that I was without a doubt going to be his wife, and the mother of his children. He had probably even fast-forwarded his imagination to the day we would be bringing our kids to the island.

I had partnered with Kemueli Naqau on that particular cross-country flight to Cicia. Kemueli was one of the boys I started with and we had Tevita as our passenger. Kemu had that brotherly persona and would always look out for the girls in SSQ. His room was right opposite ours when I was still sharing a room with Vena. Every morning he would blast his radio so loud to wake everybody up in the dorm, and I can testify that was better than waking up to a boring, annoying alarm tone. He had a good, kind heart and always seemed to have enough money to buy us bread and tuna. A very neat guy who always kept his room clean, I'd see him with a broom, sweeping his room every now and then.

It was a beautiful, pleasant day to fly, with no clouds and just enough wind when we took off from Nausori in a small Cessna 172, landing on the grassy airstrip in Cicia an hour later. One of my uncles picked us up from the airport and drove us to my village of Tarukua, which was fifteen minutes away. There I introduced Tevita and Kemu to my parents, without revealing that Tevita was, in fact, my boyfriend. A few minutes later Tevita was enjoying his first meal as a guest in my father's house. If my father actually knew, I don't know what he would have done. I had flown him hundreds of miles over water just to go and meet my parents in the village, but without them knowing of course. I wanted to make him feel special, without getting myself into trouble. I was still Mummy and Daddy's little girl or Pei, and the last thing they wanted was some distraction in the form of a man. They had paid a huge sum of money for me to pursue my dreams, so undoubtedly it would naturally frustrate them to see it all go to waste. I can recall reading my mother's letter from her sick bed a couple of months after that trip. She was so sick that she thought she was not going to make it. I remember reading from the few pages of her letter of last wishes to me. She had wanted me to make sure I completed my studies, and among other things, she emphasised, 'No boyfriend until you're twenty-one!'

I read that with such guilt; it was too late, I was already in love at nineteen. I could not imagine getting myself to unlove Tevita, or to even wait for another two years. We were not able to wait around much longer at the pace we were going in our relationship. I knew my mother's old-fashioned beliefs would not accommodate me having a boyfriend at nineteen. Regardless, I was in love and prepared to break the rules for the sake of love.

A couple of days later, she flew into Suva, and I went down to visit her. That was the first I was going to be away from Tevita for several days. Although it was only five days, it felt more like five months. I saw my mother and was relieved to see that she was recovering well, but at the same time, I was feeling sick inside for going against her wishes of no boyfriend until twenty-one, and feeling lovesick from being away from Tevita that long. I knew I had to tell her, and so I did. In my faded memory, I cannot recall exactly how all the words came out but I do remember clearly how she firmly commanded me, 'You must go and break up with him.'

'What?' I stared back in shock with tears welling up in my eyes. Those words felt like someone had reached into my body and pulled out my heart, and was asking me to tear my own heart in two. The long lecture after that was just going in one ear and out the other as I sat staring back at my mother with a blank expression. A mixture of hurt, anger, and sadness started to boil inside of me and physically hurt my chest right where my heart lay.

After being lovesick from missing him so much, there was no way I was going to go back and tell Tevita, 'I'm breaking up with you.' My mother had commanded the impossible.

I excused myself, went behind the house and flopped down crying and sobbing like a baby. A teenager crazy in love, I had just experienced the closest thing to heartbreak for the very first time. I was not going to give Tevita up that easily, especially after the many boxes he had ticked on my wishlist. I quickly dried my eyes and devised my plan to elope with him. Whatever the consequences, I was ready for them. I was prepared for anything else but not ending my relationship with Tevita.

I gathered myself together, wiped off my tears once more, and made my way back into the house to pack my bags and leave for good. For the first time, I was putting someone else above my beloved mother. I was going to run away to be with this man that I had fallen head over heels in love with.

To my disbelief, my mother called me back to the house, and in a soft voice she gently told me that she had changed her mind, on the grounds that I must not let it affect my studies. I could not believe what I was hearing and wondered if it was because she was sick, and not thinking right. It would have been a different story if she wasn't sick. My mother is known in our family for ruling with an iron fist most of the time. I've witnessed it many times with my older siblings when she would belt them up good for getting into trouble with boys. Maybe because they had always tried to hide it from her and for some reason she would always find out. In my case, I had been honest and upfront with her. I'm glad she did change her mind, otherwise I realised I would have eloped only for her to track me down and drag me back home for a good belting session. I knew that that would most probably have been the case but I bravely chose still to elope and the bashing could come later.

My visit to my mother ended and I returned to Nadi in high spirits and happy with good news to share with Tevita. 'I told Mum about us and she's okay with it,' I eagerly informed him. I saw relief and calm spread across his face as I relayed the whole story to him. 'Yes, I was going to call you to say, let's elope,' I said with a cheeky grin. 'Where do you think we could go to?' I curiously asked.

'Wherever you want to go,' came his reply.

His mother, on the other hand, had known about us way earlier than mine did. It was just a few weeks after we had started our relationship that we went on one of our weekends to Suva. We left Nadi late in the afternoon and arrived in Suva around 9 o'clock at night. The moon was out and the stars were shining peacefully in the dark of night. Lampposts warmed the quiet, empty streets of Suva city. Tevita suggested we take a taxi to their house and then he would drive me home from there. Mobile phones were not as popular then as they are now, so we made our way around to the nearest phone booth. I stood on the side as he dialled their home number and I overheard him talking to his mother.

'Mum, I'll be there soon and I'm bringing a friend with me.'

He had told me so much about his mother, so naturally I felt like I had known her for a long time already. I was not nervous, as others might have been, to meet their future mother-in-law for the first time. Instead I was full of respect for her and was secretly looking forward to the meeting. After all, she had done an exceptional job of raising the kind, loving gentleman that I had fallen deeply in love with.

We arrived at their house and she happily greeted us with a beautiful, glamorous smile. I shook her hand and immediately noticed the sweet kind-hearted lady she was, so full of love and adoration for her son, her Pei. She had prepared a delicious dinner, which was when I saw where Tevita got his cooking skills from. He shared with me how he never liked to see his mother alone in the kitchen and would keep her company and help prepare meals. In the process, he had learnt how to cook many dishes at a very tender age.

Not long after our hearty home-cooked meal, we were on the road in the same car where I had turned him down. The ride created a sense of déjà vu. This time though, without the awkward turning of wheels, gears and lights. Instead of me turning him down, we said our goodbyes and parted ways with a sweet little kiss.

That weekend we spent more quality time together, watching movies, lunching at the seawall and simply getting to know each other better. It was one of the best weekends of my young life, mostly because I had the privilege of meeting his mother. I don't recall precisely the events that led to my meeting his father for the first time, but I do recollect him being funny and cracking jokes. His father was generally friendly in nature and at the same time often a little intoxicated. Tevita had briefed me that his father loved his beer and a little bit too much sometimes.

Returning to SSQ, we had grown fonder of each other. I remember the first time he came and slept in my room. He had gone to drink kava with some other students that evening and returned around 1 o'clock in the morning. His distinct drumbeat on the door gave away that it was him. I jumped in excitement from my sleep as it had been hours since I last saw him that day. Deeply asleep, I was still expecting that knock. He seemed a bit groggy and asked for some space on the floor. My heart was pounding with butterflies going wild inside me when I offered him the only pillow I owned. He, however, kindly declined. I noticed him remove his silver-banded wristwatch before he got himself comfortable on the Fijian mat on the floor. One thing I learnt about my future husband that day, was that he never slept with his watch on his hand, no matter the circumstances or setting.

I lay there on my bed staring down at him sleeping peacefully on the floor. It was a wonderful, peaceful sight. I had never had such a charming individual sleep gracefully on my floor – so delightful to watch – as I did that early morning. I gazed at him, taking all that scenery in until I myself fell off to sleep.

Each day, after that, we kept falling madly and more deeply in love with each other. Each minute away from him seemed like hours. Hours felt like days, and whenever we were together we would spend hours and hours on end together in my room.

On one funny occasion, we had left the door closed but unlocked and were both seated on my bed holding hands. By now it was not uncommon for the other boys to stop by my room, eye my cupboard first for food, then ask for whatever they had seen. I couldn't say I didn't have any noodles or tinned tuna, as they would say, 'Then what's that in your cupboard?' while pointing at it. On one occasion, Taraiasi, nicknamed Tarz, had walked past my room and noticed that I had left my door ajar, not knowing that I was inside. He slowly pushed the door open, only to find us staring right back at him with 'what are you doing?' looks. He looked down at our hands and saw Tevita's holding mine, then he embarrassingly yelled, 'Get a room guys!'

We both raised our eyebrows, looked at each other and burst out laughing. 'No, you get a room,' was our reply. Tarz then slowly walked away, giggling to himself. From then on we would always greet Tarz with the teasing remark, 'Get a room.'

We would occasionally go out for dinner whenever we could afford it and sometimes a movie date. The best part about going to a movie was that it was all the way in Lautoka, and that was quite a long drive away. I would normally fall asleep on his shoulder on the way back. In those first few months, I even met a few of his cousins and relatives. They were all very kind and caring people. One thing that stood out to me was how he adored his little nieces and nephews. I loved how they would run to him screaming, 'Momo Pei! Momo Pei!' as if they had not seen him in years. He would lift and carry the little ones while the rest would follow him around. They loved and adored him dearly and from my observations, I knew that he was going to be a great father. But I was yet to introduce him to a family member from my side.

The first person I introduced him to was the one that I was the closest with – my dear sister Luseane Annie, who I lost to breast cancer in 2013. We were a good few years apart in age and had two other siblings between us, but we shared a special sisterly bond. I had only mentioned Tevita to her over the phone, just before meeting him for the first time on a double-date. She showed me a photo of her boyfriend on one of my weekend visits to her and I showed her a photo of my Tevita. We sat there giggling to ourselves, while comparing and inspecting one another's boyfriends. She told me that her boyfriend was in the army at the time and held a responsible position in the Fiji military. I saw her face light up with excitement when she was telling me about him, but then after a while she said, 'We had a big fight last night and I chased him out of the house. He called this morning to say sorry, but I just swore at him, told him to come and take his uniform away,' she continued.

I knew my sister well and just burst out laughing. 'Oh, you're such a liar,' I accused. 'You're just using the uniform as an excuse, you miss him and want him to come home,' I laughed, teasing her. We loved spoiling and teasing each other just to have a good laugh out of it.

One thing I loved about her was the uniquely honest and loving personality she possessed. You will know she is mad because half the words coming out of her mouth are swear words, which I always found funny. Annie always wanted what was best for everyone. She was a genuine, good friend and sister.

Her boyfriend later went on tour in the Solomon Islands during the crisis. A few months later he returned and we had a huge feast at one of the restaurants in Nadi. That was the first of many double-dates we shared, and we ended that night dancing in a bar inside the Mocambo Hotel now known as Novotel.

Flying School, on the other hand, was on a roll. We immediately became study buddies and didn't mind the long hours, since we had each other for company. We helped each other out in whatever way we could and would celebrate together whenever one of us passed an exam.

As the days flew by, as they do when you're having fun, I learnt more about flying and also about Tevita. He was a true loyal friend not only to me, but also to his friends and cousins. I got a bit jealous over his cousin Seru at one point, as he was always taking Tevita out and away from me. I could not stand to be away from him for too long, for he had become like the air I breathed and survived on. I felt like I was suffocating whenever he was away from me for too long. I wondered if that was a normal part of falling in love or if it was just me?

One day I decided to put my foot down and tell him exactly how I felt and that I didn't want him to go. Seru turned up with a few boys that afternoon and managed to get Tevita all psyched up and excited to go for a few drinks. I surprised myself and firmly said to Tevita, 'No, I don't want you to go.' He was shocked, and so was I, as he wasn't expecting that from me at all. I missed him every time he would go, but I didn't know how to tell him without embarrassing myself. So, I just plainly told him that I didn't want him to go. He ended up sacrificing a good fun time with his cousin and friends to be with me. That very act stood out to me and I was gratefully impressed. He cared about my feelings. For a while there I thought Seru was more important to him than me. Oh, they were inseparable and close too, but I wanted to be the closest one to Tevita.

In later years we all became close friends. Tevita later told me about how he felt that day. It was the first time he had ever been told by a girl not to go with his friends when he wanted to badly. He admitted he was infuriated by it, but this eventually melted away after seeing the smile on my face. 'It was all worth it,' he said. He knew then what it felt like to sacrifice his time with his friends for the happiness of the one he loved. It wasn't easy that first time but he got used to it. 'To me that is pure love, to sacrifice your own happiness for someone else's,' he later shared with me.

For the next twelve years of our lives together, he continued to love and adore me. Despite all my shortfalls and many imperfections, he never once loved me any less. He was my one true love. He taught me what love was. It was through him I got to experience God's unconditional love, God's unwavering love.

I got to meet his mother several more times. One day, she excitedly told him over the phone that she had made some calls to Vatulele Island. The ladies there are well-known for making fine masi (tapa cloth) with their unique prints. When Tevita curiously asked what the call was for, she responded with a firm reply. 'Where else do you think that relationship is heading?'

His dear mother had gone two steps ahead of us and ordered masi for our wedding before Tevita had even proposed.

We were a happy couple. We were young lovers. We were partners and the best of friends. Yes, we were Bogi and Te.

5

I'm Pregnant

It's not what we have in life but who we have in our life that matters.

ANON

'You are going to be my wife,' Tevita whispered softly as I lay in his arms one night.

We had fallen so deeply in love within the first six months of dating.

The determination in his soft, deep voice was so evident that it somehow ignited a spark of strength and courage within me. I lay there speechless while blushing in the dark of night.

That was the closest attempt at a proposal he ever made. He never asked the celebrated, 'Will you marry me?' question. Instead he answered the rhetorical question on my behalf, as if implying he knew the desires of my heart towards him. Years later our kids would see people proposing in movies and would ask me just how their father had proposed to me.

'Na, how did Ta propose to you?' they'd ask with a gleam in their innocent eyes, expecting a grand fairy tale version of how it unfolded, just like in children's stories.

At first, I could not find a single suitable explanation or answer to their question and would simply delegate the task of explaining to their dad by replying, 'Ask your father please.'

When they did, he would bluntly tell them, 'Oh you know, we Fijians don't do that kind of marriage proposal.' At that, I would look at him and smile and he would cheekily smile back with his famous double-wink.

It was obvious that he did not want to wait around and waste time at the beginning of our relationship. I was hearing things again that I thought were a bit too early to hear in the first six months of our relationship. Since this was my first real relationship, I had no yardstick to measure by, and most times, in total contrast to Tevita, it was a learning curve and journey of discovery for me. I wondered why he was not taking things slowly; it was as if he knew time was not on his side. Sometimes I look back now and wonder if something in him had known his days were drastically numbered.

During those six months, we were so head over heels in love that we would even talk about how many children we planned on having. I wanted a big family with a lot of kids, so I told him I wanted seven. It's interesting how this was a special number in my father's family, and became even more meaningful after his passing as our first love song, just released, was fittingly entitled 'Seven'. He, on the other hand, wanted three. He grew up in a family of three, and naturally thought that was a perfect number to manage and raise. All this time I was cautious, however, and there was something in me still questioning the genuineness of all he was saying to me.

'You are going to be my wife,' resounded his words of affirmation as we lay there one night.

What does he mean by that? Does that mean that he really loves me? Does he want to marry me? Among these uncertainties, I'd ask myself, What is love and what do I know about love? I was only nineteen, and as a teenager, I still had all these questions running through my head. He was my very first serious boyfriend, the first person I was exploring love and diving deep into a relationship with. I had a lot to learn and a lot to learn fast. In the midst of this, I feared one thing, and one thing only: that he might just break my heart. I had seen it so many times with my friends and close family. Guys just up and left for no apparent reason, claiming to have loved them, yet just when things looked promising, would turn around and dump them for someone else. My greatest fear was getting my heart broken, and feeling intense and unimaginable pain after I had plunged so deeply head over heels for Tevita. Eventually, I slowly learnt that he was indeed different in his unique way. He was kind, considerate, and honest; very understanding, patient, and full of respect for me. He was a gentleman with a big, kind heart. Sometimes, in my opinion, too nice, and too kind, which was the reason for our first fight.

We were young and joined friends who were in a club in Namaka Nadi. From memory, there was a girl whom he knew from their church youth days in Suva. What an odd place to run into another church member, I thought, but quickly brushed the thought aside, thinking we were young and were just out having fun. She asked if they could dance, and as boldly and as calmly as I could, I said yes, pretending that I didn't care. Inside, however, a bubbling cocktail of emotions was rising. I was not ready to see my man dance with another girl and felt a pang of jealousy. All was tolerable and contained within me, until I caught a glimpse of them through the dense crowd having fun, laughing and dancing to the happy beat of the song.

'Why on earth is she holding his hands?' I asked myself.

I was hurt and angered, yet Tevita seemed not to have a care in the world as he continued to dance away. It felt like a volcano of anger was starting to boil inside of me, waiting to explode. I was sober, as I never liked the taste of beer, and simply went out for my love of dance.

We returned to stay the night in his room. Tevita had moved back into SSQ at that time and I had moved out, staying with a cousin who worked as a traffic controller. When we reached his room, the feelings of jealousy and anger boiled over inside me. I was fuming with anger at Tevita because of a girl I didn't know and some stupid dance moves. I hated what I was feeling, and I feared that I was turning out to be the kind of jealous girlfriend I never wanted to be. If that girl's intention was to make me jealous, it sure did work. I finally exploded in a yell as soon as the door closed behind me.

'What kind of dancing was that? And holding hands? What the hell?' I screamed.

I was determined to walk away from our relationship that night merely because I was afraid of the kind of person I would turn into if I continued. I saw a little bit of what I loathed that night, a jealous version of me and I despised it. I had imagined how awful life would be if it was filled with insecurity and jealousy. I wanted to be secure in love and happiness. In that instant, without thinking it through, I yelled, 'I cannot continue like this. This is it. I'm leaving.' And with that I headed for the door.

In shock, he caught me off guard when he jumped in front of me and the door. He pushed the door shut and turned his back to it, to face me. I had never seen him so serious like that, and I'm sure he was shocked to see the crazy, mad version of me for the first time too.

'You're not going anywhere,' he ordered.

That angered me even more. Who did he think he was? I thought. 'Let me go,' I demanded.

'No!' He shook his head. 'You will thank me later,' came his reply.

I continued yelling and screaming nonsensical words at him. I was still mad and had even thrown some girly punches at him while demanding he open the door. 'Let me out! Let me out!' I demanded.

Instead of opening the door for me, he caught both my hands, which were throwing punches at him, and tried to calm me down by pinning them. He looked straight into my eyes and with his voice trembling and serious, he said, 'If you go, I might as well die. What is the point of me living if there is no you in my life?'

Oh, those words were like a scalpel cutting into my anger. They immediately calmed the wrathful storm that was raging inside of me, miraculously replacing it with peace again. I saw truth, honesty, and pure love in his eyes, as I knew that he meant every word he said.

I am one person who cannot bear arguments. I'd normally freeze and no words would come out. I always found it easier to walk away and cool off before resolving conflicts. One can say I did my fair share of walking out to calm me down, during those early years of our relationship. This came at a testing time of reshaping one's habits and personality to cater for the other special half. As I discovered, Tevita was more into confronting problems and dealing with them right then and there. Talk it out, solve it, forget it, and carry on happily, he would reason.

Over the years of being married, we continued to learn more about each other and from each other. One vital lesson he shared with me that helped to keep our relationship strong, was how one must dig deep within, and find love when at one's angriest self, either with a spouse or the one we love. To humble ourselves and be the first to apologise even when one thinks they're right. He was wise, mature, and responsible, and I learnt to be confident that I was in good hands.

I was deeply in love with Tevita but very naive about birth control. We were in love, and discovering love without taking precautions. Six months into our dating I found myself worrying for a few days, as I was late with my period. I would normally be two or three days late but never by a week. So that scared the daylights out of me. Eventually, I decided to take a pregnancy test.

The first one came out positive. Oh no! I thought, My father will kill me! On second thought, my mother would kill me first. I was frantic. I did not want to believe it, so I went and bought another one just in case the first one was wrong. It still came out positive and it was confirmed: I was pregnant. I immediately saw my future as a pilot slowly slipping away before my eyes. Oh Lord! What have I done? I imagined the very worst that could happen … a good bashing from my mother, then from my father. Tevita would probably dump me and then I'd have to face all the sarcastic comments of wasting my parents' money, for getting pregnant way too young, and being an embarrassment to my family. With all that running through my mind and with the thought of a human being forming inside of me, I was terrified to the core. I was not ready for a drastic change like that, and to be responsible for another human being!

I was even scared to tell Tevita, but deep down I knew I had to. Ironically, I broke the news to him in the Pacific Flying School tearoom where we first met. For a long time, I wondered why he never seemed shocked or surprised when I broke the news to him. In contrast, he was cool, calm and collected, while I was completely terrified, and confused about what to do. It was only after we got married that he finally told me how happy he was when I broke the news to him. I had no idea that Tevita had secretly been meaning to get me pregnant. He had made a conscious decision to get me pregnant way before I had any clue. He sat there with inexplicable joy, while I poured out all my agonising worries to him.

'My father will send me back to the village now for sure,' I gasped. Meanwhile, Tevita was screaming in his head, Yessss! She is all mine now.

That afternoon I returned to SSQ and confided to a mutually concerned friend of mine, who suggested that I should abort the baby. I was petrified, so at that point, abortion sounded like the best solution. I headed to the doctor with this friend of mine. I became even more terrified when I heard about how they were going to scrape the foetus out of me, if we left it for too long. With my worry and confusion, it was a blessing in disguise that when we arrived at the doctors that day I was short a few dollars and could not proceed with aborting the baby. Looking back, it was a decision I would have regretted terribly. I told Tevita my decision, that I was going to abort the baby and I then noticed the same sad look I saw when I turned him down. It was obvious that he was not happy with my decision, but he still respected it.

That same day I sought advice from another friend with a totally different opinion and perspective on my situation. I am so glad I went to see her, because she knocked some good sense into me and gave me some very good and hopeful advice.

'What's done is done, Bogi. Don't abort that baby. If you do, you will regret it for the rest of your life. Your parents will only be upset with you for a little while, but not forever.' That was one of the best pieces of advice I ever received from a friend regarding my situation of falling pregnant too young. She was absolutely right.

Melaia, our firstborn, was a true blessing. She was such a sweet little cute baby and has now grown into a beautiful young girl with a caring, loving heart just like her father. I never regretted keeping her, nor having her in my life.

The first person in my family that I broke the news to was my sister Luseane Anne. As my big sister, she was always protective of me, in her own loving and caring way. She was honest at heart and her ways would sometimes involve swearing too. She was also someone that I looked up to, someone I could comfortably share anything and everything with, without any worries of being judged. I remember that it was late one afternoon when everyone had left the SSQ that I decided to call her.

'Anne, there's something I need to tell you,' I whispered over the phone.

'What is it? Is it good news or bad news?' she immediately asked, getting closer to the phone in excitement and anticipation.

'I don't know,' I started to whisper before blurting out, 'I'm pregnant.'

'*****jinanaaaaaaa*,' she yelled (a nasty Fijian swearword). She was not expecting that at all, hence the obscene response I got from her. 'Don't you dare abort that baby,' came her stern command.

I did not have to tell her much, for she knew me too well, and gathered that I was scared. Being the loving big sister Anne was, she reassured me that all would be okay. Now came the difficult part of breaking the news to our parents.

Tevita was sure that his parents were not going to have any problem with it. In fact he was confident they would be happy, if not thrilled, with the news. I, on the other hand, was certain the world would come to an end the minute I told mine. We decided that we were going to tell them in person, but first his parents and then mine.

Strangely it didn't go quite as we planned with his parents. His mother found out over the phone, after asking a few concerned questions. I was a few weeks into my first trimester and was throwing up most of the time. I would give excuses and avoided going to Suva for weekends or to family functions. My mother would call and I would tell her that I had to fly, study for an exam, or was unwell. Giving all sorts of excuses was how I progressed through my first trimester of pregnancy. Tevita's mother, on the other hand, a nursing matron at the Colonial War Memorial Hospital in Suva at the time, immediately suspected something was up when Tevita told her on the phone that I was sick and throwing up.

'Pass her the phone, let me talk to her,' she insisted. 'Bogi, have you been throwing up?'

'Yes,' I whispered over the phone.

'Have you had your period this month?' she hastily asked.

'Ummm, no,' I shyly replied.

'So, you're pregnant, *matavasese*,' she yelled, and I recognised her excitement over the phone. *Matavasese* was one of her favourite teasing phrases, translated as 'clown-face' in English. The next thing she said after that was, 'Don't you try to do anything to that baby.' It sounded as if she suspected that I had thought about aborting the baby. To hear that from her was huge reassurance that I was doing the right thing in choosing to keep the baby. A load was now off our shoulders, like a tonne of bricks, but the big one was yet to come once we got around to telling my parents.

Three months passed and I somehow managed to hide my pregnancy from my parents, relatives and the school. In those three months, I continued my studies and flying. Luckily for me I was only doing flights on a flight trainer that simulated flight conditions, on the ground. It was easier for me to just excuse myself to the bathroom whenever I had the urge to throw up. I watched as my little belly slowly start to grow to a point where I could not button or zip my uniform trousers. I eventually ended up going to school with my shirt untucked.

By December 2004 I was already three months pregnant and Christmas was fast approaching. Our Christmases from when I was little were always spent with our family in the village. I knew I would have to break the news one way or another. Luckily my mother was already in Suva, and I was due to travel with her to the village where my father was, and arrive just before Christmas. That lightened the load for us, as we thought it would be a good idea to let my mother know first, then she could help with breaking the news to my father. From memory, I think it was a Tuesday night in Suva, two days before our flight to the village and three days before Christmas. Tevita and I had gone to a movie that afternoon before returning to his place where we enjoyed a delicious dinner prepared by his mother. Tevita then proudly informed her that he was going to tell my mother on my behalf that I was pregnant.

Knowing full well how my mother would react, I had told Tevita that there was no way I was telling her alone that I was pregnant. He took it like a man and said, 'Don't you worry, that's my job. I will tell her.' That night he insisted we pick up Suli Ravunikau, who Tevita was very close to at the time, for support, and as he had said it himself, 'Just in case I get chased out of the house at least I have someone with me to witness the occasion.'

We got to our house and were eager to get it over and done with – we had been putting it off for months. I called my mother and asked her to take a seat as Tevita had something to tell her. In our Fijian way of respect, Tevita was already seated on the mat not far from the main door. My mother sat down on the other side of the living room facing

Tevita while I made sure there was some good space between me and her, just in case she pounced. I imagined and was anticipating that she would go ballistic and go into kung fu mode on me. Suli was a bit shy about joining us in the house, so he waited outside on the porch. I made sure the door was left open, so if I needed to, I could run for the door. After she was seated, Tevita did not want to waste any more time. I sat there fearing what my mother's reaction would be, but at the same time in full admiration of how Tevita was man and brave enough to come and face my mother as he did.

Being the considerate, well-mannered person he was, he eloquently addressed my mother with full respect before breaking the news. 'Galuoko's mum, I am here to kindly inform you that Galuoko is pregnant.'

I remember having my head bent, anticipating the worse to come. There was about a minute of silence, which seemed to stretch forever. I heard a soft voice almost like an echo breaking the stillness. 'Galuoko, is that true?' she stammered.

I looked up and our eyes met; instantly I saw that she had tears in her eyes. I was sorry and I felt deep sadness, and with my head lowered I slowly nodded and answered, 'Yes, I am pregnant.'

That affirmation brought her to tears again, and she broke down and softly cried. Her baby was now expecting a baby. We sat and waited patiently while she cried, her heart in pain and despair. Moments later she finally spoke, after wiping the tears from her eyes.

'Well, there is nothing we can do now,' she concluded. 'What's happened has happened, and there is no point saying things that won't change anything. We will just have to accept this.'

My mother only calls me Pei, unless she has something serious to tell me, or worse, and when I am in trouble, she calls me Galuoko. I never dreamed that my mother would be in tears after hearing that news. The only way I had imagined my mother would react was by chasing both Tevita and I out with a broom, with Suli if he was still on the porch. Who is this lady? I wondered. I had witnessed and heard stories of how she belted up my older sisters and cousins for getting into trouble with boys. That, I believe, was common in our Pacific Islander way. I honestly had anticipated the same thing would happen to me.

It was only after Tevita passed on, that my mother opened up and told me that it was the way Tevita had presented himself that brought her to tears that night. She saw someone full of respect for others, for himself, and for her daughter. She saw a real gentleman who was brave and man enough to tell her in person that he had gotten her daughter pregnant. He managed to calm the storm in my mother by simply being the gentleman that he was.

After a few minutes of talking, I noticed that something was now troubling my mother. I knew her well enough to guess it was my father. She turned to Tevita and said, 'Now you will need to tell Galuoko's father.' I could see Tevita did not give it a second thought. He was determined to go as far as flying to Cicia, to face my father, like a man. That melted my heart even more. It was a huge relief for my mother, when he agreed to go with us to the village.

The next morning I got a call from his mother. 'Tevita wants to go with you to Cicia to tell your father in person that you're pregnant.' She sounded overly concerned. 'I'm sorry, we told him there's no way that we're going to let him go alone. I don't know what he was thinking. As all your brothers are there we are afraid he may be setting himself up for a trap.'

That thought had never crossed my mind, as my brothers were not those types. They respected guys who respected their sisters. I guess a concerned parent would normally be worried about their son's safety, especially in situations like this. His mother then assured me that Tevita would not be going with us, but that they would honour the proper traditional Fijian way of announcing he would take care of me and our baby. This was customarily done by a man being accompanied by his father's people to present a whale's tooth, known as a *tabua,* to the father of the woman he loved. This was a dowry signifying his acceptance of responsibility that came with their decision to be together as a couple. The more *tabua*s were offered, the better his chance of approval as it represented both the wealth of his family and the greater his love for the woman.

We arrived at Cicia airport around midday the next day with my father waiting to pick us up. That night and the following one I kept running outside the house to vomit. For the first time, Tevita was not there to massage my back, like he had been doing for the previous three months. I was alone, throwing up quietly behind our house, fearing that my father might hear. Saturday, which was Christmas Day, the festivities finally came around and everyone was busy preparing food.

Around 9 o'clock in the morning, as I was getting ready to join the rest of the family for church, my mother called me and said, 'You stay back, we will tell your father today.' I had never been so scared in my life as I felt that day. All different kinds of emotions combined suddenly to engulf me. I was utterly in fear of my strict father and at the same time saddened for letting him down. I found myself continually trying to catch my breath, talking to myself, saying, Just get it over and done with, Galuoko.

My father's routine on a Sunday or any other church day was to lie in bed listening to church sermons on the radio. He had his own reasons and preferred that to the rituals of going to church. Finally, the moment had arrived; I found myself walking towards their room behind my mother with my head bent.

A Fijian man's deep voice echoed in the room as we walked in. I saw him lying face up, with his eyes closed and his small radio beside him. He was intently listening to the man preaching on the radio, so he did not hear us walk in.

Our brown wooden house was up on a hill with a nice ocean view from their master bedroom. They had an extra main door in their bedroom facing the sea that he normally liked to leave open for a nice cool breeze. We walked in from the sitting room and I sat myself on their room's doormat – to my right was the foot of their bed. I could hear myself trying to calm down as I panicked, and my heartbeat increased as if trying to escape my caged ribs. My mother took a few steps further and sat right next to the other door but facing the bed. In her soft voice, she called out to my father.

'Drani,' she called. 'Drani, please, we have something to tell you.'

My father turned and saw us both seated on the floor – he must have known in that instant that we were about to break some serious news to him. He turned his radio off and I watched as he slowly sat up, and rested both his hands on the bed before looking back to my mother.

'Yes?' he asked.

'It's Galuoko,' my mother continued. The fact that she said my whole name instead of my pet name confirmed to him that the matter was serious.

'What about her?' my father asked.

In the softest, most humble tone I've ever heard my mother use, she downheartedly replied, 'She is pregnant.'

At that very moment, my breath was right up to my throat – I was parched, too scared to even look up, let alone speak. I did not hear a single word in reply, but his heavy footsteps now echoed in the room, which made it even worse. I could not help myself and looked up to check where he was going. I thought he was coming to belt me.

Instead, he went straight to the door facing the ocean. I looked on as he gazed out with both of his hands braced on the doorway as if to help him stand, as the disturbing news he was just given slowly settled in.

In my head, I was prepared and anticipating a good telling-off from him, but to my utter surprise, my mother got all of it. It's funny, looking back, as she did nothing, but she got the hard blow of my father's reaction to my pregnancy.

My father spent most of his time in the village and hardly travelled to Suva, so it was my mother who was always going back and forth to check up on us. In my father's eyes, she failed in watching over that part of my life as a young girl. A careless mistake? A mother's failure? Whatever you wish to call it, eventually something beautiful came out of it – our beautiful firstborn, Melaia Tubuna Secivo.

We listened, as to our surprise he continued, 'I knew she was pregnant the moment I saw her stepping out of the plane.'

That was a total surprise for me; he knew all along? But I never suspected, from how he had gently spoken to me at the airport and over the previous two days, that he knew.

'I was just waiting for the two of you to come and tell me,' he continued. Then he finally turned and asked me in his most serious, concerned tone, 'Will this guy marry you?'

'Yes,' I gently, yet firmly replied.

'He'd better!' my father warned.

That tone alone made me feel like Tevita would be in real big trouble if he decided against marrying me. I later relayed my father's warning to Tevita, which he just laughed off, telling me, 'I was going to happily marry you anyway.'

All through my pregnancy, Tevita never failed to be by my side when I needed him. From constantly running out to empty my bucket when I puked, to walking to buy potato chips for me in the middle of the night during my cravings. Tevita would iron my clothes, cook, and massage my aching body as my pregnancy progressed. A sweet, caring and loving father he was, from the moment he knew he was going to be a father.

The brave man that he was and the lives he touched are reasons enough to miss him dearly every single day. Yet I celebrate how beautifully different life's course has been, despite falling pregnant as a teenager, simply because of the beautiful soul my Tevita had.

6

Memories Before PNG

The greater your storm, the brighter your rainbow.

ANON

I fell in love all over again the first time I laid eyes on our firstborn. It is a day forever etched on my heart, including the memory, of course, of the excruciating pain of labour. As my contractions were intensifying at one point, I thought my backbone was shattering into a million pieces. I told myself, never, ever will I go through this again. But the moment I saw her, my heart melted – it was absolutely love at first sight. There she lay, cosy in the blanket that wrapped her, a tiny little being who looked just like her father. She was handed to me to hold for the first time, graduating me to my new status as a mother. Exhausted, but ecstatic, I took her in my arms, and my eyes suddenly welled up with tears of joy. For the first time, I felt a whole new, different kind of love – a mother's love. I never believed in love at first sight until that very moment. It was a love that made me forget all about the pain that I had just endured and made it all worthwhile.

Melaia Tubuna Secivo was born just after midnight on the 12th of June 2005. She weighed 3.3kg and was named after my mother-in-law, who was just excited as we were. A few hours had passed when

I introduced Tevita to our daughter, who was now fast asleep. She instantly became our new love. He simply could not stop smiling the whole time he held her in his arms. The first thing he did after putting her down was count her fingers and toes. As a first-time father he had been worried that she might have been born different.

We spent the following month together at my parents' place in Suva before Tevita returned to finish his studies in Nadi. I missed him the whole time, and he would visit us whenever he could.

I recall one early morning at about 3 o'clock after our newborn and I had moved back to his parents' house. I woke up to find a figure of a man standing in front of our bedroom door. I was just about to scream out for help when I finally realised who it was. Tevita had come to surprise us, which he did. I had to pinch him several times to make sure he was not a ghost.

Melaia was our little pride and joy and I loved every second of every minute with her. She was growing up fast and days turned quickly into weeks and months. I was dreading the day that I would have to return to the flying school, as I felt my heart torn in two. She was three months old when I went to join Tevita back in Nadi, and her grandparents took over the joy of looking after her. They adored and loved her, leaving me with the peace of knowing she was in very good hands. For three months, my life had revolved around her and she was my world, but now I had to leave her, which was my first real test as a mother.

All was well on my first day back in Nadi, until I tried going to sleep that night. I missed her so much that I literally cried like a baby, sniffing and sobbing. I couldn't sleep a wink and poor Tevita had to take me for a walk to cheer me up and wear me out enough so I could finally get some sleep. It was the same for the following few nights before I got a little used to the separation from my baby. At six months old, we had her over at SSQ for one week. As this was the only boarding option available to students, we still resided there. It was not much of a big space for a small family, but we loved it. To us, we were together, and that was all that mattered. We took turns looking after her when one had to go to school. She was always up early, so we would take her for a walk. We would stand and show her planes taking off and landing, and she loved it.

Her first birthday celebration had all our relatives gathered together for a wonderful feast. She was dressed in traditional Fijian attire by my side of the family, as is the custom, and presented to Tevita's relatives. She wore a beautiful garland but cried the whole time she had it on. There was a lot of delicious food and laughter all around with happy vibes from friends and loved ones. It was a memorable time indeed for us, which we thoroughly enjoyed. We finally went home that night with a lot of gifts to open for Melaia. It was obvious that she was tired and exhausted, but she did not want to rest until she had checked all her presents. One thing I noticed was that she enjoyed other kids' company and seemed lonely as soon as we got home.

Happily, nine months later, I found out that I was expecting again. Tevita was thrilled that he was going to be a father again. Before Melaia was born, he had picked almost all the baby stuff in blue, hoping that it would be a boy. Now that we were expecting again, he was determined that this time it would be a boy.

March 14th 2007: he had been with me all day at the Nadi hospital while I was having contractions. This time the same thoughts crossed my mind that I would never go through this again and this was definitely my last pregnancy. By ten that night we were both tired out and exhausted. I just wanted the baby out. There was a bench outside the maternity ward where Tevita took a nap. The baby was going to come any time now, so he wanted to be close by when it did. The nurses were very nice and did an incredible job of monitoring the baby and me. I was ready, they were ready, and everyone was prepared except the baby, who decided to take its time. My waters had not even broken yet. I asked one of the nurses to call my husband to come and he walked in just in time for my waters to break. The nurses immediately remarked that maybe the baby was waiting for the father.

The baby arrived a few minutes later and the nurses informed us she was another girl. Tevita proudly took up the offer to cut the umbilical cord. That was a glorious moment of meeting another little human who had both of our looks and features. We named her Olimaipa Sese Atelea Secivo, weighing 3.6kg.

The next morning I told Tevita, 'This is it for us, no more babies. I am done dealing with the labour pain.'

'One more please, a boy,' he pleaded cheekily, with a wink.

I knew that he wanted a son and I just couldn't refuse him. Surprisingly, nine months later I discovered that I was late for my period. We decided to take a pregnancy test, which came out positive. Here we go again, I thought, so much for saying I wouldn't go through the painful process again. Nonetheless, I was enjoying motherhood and raising our two daughters. They just seemed to brighten up our days.

After having two girls, we were desperate that this one be a boy. Tevita would constantly joke to his friends that we wouldn't stop trying until we had a boy. Someone even suggested that we go and see a lady who gave herbal medicine to pregnant mothers to have a baby boy. I was a bit reluctant, but we desperately wanted a boy and went anyway. When we got to her place and she was not there, I said, 'That's a sign. Let's just pray and ask the Lord, our maker, for a son.'

Now I was born into a strong Methodist family, but by that time I had converted to his faith as a Seventh-day Adventist. Tevita would join me on a few occasions in our Methodist church, as deep down I had wanted him to convert to my faith, not the other way around. One thing that stood out to me was that he never forced me to join him, or brought up the subject of converting. He respected my faith as much as he respected his own. I had been observing and had a lot of questions as to why they didn't eat certain foods and why they worshipped on Saturdays. One afternoon my many questions were answered. He had one of his brothers over for a Bible study session at home. His brother was Pastor Epeli Saukuru. Many years later he would be the same brother who would deliver the sermon at his funeral service. The study was mainly for him, but he invited me. Being open-minded I thought, Oh well, I might as well ask all my questions here. I did and was amazed at how all my answers were right there in the Bible. I chose to continue the study for the following weeks and ended up converting. I did not want to rely on the herbal medicine or the lady. If we were to be given a son, I wanted him to be from God and not because I drank some herbal medicine.

A few months later when I was heavily pregnant, we decided to go for a scan for the first time to find out if it was another girl or a boy, to satisfy our curiosity. I recall lying down with 'Tevita standing next to me, both looking at the screen when the doctor asked us, 'How many girls and boys do you have?'

'Two girls,' we answered in unison.

'Any boys?' she asked with her eyes fixated on the black-and-white smudge moving about on the screen.

'No,' we replied as she sensed our disappointment.

She flashed a little smile at us and finally said, 'Well, congratulations, you will be having a son!'

I was so happy I cried and for once looked forward to going through labour, to cradle our son in my arms.

On September 14th 2008, we welcomed our one and only son. He was his father all over again, and Tevita would not leave his side. He watched as the nurse rubbed oil on him before wrapping him in a white blanket. He proudly carried him over to me to be fed, as the doctor and the nurses left the room, and then it was just the three of us. He continued to watch us the whole time and couldn't stop smiling. Our son had finally arrived. We named him after his father Tevita, which is why we call him Yaca (namesake). We had wanted to include a name that would symbolise our love for each other and for him. The Greek word Phileo, which means 'love', stood out for us. We both loved it so we included it. Sovau was from Tevita's cousin, Seru Sovau Saukuru, who shared a close bond with Tevita so he also named our son after Seru. The name Lisala was from Tevita's namesake, his father's younger brother. My husband did not get to use that name himself but used his maternal grandfather's middle name of Tiko instead. To keep his uncle's name, he decided to give it to our son – Tevita Phileo Sovau Lisala Secivo. It was a long name for a small boy but it was significant and we loved it.

The following day we were discharged and the whole routine of nursing a newborn started all over again. My mother took months off from work to come and do everything for me. For one whole month, I had all my meals in bed. All I did was eat, feed the baby and sleep. My weight ballooned and I felt like a gigantic whale.

It was frustrating trying to find clothes that fit when I had to go back to work. I would get discouraged and disheartened every time my clothes wouldn't fit. My husband, being who he was, would say, 'I don't care if you're fat or skinny, it will never change how much I love you.' Even now, I still carry some weight that I piled on during my three pregnancies. It becomes an interesting topic of discussion, each time one of them asks why I have stretch marks on my tummy.

At the time, I was working with Pacific Sun Ltd, and they were kind enough to give me ample time to recover. As my days consisted of me lazing on the bed with my baby and being fed by my mother, I had not been flying for months, and I missed it. Upon return I had to spend a few weeks working in the office first. All my checks had expired and so had my medical. I was obviously overweight and was worried that I was going to fail the medical.

At home, our two girls were happy and proud to have a baby brother. I recall one day we were all in the living room, while baby Yaca was asleep in his cot in our room. Ipa, who was now aged two, had been playing with her doll, which she called Papa, and somehow misplaced it. I assumed that it was in the room so I asked her to go and get Papa from our bedroom. Everyone in the living room was shocked when she emerged from the passageway carrying her little brother instead of her Papa. I'm still puzzled to this day about how she managed to carry him from the cot without dropping him.

We were one month away from Yaca's first birthday when sadly Tevita's mother, my mother-in-law, tragically passed away. They had just moved in to live with us a few months earlier, after she fell ill. She was a strikingly beautiful woman and had the most loving and kind heart just like Tevita. I easily saw whom Tevita got his elegance and neatness from. His mother would not step out of the house dressed just any way. She always dressed up exquisitely, neat and stunning. Her hair was always tidy, and her sweet scent would turn heads when she walked past. She loved to cook, so most of the time she would refuse to let me cook or even wash the dishes occasionally. She was a very good cook and that saved me some embarrassment since I was the opposite. She would take me shopping and buy special things I would not dream of buying for myself. I always felt a bit spoilt, and I guess she was treating me like the daughter she never had. She would tell me stories of her young days, how she met Tevita's father, their fights and we would have a good laugh about them. She was a more loving mother-in-law than anyone could ever ask for. I am glad for all the memories I shared with her and miss her dearly to this day. The kids do too, especially her namesake Mela, who would remark at times, 'I miss Nau Mela and her cooking.'

Just a few months back Yaca begged me to tell him more about his grandmother. Their little minds remember the events of her passing. They even recall some parts that I had forgotten. Ipa was telling me how she went with her father to see her at the funeral home, and she couldn't stop crying. She was only two at the time, but she remembered this clearly. I had left for work that morning when she passed away in our home. I remember walking past their room and noticing that it was unusually quiet. She was always up early, but not that morning. I finished work after midday, called home and the house girl answered. The news was then relayed to me, and I was shocked to hear that my dear mother-in-law had left us. I was standing at the domestic check-in desk at the Nadi airport, overcome with grief and shock. I suddenly sat myself down on the floor. The news was still slowly sinking in, and I hated that I had to hear it over the phone. I still could not believe this and I made a few more calls before I finally spoke to her younger sister who confirmed the terrible news. That day my heart sank, and I felt I had just lost my own mother. We had such great support from families, friends, her nursing workmates from the hospital, and our colleagues during her funeral service. She came from a large and loving family, and it was sad to see all her brothers and her sister surrounding her grave weeping for her.

Her absence in the house was greatly felt at home in the following month, and we witnessed how it had taken its toll on my father-in-law. It wasn't easy for him, but he was strong. Tevita grieved in his own way and preferred not to see pictures of his mother from when she had been sick.

We would talk about her every now and then – even during my husband's last few days as he lay in the Port Moresby General Hospital. Despite the cancer, Tevita found comfort in the thought that in the end he would no longer be in pain and would someday be resting close to his dear mother.

We celebrated Yaca's birthday the way his late grandmother would have wanted. She had been looking forward to it being another big celebration with lots of food and presents. One of his aunties baked a really yummy birthday cake for him, and to this day, it remains my favourite.

By Yaca's second birthday, our small family left Fiji for Papua New Guinea. Life before PNG was pretty much family, church, school, and work. We would get ourselves so busy with other things that we often forgot to have quality alone time together.

I remember one Valentine's Day in Fiji, we were both at work and ended up flying together. Tevita was a captain and I was a first officer on the Twin Otter at the time. The company advised that it was best that we did not fly together, for the kids' sake, in case something happened for the worst. But that day, there was no other first officer available but me. Flights would have been cancelled had I refused to fly with my husband. I had the right to refuse to operate the flight, but fortunately for the company, it just so happened it was Valentine's Day. The rebel in me thought, Why not spend the day with my husband and make this a memorable occasion. The day boasted a clear blue sky with hardly any clouds en route. Just perfect for an easy, smooth day of flying. I think we did four sectors of flying that day and managed to keep it at a professional level, with some jokes along the way. Tevita was always professional, committed and a hardworking pilot. I was truly proud of him and for being my captain that day. A day I hold dear to my heart.

Our spiritual growth continued as we did more Bible study. I was baptised into the faith while Tevita went on to preach for a bit. I used to also help out with the Sabbath school classes for little kids. My husband used to love singing in church, and I must say, he had quite a beautiful voice. I never got tired of listening to him sing.

One Sabbath in church, when we had just joined a church that was closer to where we lived, Melaia came running to me yelling something about her late grandmother. 'Nau Mela is alive again!'

I could see the glow on her face as if she had just seen her beloved grandmother again. I was puzzled and asked her what she meant. She turned and pointed to a lady seated across from us. She had the same Fijian hairstyle as her grandmother, was about the same age, and wore similar reading glasses. Mela begged to go and sit with her, and she did for the entire service. We ended up visiting her grandmother's grave after that. It was both sad and heartwarming at the same time.

The kids were growing up quickly, and I loved watching them play. I noticed their different interests and their characters begin to develop. Even before she turned one, I knew that Mela was going to love drawing. She was always seen around the house with a pen in one hand and paper in the other, scribbling. She would even draw on the wall whenever no paper could be found. It was like drawing was a part of her life she couldn't live without. Even to this day, she still loves to draw and does a great job, way better than I could ever do. Ipa, like her father, loves to sing and be in the kitchen baking and eating. Yaca, on the other hand, was into books long before he could even recognise the alphabet. I would find him around the house lying with a book in front of him, pointing and mumbling, obviously imitating how he knew reading was done. His favourites were comic books, and sometimes I would even catch him with my *Women's Weekly* magazines.

To correct and discipline our children, we used the old method of spanking as we were raised with the friendly wooden spoon. The naughty chair for time-out was another and Tevita's brilliant suggestion was one big cup of water for every time they were naughty. He said his mother as a nurse used to do the same when they were younger, and it helped keep them hydrated in the process of being corrected.

It was not easy juggling work and three kids but we had a good helper, Kelera Biu. A tall, slim middle-aged lady from Cicia, where I come from, and who grew up in our village. She was an honest, hard-working lady who had never been married nor had any children of her own. She was just what we were looking for. We organised for her to come over and she flew in from the village. She arrived to stay with us from when Ipa was only two months old until the time we moved to PNG. Our children adored her, and she treated them as if they were her very own. She helped immensely in the house, and with raising the kids. Quite often they would prefer to sleep with her than with us, especially Ipa.

Apart from work, we tried organising family time and loved taking the kids for an afternoon stroll and to the park. I remember one day when Yaca was only one-and-a-half. It was a perfect day for a family picnic, so we decided to take a drive down to a park where we spread our mat under a tree and enjoyed our lunch. Yaca decided to take a little adventure exploring the park, picking up whatever caught his attention. He picked up something that looked suspicious, so his father yelled out to him to throw it away. Instead of throwing it away he threw it straight at his father. It was dog poop! We had a good belly laugh at that and rushed him to have a good thorough hand-wash.

My husband Tevita was a man of his word. He had a lot of respect for others and he always believed that respect must first be earned. He was someone who was always true to himself and very well-mannered, with respect being one of his characteristics that stood out to people who knew him well. Others who got to know him often admired this quality. On the other hand, the opposite was true when someone dared to disrespect or belittle him. This in itself was an intolerable thing to my husband and something he just could not stand it, almost as if a version of the Hulk emerged from him.

One vivid incident was when we were driving into Nadi town one afternoon during peak hour. There were many cars on the road, as well as people walking on the side of the road. An Indo-Fijian middle-aged couple decided to cross the road right when the traffic light turned green for the vehicles to go. Tevita could have bumped into them, if it wasn't for his quick reaction. Instead of apologising, the guy yelled, tapped on the car bonnet and pointed at Tevita as if he was the one at fault. Needless to say, we did not move an inch forward after that. He pulled the handbrake, stepped out of the car, and walked straight at the guy. Next thing I knew I was alone in the car looking out at Tevita yelling at the guy with his finger on the man's forehead. People around were now staring, and I just wanted to shrink and hide. The poor guy was obviously now scared of the enraged Tevita, so he did the right thing and just walked away.

Another similar incident was when Mela and I were sitting in the back of our car. We were just pulling up in front of a supermarket when Mela opened the car door, almost scratching the taxi next to us. She was only four or five at the time, but it was our fault. Tevita didn't see what happened but only heard the taxi driver yelling out to us, 'You fool.' I think Tevita must have thought that it was meant for him. He again pulled the handbrake, got out and before I could even process what was happening or try to explain, Tevita was yelling and screaming at the taxi driver. Again, I wanted to shrink and disappear from embarrassment into thin air.

He returned moments later, and I told him, 'You know it was our fault.'

He replied, 'No, he should have never yelled at my kid like that.'

I admired that he would stand up for things I wouldn't normally stand up for myself. I was also worried that it would get him into trouble one day. It was his temper that played an important role in his seeking a job outside of Fiji, which is eventually how we ended up in PNG.

It was early 2010 when he had just finished a long day at work. Pilots would normally hang around the check-in counter while waiting for their taxi to go home, and chat with the ground staff if they weren't too busy. Another trait of my husband's was that he loved to crack jokes and had one of the loudest soulful laughs to accompany them. That afternoon he came home and told me that he might be losing his job.

When I asked why, he replied, 'It wasn't even a slap.'

While waiting that evening for his taxi, he must have been laughing loudly, and one of the girls at the desk hushed him to be quiet and must have said something else that pissed him off. He continued trying to make his case and said, 'She could have just asked me politely to be quiet and not treated me like some little kid. It was just a tap on the cheek,' he stressed. 'If it was a slap she would have been unconscious.'

According to the lady, it was a slap on the face and she went and complained to her boss who approached our boss. Tevita was told that he would be suspended without pay, while awaiting their final decision on the disciplinary action to take. The following weeks were a big challenge for us, as we had to adjust to living within our means on a single income.

Among other challenges during the time Tevita was suspended, we found out that the second-hand four-wheel-drive vehicle we had just bought had a faulty engine and wouldn't go up a hill. It was practically useless and a waste of our money. The seller really did a good job of deceiving us that it was a great car. We also had one of our two vehicles that were on hire break down, and our house was also broken into.

'There goes our rent money,' I said exasperatedly. 'This is just great! What else is next?' It felt like God was testing us. Now on only one salary, and after all the bills and payments, there was almost nothing left to save. We had to walk for about ten minutes every day, from where we lived at the time, to catch the bus while our second-hand car lay at home, useless. Sometimes we would walk all the way to the closest supermarket, which was about twenty-five minutes away. Four weeks passed, when I woke up early for work one day, only to find out that we had no running water. I do not remember if it was because we had not paid our water bills, but I recall ending up having to wash using two standby bottles of water.

That very afternoon Tevita was called in for a meeting with our bosses for their final decision. We had expected the worst – that they would probably fire him. He returned and informed me that they were going to put him to work for three months on the ramp, which was a huge demotion, and additionally there would be another three months as a first officer. During this struggle, we reassured and kept reminding each other that there would be light at the end of this long, dark, winding, and testing tunnel.

Two dear friends in particular, to whom I feel forever indebted, came and visited us during those days – Kris Mundri and Ului Katia. Tevita never forgot their good, kind gesture of support at the time. Both were real, true friends to him and he really appreciated all they did. At the time, the pilots' union rep, Jerry, was also of tremendous support, arguing that it was unnecessary for Tevita to do three months on the ramp. Such warm hearts have been a blessing to us and for that, we are truly grateful.

During those weeks of being under suspension, jobless, with no pay, my husband was also busy looking for a job online. He had sent his CV to almost all companies that had Twin Otters around the globe. I remember him sending it to companies in Canada, India, Africa and Papua New Guinea. He later apologised to the girl that he had slapped and was back at work in the weeks that followed. From the efforts of the pilots' union rep, he was not put on the ramp but assigned as a first officer on the Twin Otter. He admitted that it was a hard but humbling lesson. A few months later, we finally got to see the light at the end of our tunnel. Tevita received an exciting and promising email from Airlines of PNG where he was offered a very attractive contract.

This marked the beginning of the next phase of our lives in the exciting and renowned land of the unexpected, PNG.

Looking back, of course, we sometimes do not understand or fathom why bad things happen to good people, but from this experience, we do know that at the end of rain and storms, there is always rainbow and sunshine awaiting.

7

Arriving in PNG

Don't be afraid to start over.

It's a brand-new opportunity to rebuild what you truly want.

ANON

One afternoon we were driving back to Nadi from Suva. It was a scenic, relaxing drive passing the villages along the Coral Coast with views of endless coastlines to our left. It was sometime around the end of November 2010, when Tevita received an email from Airlines of PNG, now known as PNG Air. In the email, he was asked if he was still interested in joining the company as a full-time pilot based in PNG. He had applied for a job with this company a few months earlier, and after several follow-ups, had lost all hope of ever receiving a job offer in PNG.

In our excitement we immediately pulled to the side of the road so he could make that call. A few minutes later it was confirmed. He was all smiles and getting excited about his new job offer. We had just over a month from that day before he was to leave for PNG. He flew out in the first week of January 2011 and stopped over in Brisbane before continuing to Port Moresby, PNG. It was the first time that he'd left Fiji, so he was excited. He later told me how much he missed home and us, after just a few minutes into the flight to Brisbane. All the excitement was now gone, and he was homesick. He even said, 'I was never so happy to see Indian people in my life as when I saw them at Brisbane airport. They made me feel like I was still in Fiji. They must have thought I was crazy because I was just smiling at all of them.'

On the other hand, my children and I got home from the airport heavy of heart. I went straight to our room, locked myself inside and cried my eyes out. We had always been together, and he had always been there for me. It was the first time that he left me, made worse by not knowing when I would see him again. I was eagerly awaiting that phone call, to hear his voice telling me that he had reached PNG safely, and he was okay.

The phone call finally came through and I was able to breathe again. For the next few days, he kept updating me with his daily experiences of PNG. The first few nights he told me how he had heard a few gunshots from his room. Later someone broke into one of the other pilot's rooms. He had also met two Fijian families, which was nice. This occurred just before they heard gunshots when they were on their way to a supermarket. Apparently, a fight broke out at a market over a phone and ended with someone being beheaded. While they were on the road, the police got involved, and they had to immediately turn around for their safety and drive back. All this was his orientation to PNG during his initial days. Even though I wasn't there, it sounded so scary that I wanted him to return to Fiji the very next day. A few weeks later he told me that they would be sending him down to Brisbane for a few days and we quickly agreed to meet there.

It was April when I flew to Brisbane from Fiji. That was one of the best weekends ever and I am grateful that I went. After our sweet time together, my husband again departed for PNG, and I returned to Fiji.

We hated being apart. After a few days back in Fiji, Tevita called one day asking me to tell him what my total flying hours were. It never occurred to me what he was doing, until I received an email from Airlines of PNG a couple of days later. I was being offered a job with them as well. He was writing my CV when he called asking for my hours, despite my having told him boldly that I would never fly in PNG. After all the terrifying stories and the number of crashes I had heard about, I was too scared. I told him I would come and be a full-time housewife while he worked. I obviously doubted myself, thinking I did not have what it took to be a pilot in PNG. My loving husband thought otherwise, and believed in me.

The following month in May after four months apart, I was checking in with the kids to take the same flight that Tevita took a few months back. Travelling with three young ones was not easy on my own. I had our five- and three-year-old girls walking in front of me on the plane while I was carrying our two-year-old son, trying to locate our seats. We finally did, just about halfway down the rows of seats, and both my girls ran for the window seat. There were three seats on each side, but there were four of us, so one had to sit on their own on the other side. I managed to talk our eldest daughter Mela into taking that seat and thank God, she agreed. Both Ipa and Yaca raced for the window seat. Ipa beat Yaca to it, and he ended up screaming at the top of his lungs. I turned away just for a few seconds and looked back to witness Yaca biting Ipa's arm. Now I had two young children fighting and screaming on the plane. Yes, we were turning heads, but these two didn't care. A young lady noticed how I was struggling to calm them down, so she offered her iPad to Yaca to play with. What a relief!

There were no other dramas after that, all the way to Brisbane. We got through customs in Brisbane fine and had to spend a night. The kids were a little excited at first and then shocked to see so many white people at the airport. Especially Ipa and Yaca, who would not leave my side. I was pushing a trolley full of suitcases with one hand and carrying a two-year-old with the other, a three-year-old clinging on to me on one side and my five-year-old pushing another trolley full of suitcases on the other side. It was literally a handful.

I thought that it would be easier to take the elevator down to the taxi bay. We all got in fine and it was just the four of us with our two trolleys of suitcases. Then the silver elevator doors slid open. I was the last one to get on so I had to be the first one to push out the trolley with two little kids clinging on to me. I looked over my shoulder and was shocked to see only a little bit of Mela through the elevator door gap before it finally slid shut. 'Oh, my Lord. I'm going to lose my daughter,' I cried in panic. I got paranoid all of a sudden and thought of movies I've seen with kids disappearing in airports and shopping malls. It might sound crazy, but in that few seconds, I was really convinced that she was either going to get lost forever or someone was going to kidnap her. I couldn't run up the escalator, or anywhere for that matter. I was stuck with two kids clinging on to me and a trolley full of suitcases. I could feel my heart beating and starting to palpitate. Then I thought, No, calm down and just wait here. Maybe she will decide not to leave the elevator and will still be in it when it comes down again.

I was still running through all the possible scenarios in my head when the elevator door started to open. It was empty, not a sign of Mela. Oh my! We were at the lowest level, and there was not a soul around. I felt helpless just as a young lady wearing the red Virgin Australia uniform emerged from the hallway. I yelled out to her in a worried and desperate tone, 'Please help me, my daughter went up the elevator alone, and I'm stuck here with my other two.'

It must have been my tone that set her off running up the escalator like wildfire. I watched her red dress disappearing around a corner just in time for the elevator door to open again. There stood a female airport security guard with little Mela beside her. I uttered a huge sigh of relief. 'Thank you, Jesus,' I said. 'I've got my daughter back.'

The next day we finally arrived at Jacksons Airport at around midday. My eyes almost popped out as I saw the long snake-line of people in the customs area. I was still carrying Yaca, just changing from one hand to another with my back just resisting breaking in half. The two girls walked beside me. We must have waited in line for at least half-an-hour before we were finally attended to.

The kids had not seen their father for almost four months – we walked out of the arrival hall pushing our two trolleys and there he was. He was standing in his handsome pilot's uniform, and greeted us with a big smile. He looked so happy to see us, and I was so relieved for my back. I could not wait to hand our son over to him. At first Yaca was a bit reluctant, like he did not recognise his own father, or maybe he was just being shy. I did not blame him, it had been a long time since he last saw his father.

I recall my first reaction when we stepped out of the airport. I looked to my right towards the domestic terminal and there were hundreds of people waiting outside. With all the scary stories I had heard about PNG, it felt like all of them were staring at me. In a shiver, I had goose bumps all over. I looked straight to the other side of the road and saw a big board that said *Welcome.*

This was to be our home together for the following five years. Despite all that we had heard about PNG, we were prepared and happy to face this land of the unexpected, as long as we could be together again as a family. Our little family stepped out of the terminal, excited and ready to explore and experience all that life had to offer us in PNG, but most of all we were eager to make memories.

8

You Have Leukaemia

Cancer is only going to be a chapter in your life, not the whole story.

JOE WASSER

Our little family got busy with our lives and time sped like a plane across the clear blue skies. Soon enough we found ourselves mid-2012, a year that completely changed our lives and one year after moving to PNG.

I do not exactly remember the day, though I recall clearly that it was my day off. It began warm and beautiful, bright and sunny outside. The sun was streaming right into our bedroom with just enough breeze blowing the white window curtains, adding serenity. It was around nine in the morning when Tevita stepped out of the shower with his towel wrapped around his waist. I couldn't help but notice immediately the lines of worry on his face and could tell that he was in a bit of pain. He went straight for the bed and sat down with his head hung low as if his neck could not support the weight anymore. I asked what was wrong and he lifted his hand up and touched his chest. 'My chest hurts,' he replied softly like every word coming out required a lot of effort, and added to his discomfort and pain as he spoke them. I thought, Dear God, he's having a heart attack! What do I do? I panicked and started Googling for symptoms of a heart attack. For a minute there I sounded like a doctor asking question after question. He complained that the pain was intensifying and the look in his eyes confirmed it. It hurt more when he tried to move, so he just sat there stiffly, with fear of aggravating the pain. I was worked up, just wanting to take him immediately to see a doctor, but there was no way I was going to be able to carry him downstairs and into the car alone. He was much bigger than I, not to mention heavier. He was soon feeling tired again with his body begging him just to lie down and rest. I was also disoriented. After about fifteen minutes, he was feeling a little bit better and was able to get himself dressed.

At the time, my husband was working with Hevilift, so I called and explained what had happened and that he would not be able to come to work. I was terrified by what had just happened. This was the first time I experienced something like this, and I remember fighting that terrible gut feeling deep down that something was seriously wrong.

We drove straight to a private hospital about ten minutes away from where we lived. We were soon directed to a doctor who asked him a few questions and went through a routine check-up. I was waiting for the doctor to give me a name or a term to satisfy my curiosity as to what all this was – to explain what my gut feeling was telling me. The doctor had a listen to his heart, took some blood tests, gave him an ECG and later an X-ray. His heart was okay. It was healthy and pumping fine, and they did not find anything wrong with it, which was a relief. I crossed off heart problems and heart attack from my list of concerns. We went home somewhat relieved as our worst fears had not been confirmed. We were asked to return the following day for the blood test results, which I felt deep down would be nothing major.

The doctor sat us down, holding a tiny piece of paper in front of him; paper that would redefine how we saw life from that day on. It was Tevita's blood test results. The doctor reminded us that my husband's heart was perfectly fine from the X-ray and ECG results but he was still puzzled about what could be the the cause of the heartburn and chest pain. 'We have picked up something else that is not related to the heart,' he began cautiously, like he was skilled at breaking down bad news into bite-sized chunks. The doctor put it to us in such a subtle way that everything that he explained to us did not prepare us for the ultimate reality that Tevita could have cancer. He explained that they had detected some abnormal readings in Tevita's white blood cell count (WBCs). It was abnormally high. He continued that the normal number of WBCs in the blood was 4500 to 11,000 white blood cells per microlitre (mcL). Tevita's WBC was 86,000 – way too high. He continued that the results could be indicating other problems, but they were strongly suspecting that it was leukaemia. However, at this stage he could not confirm the diagnosis of leukaemia. He suggested that we take the result to an oncologist who specialised in cancer treatment to confirm it, as soon as possible.

We just so happened to be travelling to Brisbane the following week and decided to see an oncologist while there. The doctor was very straightforward and informative. He confirmed, with a stab to the heart, that Tevita had leukaemia. While we were hoping that it was not that serious, we had walked into the doctor's room with an open mind, and were also prepared for the worst. 'There's good and bad news, which one do you guys want first?' the doctor casually asked in his distinct Australian accent.

I looked at Tevita, and I remember him saying, 'Bad news first, so the good news will make us feel better.'

Then the doctor continued. 'Well, there's a medication for leukaemia but it's bloody expensive. You'll be spending about at least AUD $30,000 a year on it.' We did some quick math, converted it into Fijian dollars, and realised that it was a lot of money. I felt really depressed with the bad news and was lost in my thoughts when he continued, 'The good news is, you're still at a very early stage and as long as you keep taking your medication you'll be fine.'

After realising that we were from Fiji but living in PNG, he gave us an unexpected piece of good news. He informed us that both countries were under a funded program that gave out this exact medication for free. The doctor had told us that the medicine was called Gleevec, and Tevita was to take 400g every day. What a huge relief that was, as if our scales to assess our situation had shifted to almost being relieved that he had leukaemia, since there was free medication for it just like for some other diseases. All in one conversation, we had been taken on a roller-coaster ride of emotions, but with this new information things were put into perspective for us. We left the doctor's room feeling determined we would manage the cancer instead of it controlling us.

We tried to ignore the fact that Tevita now had leukaemia. The doctor had confirmed this and we now knew exactly what was wrong. All we wanted to do was lift our spirits and enjoy the rest of our stay in Brisbane. We gathered some new beautiful memories visiting a few theme parks, families, and friends.

It was not until we got back to PNG that I started to really get worried about his condition. While I remained optimistic, I would find negative thoughts creeping in, reminding me of the uncertainty of our future together. There was the fear of the unknown that I might not get to grow old with him. This led to my search for answers, and I started to do my own research online.

The first thing that I searched for was the lifespan of leukaemia patients. I found reassurance in the knowledge that most of them lived for over five years while taking Gleevec. That was good to know, but I always had that horrifying, worried feeling at the back of my mind, that anything was possible, even the worst.

We also found out the cause of the heartburn he had that morning when we drove to the hospital. It was gastro-oesophageal reflux, a common condition, where the lower oesophageal sphincter is weak or relaxes inappropriately, allowing acidic stomach contents to flow up to the oesophagus, causing heartburn. To prevent the heartburn, he had to avoid eating certain foods. We were lucky enough to have detected the leukaemia at that early stage because of the gastro-oesophageal reflux. Heartburn often comes early in the morning after having a big late dinner the previous night. It would normally last about twenty to thirty minutes before the heartburn pain would subside. I remember a day when it lasted longer, about forty minutes. He complained that his jaw grew a bit numb, which got me worried. I broke down and cried next to him, feeling it was not fair for him to bear this alone and feeling helpless that I could not take his pain away. 'I don't know how I will ever survive if anything ever happens to you. I'm scared Ta. I'm terrified.' It was upsetting not to be able to do anything to ease his pain – we just had to wait.

For the four years of him living with leukaemia, I never saw him worried even a little about it. I admire how he refused to let it dampen his spirits or lose hope in our future together. Instead, he braved the uncertainty of the future and lived his life to the fullest. He trained harder, worked smarter and loved fully from the day the doctor said, 'You have leukaemia.'

9

Flying and Surprises

Let your dreams take flight.

ANON

In my younger years of daydreaming of being a pilot, I never dreamt that one day I would be flying in one of the most dangerous flight environments in the world – Papua New Guinea, the land of the unexpected, as it is famously known to many. I was given a start date and was to attend a ground school for two weeks first. Basically, a revision for me, studying the same aircraft type I had been flying in Fiji – the Twin Otter, a high-winged unpressurised aircraft with two turbine engines and fixed tricycle landing gear. It could carry up to nineteen passengers and is well-known for its short take-off and landing capabilities.

There were ten pilots in my lot: Three Fijians, a few Kiwis, an Aussie, and one South African, and I was the only female. We had a very experienced ground instructor who did a bit of my flying training as well. The two weeks went by quickly, and we were itching to get our hands on the aircraft – to finally experience what flying in PNG was like. We all passed our ground school and decided to hit a club to celebrate.

By then my spiritual life was not at its all-time high and Tevita and I would join friends on many outings. That night Tevita introduced me to a drink (Wild Turkey with Coke) that became my favourite for a while. It was a lovely, fun night, and I enjoyed a lot of dancing with Tevita. He knew I loved to dance and I kept dragging him to the dancefloor. The fun lasted until they closed the club, and it was back to work the following week.

My first flight was as a passenger around the Gulf Province with seven stops along the way then back to Moresby – familiarising myself with the environment, the weather and the company procedures. I went prepared with one big bottle of water to keep myself hydrated. Our first stop was at Kerema, about an hour from Port Moresby. The airstrip was close to the sea, in the middle of a few houses and had a small terminal on the side. We took off a few minutes later and tracked inland towards Sasereme, still further from the highlands. Halfway through the flight and after a few gulps of water, I felt the urge – I needed to pee. Unlike the bigger aircraft, the Twin Otter wasn't equipped with a toilet. So, there was nothing else I could do but hold it until we landed. I remember the Sasereme airstrip was just long red soil stretched across an area with lots of trees. There was a logging camp with a red-roofed house close to the strip that would help us locate it, especially in bad weather. We landed, and I rushed out of the plane to look for a restroom, only to find myself surrounded by thousands of tall trees. We were in the middle of the bush. I needed to relieve myself, but I couldn't find a single house or terminal. I thought of going into the bush but then I was scared that I might run into some wild animals or worse, a snake. That terrified me, and I decided to ask how far it was to the next stop. 'Only a few minutes away, it's not far,' the captain told me. So I decided to wait until the next stop.

We took off and landed twenty minutes later in Balimo. They had a nice long grass airstrip, well-fenced and again, not a sign of any terminal. You can just imagine the look on my face when I glanced around, desperately trying to find even a house I could run to. Why wasn't I told this? I thought. This is so unfair. Obviously it wasn't a problem for the male pilots. They could do it easily anywhere – even on long flights.

I had one captain who couldn't hold it any longer and ended up using a bottle. I had to look away of course so he could do his private business. It's so easy for men. I'm glad that we women are blessed with the ability to endure and hold.

I made it to the next stop, Daru. And finally, a huge terminal was waiting for me with open arms. My first flight and it was quite an experience. I was ready to commence my training.

A few months later, just immediately after lift-off from Daru, I felt someone tapping me on the shoulder. We were at a very crucial part of the flight and I needed to concentrate on flying. A quick glance back; I saw the guy seated in the front row pointing at my bottle of water next to me. He wanted to drink, that could wait. I turned back and continued to fly, but he kept tapping me and I kept ignoring him. Once we were high enough, I handed the control over to the captain and turned to this guy to ask what he wanted. Would you believe it? He wasn't thirsty, he wanted to use my bottle to pee in. No bloody way!

I turned back and ignored him all the way until we landed. He ended up using one of the sick bags and left it under one of the seats. I had to yell at him to come back and collect it.

In Daru, I remember once opening the nose cargo compartment to find a crocodile about half-a-metre long crawling around. Apparently, someone smuggled it in without the proper paperwork and it escaped its box.

We had some really good training captains who had been flying in PNG for years so were very experienced pilots. One of them even had a flight bag that was older than me. They were tough, and they made us work and study hard. I completed my training and gained a whole lot of flying knowledge from them. Flying in PNG on the Twin Otter was exciting, thrilling, and adventurous. However, with its high terrain and rapidly changing weather, it could also be dangerous. We got to operate out of some short, steep, and rugged airstrips that made me a bit edgy. Some had mountains all around or on the side. My first take-off out of Woitape airstrip was 4,900 feet above sea level. I remember it as the roughest take-off I had ever done. There were patches of long thick grass on the runway that made the take-off roll very bumpy. We were almost bouncing down along the runway like a kangaroo, or maybe that's too much exaggeration, but that was how I felt. We had to keep pushing the nose down to make sure we gained the required speed to lift-off safely. A premature take-off would leave us with not enough airspeed to maintain directional control.

Our next stop was only ten minutes away. A very short flight along a winding valley to Tapini, the interior or highlands of the Central Province. Three thousand feet above sea level, it was a one-way take-off and one-way landing airstrip. Getting in could be quite tricky when you had a steep cliff off the end of the runway one would land on.

The cliff on the right had a goat track along the side that we usually used as a guide to position us at the right altitude before turning left to land. The runway was sloping up so we would normally add a bit more power to help us get to the end. Taking off was down the slope in the opposite direction, almost like falling. An immediate right turn is required to avoid the cliff. In good weather, it is a thrilling experience flying along the hills and mountains rising up high above you on both sides. On a shitty weather day, it's a different story. Flying with high mountains around, it is vital to always be aware of where they are, and always have an escape plan when caught between weather and the mountains.

Not far from there was the famous Kokoda airstrip. We did a lot of charters there taking trekkers (majority from Australia) who flew in just to walk the renowned Kokoda track. Getting there is a piece of cake on a fine day, but on a bad day it can be dangerous.

The forever-changing weather and treacherous terrain around the country provided me with some very good skills and experience. Challenging at times but I loved it. We had a few contracts at the time, and one of them was with Porgera Joint Venture – a gold mine located in the Enga Province of Papua New Guinea. The camp was based in Kairak, about 8,000 feet above sea level. Its airport was a little bit further down, with an elevation of 7,280 feet above sea level, roughly 130 kilometres west of Mount Hagen and a thirty-minute flight away on the Twin Otter. We had two Twin Otters based out of Hagen doing shuttles back and forth, bringing workers from Kairak to Hagen where they could catch their flights home. Every day workers were going home for their break. I got sent up to the highlands after attaining the hours required. From memory, we did Friday to Friday. We would get in, have Saturday off, and work from Sunday to Friday, finishing around midday, and catching the flight down to Moresby in the afternoon. We had a four-bedroom crew house in Hagen that accommodated two crews for the two Twin Otters that were based there: two captains and two first officers. It was a house located on its own in a big compound, and with a garden all around. It was homely and had a gate that was never locked and an unarmed security guard/caretaker. So different from the security we had back in Moresby where our guards were armed with machetes, so I felt a little bit unsafe. But I was told that the house was owned by a very famous and respectable man in the area, and no one would dare to disturb us. That was supposed to make me feel safe I guess.

On my first night, when we had all retired to sleep, cold and alone in my room, I decided to watch a movie before going to sleep. Then all of a sudden, there was total darkness. We had a blackout, and I was waiting for the backup generator to kick in but nothing happened. I hoped to hear some of the crew moving about, but nothing. It was like a scene from a horror movie where I was sitting on the bed with the bedsheet almost up to my eyes, peeking out and just staring at the door. A shuffling sound outside my bedroom window almost made me jump to my feet. Oh my God! Someone was outside – the thought terrified me. I was just about to yell out to the rest of the boys when the lights came back on. The power was back so I got up, plugged the iron into the electrical socket and turned it up to maximum. If anything happened, I would use it to defend myself.

I had heard so many crazy stories of the highlands and it probably made me a little paranoid on my first few days. It was extremely cold up there, good for sleeping but not for waking up early at five and trying to have a shower. Thank God there was hot water in the house.

We would normally spend a few nights in Hagen and a few nights in Kairak at the camp where it was much colder. With the regular changing of weather, I remember flying in and out of Kairak as always challenging and exciting. The location of the airstrip required manoeuvring next to high terrain. Sometimes there would be clouds sitting just on top of the runway threshold, making a safe landing impossible. We would hold and wait for it to move, or divert back to Hagen. Just like Tapini, it was also a one-way landing and one-way take-off airstrip with a slope. At the majority of times, we would have to wait for the fog to lift from the runway to allow us to take off or land.

We had another contract with an oil search company that meant spending almost a week based out at their camp in the middle of the bush. Flying often kept us busy, and we always looked forward to going back to civilisation at the end of the week. It was there that I received a call one night from Tevita, telling me that one of our Dash 8 aircraft had crashed near Madang. I was saddened – my heart cried for all the twenty-eight lives that perished on that flight. At the same time, I worried about the chances of that happening to either of us. Tevita was also flying Twin Otters at the time and doing the same things I was doing. The company was very considerate in making sure our rosters would always have one of us at home with the kids.

I recall one day Tevita called me from Hagen and he seemed not to be in his normal lively mood. He was supposed to return to Moresby that day and told me that it had been cancelled so he would fly down the following day. Later that afternoon my phone rang. 'Babe, I'm sorry I didn't tell you earlier.'

'What? What happened?'

'We almost crashed.'

'What?' I asked in disbelief after a few seconds of silence. 'What happened, Ta?'

'We went into clouds below our lowest safe altitude, and the left wing hit a tree.'

'Ta! … What if I had lost you today?' I cried.

He then told me exactly what happened. They only gained visibility just seconds away from hitting a tree right in front of them. Both their hands immediately reached for the power throttle, pushing it forward to max power, and they managed to climb up just in time.

The next day we met and hugged, counting our blessings – thankful for having another day to be in each other's arms again.

In 2013, I was offered a promotion to first officer on the Dash 8. I did the two-week ground school training and spent another two weeks in Melbourne for simulator training. It was winter in Melbourne, and I couldn't wait to get away from the cold weather. Having flown aircraft without autopilot for years, I had a little trust issue with the autopilot when I first selected it on my flight back to Moresby. The plane was bigger, more relaxing, comfortable, and faster, and I enjoyed being served coffee. Oh yes, we also had a restroom right behind us. I never missed the Twin Otter after that, except for the thrilling experience of going into small airstrips around PNG.

In 2015 Tevita resigned from Hevilift and joined me at Airlines of PNG, also as a first officer on the Dash 8. He did his two-week ground school training and left for Melbourne not long after. He happened to have partnered with Iyata on this trip and met up with two other boys from his lot, and you can guess what happened next. They had a big night in his hotel room after their flight test, celebrating their passes. He had to return to Moresby with Iyata the next morning but he ended up passed out on the floor, and they had to pack his suitcase for him. He had bought so much stuff that it could hardly all fit into the suitcase, so one of the boys had to jump on top to zip it closed. Thankfully, Iyata didn't drink much so he dragged Tevita to the hotel bus, checked him in, and made sure he got on the flight.

His next trip to Melbourne, five months later for his base check, was with a different partner. I just had a feeling something was going to happen when he told me he was going to have a few drinks after his flight test. I thought, Okay, Iyata is not there to wake him up and check him in if he decides to have more than a few. I decided to call him the next morning, knowing pretty well that he should already be on his flight home, and his phone would be diverted. I was shocked when I heard it ringing. Just as I thought, he had slept in and had missed his flight. I was fuming. I had been so looking forward to seeing him that day. He finally ended up coming back via Cairns the following day.

There were a few months when our rosters were crazy. We were short of first officers and we ended up flying long hours almost every day. Sometimes we would fly out for overnights and wouldn't see each other until our days off during the weekend. I would return from my overnight and only get to see him at the airport on his way out for his overnight. Work was keeping us apart a lot and we were missing each other terribly. So we would leave love notes around the room for the other person to find. On the bed, the table by the door, and in the bathroom. My favourite was writing *Loving you with all my heart* on the mirror with my lipstick and leaving a kiss next to it. One time he wrote me a message on the mirror too, using my lipstick. I got home and the kids were excited to show it to me. I left it on the mirror for weeks.

Surprises and gifts were things that we both enjoyed. So, we started spoiling each other with gifts to keep the spark going, and we got a little competitive sometimes. I once paid him a surprise visit while he was in Hagen. I tricked him into thinking I was flying that day. I messaged that I had just landed in Daru, which was what he saw on our roster that I would be doing. I asked him what he was doing, and then walked up to him. He looked up, saw me, and he just stood there as if he had just seen a ghost. Then he let out a noise; a burst of excitement and shock. I spent two wonderful nights with him there in Hagen before I returned to Moresby.

My other surprise was on Valentine's Day in 2014, when I made reservations for a romantic dinner for two, booked a room, and bought two tickets to a concert. I packed his bag, hid it in the car with mine, and drove him to the hotel. He never had any clue and I had the pleasure of capturing his reaction on my camera. He was completely surprised. He also spoilt me with gifts but most of the time Ipa would ruin the surprise for me. She would get too excited and spill the secret.

On my twenty-seventh birthday, I had no clue that he had bought me a gift until Ipa excitedly said to me, 'Ta bought you a surprise, and it's something you put on your finger.' I knew straight-away it was a ring.

Four years later would be the last birthday I ever got to celebrate with him. He had organised a surprise birthday dinner in a private room at one of the restaurants in Port Moresby. He had never done anything like this before, and invited my friends. When we went out I was thinking it was just going to be a quiet dinner with only the two of us. I was blown away. He didn't even ask me to dress up and because I was feeling a bit cold I had socks on with my flip-flops.

I bought him a gold chain as a surprise Valentine's gift, with an anchor, a cross and a heart hanging from it. I told him the anchor represented that he was my anchor, the cross was for unconditional love and the heart because he alone had my heart. In return, he bought me the last piece of jewellery he ever gave me – a silver chain with a little cross, and a message engraved on a round piece of silver that reads, *I am with you always*. This was a message that he left behind to give me strength whenever I am feeling down, and to comfort me whenever the loneliness gets too painful to bear.

We always looked forward to our time together during our days off and made sure it was well spent with the kids. We would take the kids out to the park, the movies, a picnic, or swimming during the day, and saved the nights for us. Dinner dates, karaoke with friends, and dancing at the club made up our usual social lifestyle with friends in Moresby. Our days off were often filled with fun activities. Sometimes we would just mix ourselves a few glasses of gin and tonic, lock ourselves in the room and laugh at each other singing karaoke. It was so nice to have grown into a relationship where we didn't just get to be each other's spouses but be crazy best friends too.

We were both doing a lot of flying on the Dash 8, almost maxing out our hours every week. We rarely got to spend an overnight together in one place. On one occasion, we were both rostered for an overnight on the same day, myself in Simberi and Tevita in Rabaul. My route was to stop over in Rabaul on the way to Simberi. We ended up diverting back to Rabaul when we couldn't land in Simberi due to bad weather. I thought, Oh, this will be a perfect surprise for Tevita. On the way I texted him, and he responded that he was in his room. I got to the hotel, asked for his room key from the receptionist and I headed up the stairs to find his room. I carefully turned the doorknob, making sure I wasn't making any sound and slowly pushed the door open. The light was off. But he had just texted that he was in his room. Then to my shocked surprise I noticed his uniform lying on the floor, shirts and socks on the bed as if he had hurriedly undressed for a suspicious purpose. Like a scene from a movie, I was shaking and couldn't believe what I was seeing.

In my fury, I concluded, He lied to me! So, this is what he does on his overnights. I was livid.

I was just about to explode when I noticed the uniform was not of a pilot but a male flight attendant – I had been given the wrong room key. I burst out laughing at myself. There goes my surprise. I had no choice but to call him and ask him for his room number. When I got to his room we had a good laugh about what had just happened.

During our marriage, we refused to let the hectic schedules of work and family keep us from sharing and reminding each other of our deep love as a couple. Surprises, throughout our life of flying, helped spice up our marriage, and were the secret ingredient to keeping our bond strong as husband and wife.

Me with my mum and dad.

The first picture of me in a plane as a pilot student in 2003.
My dreams were coming true!

In 2004, love had found me. Tevita was a passenger on my flight that day.

During one of his many visits to my room in SSQ.

His first lunch at my father's house in the village,
pictured here with Kemueli Naqau.

Our firstborn, Melaia Tubuna Secivo, just turned one.

My late sister Annie, me, and baby Melaia.

Our second-born, Olimaipa Sese Atelea Secivo.
A quick photo with *Ta* (Dad) before he heads off to work.

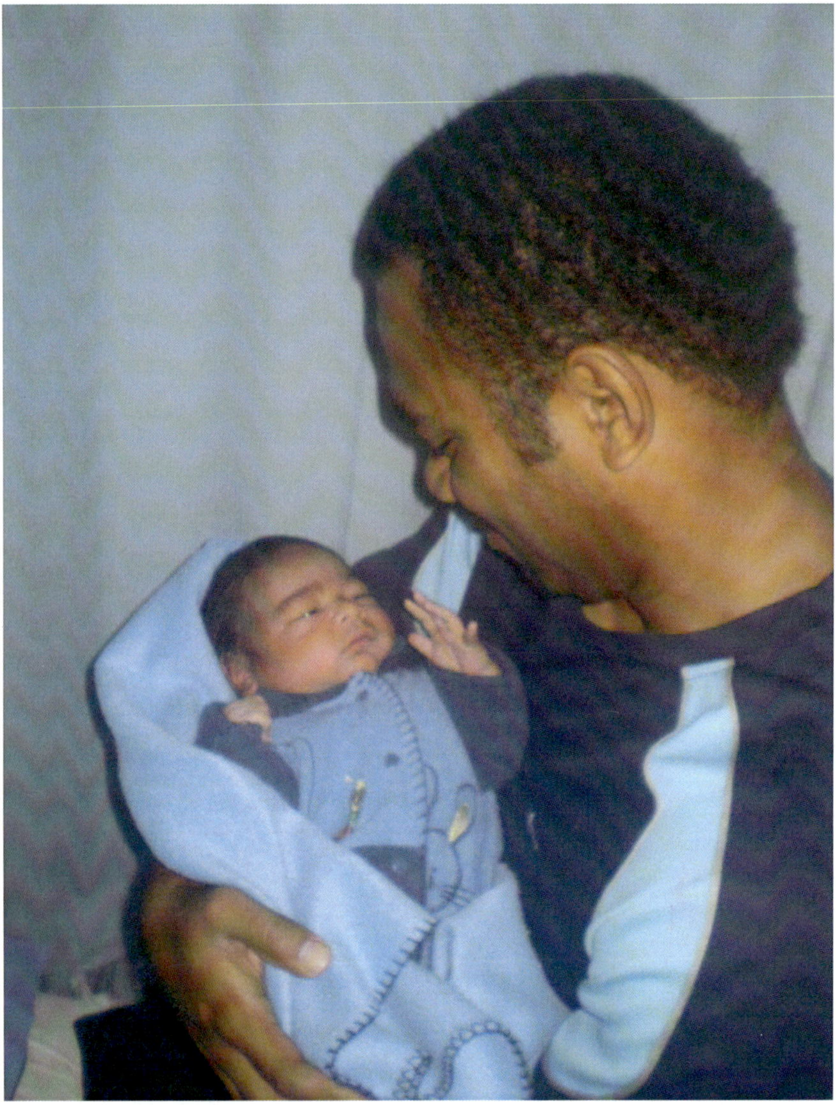

Finally, a son. Tevita Phileo Sovau Lisala Secivo.

Back to work after maternity leave. I got to fly with Tevita as his first officer on the Islander BN2A and on the Twin Otter a couple of times when we were with Pacific Sun Ltd.

Tevita (left) and the kids with Uncle Seru (right).

PNG Kairak Airport (7,280 ft elevation). On a beautiful day and on a foggy day.

At Sasereme Airport with some locals.

A baby croc on board.

Tevita starting again with Airlines of PNG in 2015, on the Dash 8. From left to right: Barry Sutton, Iyata Tavinke, Tevita Secivo (my love), Francis Chakumai, Eroli Yasi, Valentine Wyatt, Abraham Makop and Captain Adam Loughrey.

One of those mornings at work when I would run into his aircraft first for a quick kiss!

Quality time at a coffee shop before heading home.

His surprise romantic dinner!

Family photos in PNG.

Family trip to Rabaul in 2014.

Valentine's Day, 2014.

Watching the sunset at Waikiki Beach.

Waikiki Beach, 2014.

Christmas lunch at Holiday Inn, Port Moresby, 2014.

Fit as a beast! I called him 'my black panther' sometimes because of the black panther tattoo on his right arm.

This photo was taken by our trainer in the middle of doing our abs workout.

The boys on a day cruise the day before we renewed our wedding vows.
From left to right: Fotu To'ofoe, Fred Puni, Oliver Aquino,
Tevita Secivo and Iyata Tavinke.

Front: Tumai (Tevita's cousin), Tevita, and Esira Donu. Back: Oliver and Fotu.

On our ten-year anniversary, we renewed our wedding vows. As I walked down to Tevita, my feet were burning on the hot pavement, but no one knew. December 17th 2015.

Newly married again. I remember whispering to him,
'We did it, babe. Ten years and we did it!'

Pilots working in PNG. From left to right: Jovesa Lasei, Kris Mandri, Ben Baleikanacea, Kapeni Mua, Ralph Teo, Tevita and me, Oliver Aquino, Fred Puni, Iyata Tavinke, Michael Beier, Fotu To'ofoe and Alipate Vasutoga.

December 17th 2015.

My favourite moment from our anniversary.
Dancing under the stars with my love.

The morning after the renewal. Tevita and the boys enjoying their liquid breakfast by the pool.

A gift from Tevita. *I am with you always.*

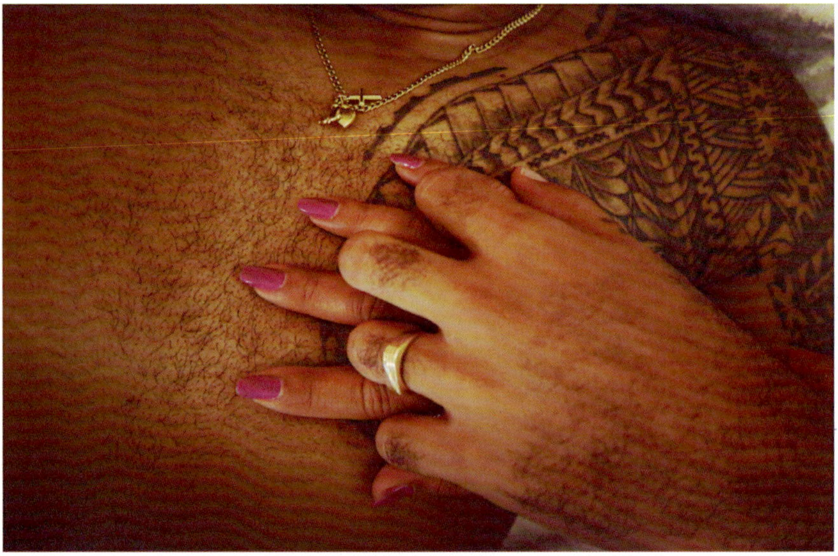

Our first night together in Singapore.

At the Marina Bay Sands infinity pool. Ticking it off the bucket list!

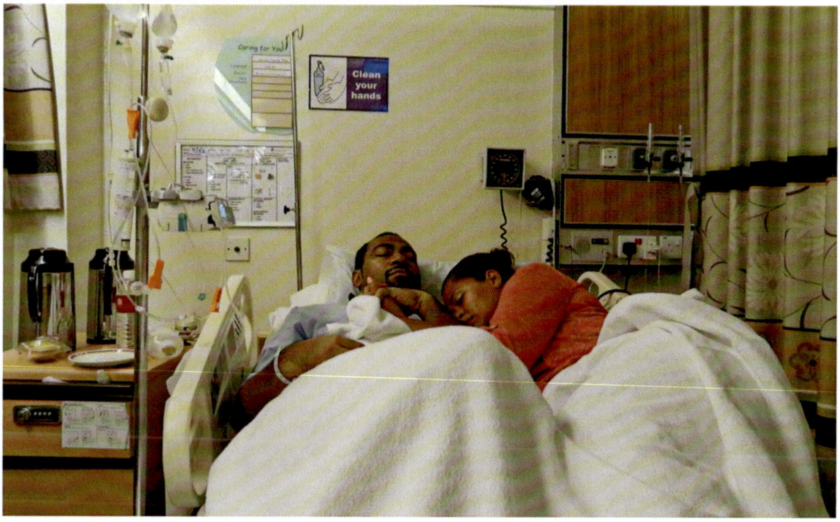

Singapore General Hospital.

The morning after Tevita was discharged from the Singapore Hospital.

The Commit To Be Fit ladies. My sisters, my family in PNG.
They have all been amazingly supportive.

Me and my Twinny. We would always turn up to meetings or functions accidentally wearing the same or similar outfits.

My beautiful late mother-in-law with my daughter Melaia Secivo.

My mum and the kids in the village. Just a few days away from New Year 2016.

In front of Tevita's tomb. Left to right: Fred, Naibuka, me and Fotu.

10

The Renewal of Vows

Loved you yesterday. Love you still. Always have, always will.

ANON

It was in 2005 that we found ourselves at the registry office in Suva, standing in front of a tall Fijian woman ready to legally declare us husband and wife. I was only nineteen, and five months pregnant at the time. Since we first found out we were expecting, our parents had agreed that despite our age we would get married with all the formalities. On the day, I chose to wear a beautiful light pink maternity dress and flat shoes. It must have cost me fifty dollars to buy the material and have it sewn by one of my aunties. It was simple and comfortable, and I loved how graceful and pretty it made me feel. There was no wedding make-up, no styled hair, no bouquet, and no beach, which were all the essential components I had always imagined my wedding day would have. Even though it was nothing close to how I had dreamt my wedding day would be, it was one of the happiest days of my life. As for Tevita, his dream wedding consisted of one thing only – and that was that he was exchanging vows with the one he loved.

Recalling the words of my father when I first broke the news of my pregnancy to him, it was of extreme importance that Tevita and

I wedded before our baby was born. My parents, who were at Cicia Island at the time, could not make it as we hurriedly organised to register our marriage. I also did not want to burden them and decided that we'd do this on our own.

My mother literally cried when she heard that I had gotten married that day. She was in the village at the time, and I laughed when she told me the story. She is a tough, confident woman, so I hardly ever saw her cry. She told me, 'I was in the bathroom when your Auntie Tale came to see me. She was calling from outside and I didn't say a word.'

'Oh, why?' I curiously asked.

'Because I was crying,' she quickly blurted out. I laughed just imagining the sight of her sobbing in the bathroom. Then she continued, 'I was crying to myself – I had worked for more than twenty years and I did not even get to spread a single mat on my daughter's wedding day. Eeeeee eeee eee.' I laughed even more when she imitated how she cried.

Tevita and I had agreed that we would get married before our firstborn's arrival. The only problem was that we were still in flying school so both our parents paid for everything and all was done their way – from the lunch, after signing the papers that day, to all the traditional stuff that was held the following year.

Growing up in the village, I naturally spent the majority of my time alone on the beach. I would either be sitting down with a fishing line in my hand or simply walking along the beach collecting shells. But my favourite thing was watching that magical moment when the sun was setting on the horizon, and I would marvel at the whole scene. To me, there was nothing more peaceful or fascinating than watching the sun and its warm dreamy colours slowly drowning in the endless sea. And the sand under my feet and the sound of roaring waves crashing on the shore made it perfect. I fell in love with everything about the beach. The scene, the breeze, the shells, and the warm feeling of sand under my feet was heaven on earth for me. The perfect venue for my dream wedding.

Tevita was a very supportive, caring, and loving husband. He knew that I had always wanted a beach wedding and when we first got married our wedding was nothing close to it. I think he always felt somewhat responsible for me not having my dream wedding. It was something I wanted to have, and something he wanted to give me.

In 2013, we decided that we were going to strengthen our love, renew our wedding vows and commit to each other in marriage, all over again. We decided our two girls were going to be our flower girls, and our son would be the best man. Tevita told me, 'Now you can finally have your dream wedding, whichever way you want.' It was said with so much love and adoration that it was impossible to disagree or contest the suggestion. We were two years away from our tenth anniversary, and we couldn't think of a more perfect time to do it than when we reached that anniversary. There was just enough time to save for and plan the big day. The planning and putting my dream wedding together was exciting. I must have gone through thousands of pictures of beach weddings, dresses, cakes, décor, and bouquets in the first ten months. He delighted in the excitement and the glow I would have on my face whenever we sat to discuss 'the day'. It was like I was going to marry him for the first time.

We travelled down to Hawaii in June 2014 for an exam and we stayed an extra few days to make it an early honeymoon. We gathered some very beautiful memories there that will be forever etched in my heart. Memories of us walking the white sandy beaches of Waikiki hand in hand and watching the sunset, and swimming about a hundred metres into the sea to watch surfers catch waves. The visit to the Pacific

Aviation Museum Pearl Harbor was very touching and we enjoyed every bit of it; we even enjoyed getting lost on the way there. It made it feel like an adventure. I can vividly recall how excited Tevita was while picking out a black convertible Mustang for us to rent that day. It was a beautiful sunny day, perfect weather to drive out with its roof lowered. He drove, and I became the designated navigator, telling him when and where to turn. Ten minutes later we were on the highway and he immediately sped up, driving at about 100km/hr. He was like a child who'd finally gotten his hands on his favourite toy. I had to keep reminding him to slow down.

I was struggling to hear the GPS instructions. We had driven past several exits, and we had no idea where we were heading. Our only option was to put the roof up again to get rid of the noise and give us some shade, so we could also see the GPS screen. We both struggled for about five minutes, trying to locate the button for the roof and when we finally did, it seemed not to be working at all. Eventually, we had no choice but to pull to the side of the highway. With cars passing us in a flash, one after another, it was impossible to ask anyone for directions. Clueless as to where we were, we stepped out feeling like we had just committed a crime. It was obvious that we were parked somewhere we were not supposed to be. Well, we couldn't have cared less – we needed to get the roof up and to figure out where we were.

Tevita decided to hit the button one more time, and hey presto, it finally worked. We later read the instructions that said we needed to stop the car first for it to work. There was a good laughing session almost all the way to Pearl Harbor after that.

Other memories that come to mind are of when we were shopping at the market in Waikiki and a starfish hairpin and earrings caught my eye. I loved them and couldn't walk away without buying them. I, unknowingly, had just purchased the first two items for our renewal.

There was not a single day in Hawaii that we did not do something fun or exciting. We thoroughly made use of our time there. We returned to PNG via Fiji, spending three nights there, then one night in Brisbane, then back to the land of the unexpected, PNG. The kids were very excited to have us back at home.

In the months that followed we progressed through our wedding to-do list and secured the beachfront bure (bungalow) at the Sofitel resort in Nadi, Fiji as our venue. We agreed our theme colours were to be purple, pink and a touch of sky-blue. We also made arrangements with Grace Creations for decorations and secured a band for entertainment.

By early 2015, I had arranged for our photographer, and ordered my shell bouquet with matching boutonnieres for the boys, together with a matching cake-topper. Guestlists were completed, and by mid-2015 I had sent out our invitations as a message in a bottle. Everything that needed to be secured was done with all orders arriving by August, three months before the renewal. Everything was ready and ticked off my list, except we all still had nothing to wear.

I was starting to panic. Luckily it just so happened I had to spend four days in Melbourne for a flight test that August. It was good timing and I had no choice but to find a dress on that short trip. On my second day in Melbourne, I Googled the closest bridal shop and found Fairytales Bridal Boutique about thirty-five minutes' drive from the hotel. It was my first time going shopping for a wedding dress. No-one was there with me for a second or third opinion – I kept telling myself that I would know *the dress* when I saw it. I walked in, and was instantly enchanted by all the elegant wedding gowns on display. A blonde lady in her mid-forties was very friendly, and she guided me to where more dresses were. In a minute, I found myself alone standing in the middle of two long racks of wedding gowns. The first six dresses made me worried about whether any of the dresses would fit a size sixteen Fijian girl.

After going through all those lovely dresses I pulled out two that caught my attention. For the first one, I was told I would need to give them at least six months to create a custom-made dress. I did not have six months so that dress had to go. The second one was a size fourteen, sleeveless, ivory silk dress with a corset back by Maria Chiodo. It wasn't in my size, but I was hoping that it would somehow magically fit me. Well, it fitted perfectly – one look at myself in the mirror, and I instantly knew that I'd found *the dress*. The next thing that the lady helping me said was, 'You're very lucky, this is real silk and it's very expensive. Do you know what the original price was?'

I slowly and hesitantly replied, 'No,' and braced myself to hear the amount. I had been too excited to even check the price tag.

She then pulled out a tag and said, 'It was AUD $3,140 and now it's been reduced to $850 off-the-rack.'

I thought, Oh wow, it must be my lucky day. It was definitely *the dress*. Though I honestly would not normally spend that much money on a dress, I could never put a price tag on precious memories, especially ones to be created on my happy wedding day with my dear family and friends.

The dress was simple, elegant, and comfortable, and now knowing how much I had saved I knew I had found *the dress* and was willing to foot the bill. I would go for anything of good quality that saved me money. The starfish hairpin would complement the dress perfectly, adding that beachy touch to the hair but still keeping it simple.

While in Melbourne I also managed to get matching charcoal-coloured pants and vests for the boys and two floral dresses from Myer for the girls as a plan B if we didn't manage to find anything else.

Back in PNG, I was overly excited to have returned with *the dress*, but I could not show it to Tevita and share my excitement. I kept it from him as a surprise. Unfortunately he accidentally saw a photo of me wearing it on my phone. However, for weeks he pretended not to have seen it until I found him going through photos on my phone one day and I warned him not to look. He turned to me with a sorry look on his face, and I just knew it, he'd already seen it. Immediately, in his defence, he exclaimed, 'It was an accident, I had no idea that you had the dress photos on your phone.' I was a little upset that the surprise was ruined, but happy at the same time that now I could ask him what he thought of the dress. He loved what he saw from that brief look.

As for the girls' dresses, I was not quite satisfied with what I bought from Myer. They were not what I wanted, so I searched Facebook and found a local designer in Fiji, well-known for his bold, tropical and vibrantly coloured designs – Hupfeld Hoerder, a familiar name in the fashion industry. I fell in love with his collections and how he blended different shades of colours together. I knew they would just be perfect for the girls' dresses and also add that tropical touch that I wanted, in line with our theme colours. I found myself sending him an email and a photo of my bouquet, and I explained how I wanted the same colours on the bouquet to be on the dresses. I pictured the dresses on the girls, and a brilliant idea came to mind. The last thing I'd been struggling to find was neckties for the boys that would blend well with our outfits and the theme colours. So I added them to my email to Hupfeld. Two dresses for the girls and matching ties for the boys with blended designs of pink and purple. The items were gorgeous and just how I imagined. As anticipated, he did an exceptional job of pulling it off.

Now everything was coming together with most decisions made – Tevita gladly allowing me to decide what I wanted. As for the song, I had pleaded that he have some say in our wedding and he accepted the task of choosing our wedding song. He took his time, and I had to be patient with him, though at one point I was feeling worried, wondering if he was ever going to come up with a song at all. Then he came home after work one fine afternoon and said, 'Babe, you have to listen to this song.' He played me a duet, sung beautifully by John Legend and Meghan Trainor – 'Like I'm Gonna Lose You'. The words – *I'm gonna love you like I'm gonna lose you* – were so true, so real, and felt perfectly right for the occasion and for us. No wonder Tevita cried when he first heard it.

He told me that our Samoan friend Fred Puni played it to him while they were in the aircraft. He had to pretend to look outside to hide his tears from Fred, and he was also glad to have been wearing sunglasses. Tevita was a tough, spirited person who hardly ever cried. With the lyrics of the song, he must have felt them hit a soft spot to have made him cry that day. 'This will be our song,' he proudly declared like he had just passed a major assignment with flying colours. I immediately loved it and could not have agreed more. The lyrics were sweet and uplifting, yet deep and meaningful, touching and heartfelt. It was many things, including a goodbye song. I remember staring at him listening to every word of the lyrics and feeling my love and yearning for him renewed and deepened. I wanted to love him every single day just like they were singing in that song, to love him like I was going to lose him. It was truly a beautiful song.

Our date of travel for the renewal in Fiji was fast approaching, and we were all getting excited. The kids were well aware that their mother and father were going to get married again, and they were just as excited as us. We arrived into Fiji just a few days before our big day. Two days before the ceremony, we got together for dinner with all our close friends from work who had travelled over with their families. I still remember it like it was only yesterday. The following day we all went our separate ways as planned. The boys on their day cruise on a private yacht and the ladies to a whole-day spa. They told us that they would be back around 4 p.m. but boys being boys, that never happened. They carried on, much to our concern, until three hours later, when darkness had settled. As for the ladies, we enjoyed a whole day of being pampered then later got together again for a karaoke session. It was a wonderful, memorable time together with friends. I saw Tevita later that night, and I laughed when I noticed his sunburnt face. I teased him, saying, 'That's from being in the scorching sun for a whole day and coming back late.' Thanks to our friends who organised the cruise, he really enjoyed it. We kissed each other goodnight and agreed that we would only see each other at the ceremony.

Despite the rain a few days earlier, which got me a little bit worried, the next day I woke up to a very beautiful, bright, sunny morning. The girls and I had our own room to get ready in while Tevita and Yaca had a room for themselves. I had hired one of the best bridal makeup artists in Fiji, Stanley Morrell, to perform his magic for my special day. His team's professionalism stood out from the moment they walked into the room. It was the first time that the girls were to have their makeup done by a professional and their excitement filled the room. It was obvious that out of our three children Ipa was a little over-excited. She was beaming with smiles and couldn't keep still or her hands off the bouquet, earrings and even the makeup kit.

After the makeup was done, we put on our dresses and we all looked very glamorous. I was overwhelmed with happiness and exuberance. It was like we were never married and I was marrying him for the first time. I was experiencing emotions I didn't have when we first got married. I even found myself asking, So this is how a bride feels on her wedding day? It was such a beautiful feeling.

We had briefed the kids on the general formalities, so they knew that we were to avoid each other until the ceremony. Their duty was to make sure that their father didn't see me before then. Well, the girls and I got a surprise when Yaca decided to make a visit to the girls' room, all handsomely suited up. He took a look at me, ready to walk out, and with a big smile on his face commented, 'Oh Na, you look beautiful. I can't wait for Ta to see you!'

Moments later I was finally walking towards a small Fijian bure or hut, themed and decorated for the ceremony. Our two girls were about two steps ahead of me, and I was following behind. I took my first step, and I almost jumped off the stone-tiled walkway. It was burning hot, and I was wearing barefoot sandals decorated with shells. I looked down and saw that it was going to be quite a long fifteen-metre walk with that heat under my feet, but I knew it was worth it. At the end our forty guests were seated, and my husband and our son were standing in the bure waiting patiently. It was now or never – hot or not, I was walking up to marry my husband again. About six steps further on I was almost tiptoeing, trying to keep my feet off the hot stone. I could feel them burning but I kept my smile on. If anyone looked closely, they would have noticed that I was not only smiling but also giggling. I just found it so funny that I was trying so hard not to jump off the hot walkway in that wedding dress.

We finally reached where the boys were standing. The girls went on and stood to my left while Tevita joined me on my right side with Yaca next to him. It was one of the most magical highlights of my life.

The moment we had all been looking forward to – the exchanging and renewal of our vows. I asked to read mine first because I was worried that I might cry listening to his and then end up struggling to read mine through my tears. It didn't make any difference. I was crying as soon as I started to read mine. It was an emotional moment – even our photographer was in tears. Unlike our first vows that were written for us, this time we wrote our own for each other. They were written from the heart, and we meant every single word.

I read my vows to my husband before the celebrant and our special guests:

> 'Tevita, my best friend, my husband, my perfect other half. You have loved me more than I deserve to be loved. You have seen me at my absolute worst, know my multiple personalities and yet you still smile and tell me that I am beautiful. I have never felt so loved, so cared for, and so cherished by someone. Thank you for loving me for who I am, Tevita. Thank you for making my dreams come true, including this special one right here. A beach wedding. Ten years, *wajiqu* (my husband). I am happy that after going through a lot of things that were meant to tear us apart, our love has only grown stronger.
>
> Today as I recommit myself to you and our marriage, I vow to give you the best of myself. I vow to encourage and inspire you, to laugh with you, and comfort you in times of sorrow, and struggle. I promise to love you in good times and in bad, when life seems easy and when it seems hard. I promise to respect you, even when I disagree with you. To respect the decisions you make for our family. I promise

to communicate with you and not to shut down. I promise to stand by you at every stage of life when things are good or bad. Whether we are laughing or crying, I promise never to leave you, whatever we may go through. I promise to be faithful and to love you unconditionally with all of my heart. This is my solemn promise to you.'

It was important for us to renew our vows in front of our children. Tevita, my husband, read his heartfelt vows to me:

'Galuoko, the first time I laid eyes on you, I was instantly convinced that my life was complete. I had to make you my wife. I had to make you my life. Achieving this huge task was difficult and I knew this, yet for all the reasons in the world, I felt that it was my calling in life to take care and love you the way you deserve.

Occasionally during the last ten years, I know I let you down and I thought I knew what love was. Nature taking its course compelled me to realise that I did not have a clue. Life with you has taught me what love is. It has taught me what commitment and dedication is, and most of all it has taught me what it is to live for someone selflessly.

It's been ten years and my love now for you is one that has been tried, weathered, and refined by the fire that is life. I now stand before you to once again commit myself to you, my best friend, my companion, my one and only true love, and my wife. I will forever continue to love you in the good and the bad times. To take care of you in sickness and in health, and to be a shoulder to cry on always. I will take care of you and our family till death do us apart. This I promise you, *Au na domoni iko tikoga Na. Au na lomani iko tikoga'* (In Fijian: I will deeply love you always Na). *Oute alofa ia oe* (In Samoan: I love you).'

We wanted our guests to witness, feel, and know how much we loved each other.

The ceremony ended and we had two hours for the photo shoot before the reception. I had been a fan of this photographer, Tara Toohey, for a long time. I loved her style and how she captured raw candid moments. I knew her through her husband Jayden Toohey, who was my pen-friend from high school, way before any social media existed. We had kept in touch since then but only got to meet in person ten years later, in 2012 during our visit to Brisbane. He was a wedding videographer while Tara was a wedding photographer. She was amazing to work with and they were a talented and gifted couple.

We finished the photo shoot just in time for the reception to start. The sun was slowly setting, radiating that warm, romantic feeling. For a few minutes, the whole sky was like a big canvas hanging from the background with a sunset painting on it. There was a live band, and lots of food, drinks, and dancing. My favourite part was us dancing to our song under the stars with sand between our toes. It was just as magical and romantic as I had wanted it to be – *I'm gonna love you like I'm gonna lose you.*

Tragically, I lost him exactly one year later. I am glad we renewed our vows and that he knew, as I did, of our undying love towards each other.

11

JustaLOv3

The sky may fall and the stars will too
but in the end, I will still love you.

ANON

The pain I suffered after losing my darling husband was beyond words. I had lost my best friend, my love, and the very person I would run to for comfort. It was a time when I needed him the most. I was yearning desperately for the comfort that only he could give, but he was no longer there. It was painful.

I woke up one morning thinking, This is how it can be done. This is how you live with the pain. You just do. You pretend everything is fine and ignore the deep cramp-like pain in your stomach. You somehow anaesthetise yourself so nothing feels that bad, but nothing feels that good either.

Deep down I also knew I needed to vent, so I took to Facebook. I turned exactly what I was feeling into words and posted them. Sometimes I even pretended that I was writing to Tevita. Anything to make me feel a little bit better. I didn't think that anybody would even bother to read my posts. But to my utter surprise, people were moved and touched. They felt my pain and my friend list skyrocketed to 5,000 Facebook friends – the friend limit. Endless messages were flooding in and I ended up starting a separate Facebook page.

Six months later I was still getting messages from people I didn't know. Encouraging and supportive ones and the majority were from women, sharing with me how they had been touched and inspired to love their husbands more dearly. To cherish every moment with them while they still could. Some were on the verge of giving up, but from the posts, they were inspired to love harder and not give up. A few shared how their love was rekindled and how they were giving their marriage another chance. A young wife wrote to me and said she had been separated from her husband and they had moved back in together after reading some posts. Reading stories like that comforted and warmed my broken heart. To know that even though I had lost my love, other loves were mended and strengthened.

Frankly, I do not want our marriage to be seen like it was perfect and that we never argued. Just like any other couple, we had our problems. There were some wonderful rows that I would also like to share here. Firstly, it would be dishonest of me not to mention that a couple of times I wanted to give up. Always in the heat of the moment whenever we argued. As for him, he never did. Not a single time. He would lock the door, and stand in front of it so I wouldn't be able to walk out. And there was something that he would always tell me: 'You will thank me later.' Which I did and he was right. He understood that I was still young and naive.

I was married and a mother of one by the time I turned twenty. Tevita had whisked me into a life I wasn't quite ready for, but somehow it felt right, and I never regretted it. I had delivered a life into this world, yet I felt that there was more I needed to know about life, marriage, and love. Tevita, my darling husband, taught me a lot. My version of a perfect happy marriage was developed from all my favourite 'happily ever after' fairy-tale stories when I was little. I used to think that happily ever after involved no fighting, no arguments at all. How wrong I was.

Our first few years of marriage were wonderful, passionate, and sweet. He was a fantastic, devoted, loving, and understanding husband. In most of our arguments, Tevita being the more mature one would just give in and be the first to apologise – even when he was right. I would find out later that he was right all along and I'd feel like a fool. That was a first big marriage lesson for me. Sometimes you just have to be wrong to be right. I was always moved by his humbleness and his love every time he would do that. So, it was very pleasing when I finally got the chance to return the love, in the same way, apologising even when I was right.

Our big issue in our first few years of being married was my insecurity. I hated that feeling – I would get so jealous, it was ridiculously unbelievable. I was shocked at who I was becoming and I loathed it. At one point, I didn't even want him to look at a girl, especially if she was attractive. I would go ballistic even if it was just an innocent glance.

There was a barrel night sometime in 2006. We were still a newly married couple and had moved out of SSQ and into a three-bedroom flat near Nadi town. We shared the flat with two other couples and we all went out that night. I must have had some red wine and was already tipsy when a couple from our flat got into a fight. I tried to help and calm the girl down but was unsuccessful. I can't remember why they were fighting, but I do remember looking up to see Tevita comforting the girl who was now crying in his arms. She was, of course, beautiful and it felt like a bomb exploded in me. Tevita could be too kind and sometimes I got jealous. We ended up getting into a bigger fight and I walked away, refusing to get into the taxi with him. I walked the other way with no money, barefoot and alone. It was probably around four in the morning when I realised that I had been walking for some time and I was getting tired. I wanted to sleep but had no idea where I was going. I was too proud to go back home, but I couldn't think of any other place to go. So I ended up stopping a taxi and bit my nails all the way back home. The first thing I was told when I got home was how Tevita was so worried about me. That was all I needed to hear to get me smiling again. He must have apologised a thousand times that day. He made me breakfast, did all the house chores, and I felt like a queen.

Another incident was on August 12th that year. I woke up around eight in the morning with him still fast asleep next to me. I lay there again for about twenty minutes waiting for him to wake up, but no. I finally got up and started making some noise around the room to wake him but still, he didn't. I knew it. He had forgotten about my birthday. I was turning twenty-one that day.

It would be a big celebration if I was still with my parents, I complained to myself. But I was married, and now my husband was supposed to be the one throwing me a big celebration, but no. He was still fast asleep comfortably in bed. I said to myself, Fine. I freshened up and took a taxi to town.

An hour later my phone wouldn't stop ringing. He finally woke up and obviously couldn't find me. I wanted him to get the message without actually messaging him, so I turned my phone off. Now I was planning to hang around town until Tevita realised that it was my birthday.

I was standing just outside a second-hand shop in town when I met a man. He was short, dark, and he had a white cap on and a scar on his face. Then he started flashing me a fancy phone that he was selling at a very cheap price. At first, I ignored him, but he kept insisting that I have a look. I thought, Oh well, I might as well buy it as a birthday present for myself – to cheer me up. I watched him put the phone back in a brown paper bag and he told me that he would give me a new one. He pulled out another brown paper bag and handed it to me. I held it in my hand, and I was absolutely sure that I was holding my brand-new fancy phone. But he warned me not to open it just yet. A few moments later he was long gone when I decided to finally open my birthday present to myself. It was a piece of soap and not a phone. Humiliated and frustrated, I just wanted to scream my lungs out and cry at the same time. I had been duped on my twenty-first birthday. How much worse could this day get? It was like I was on a prank show.

I was angry, and I blamed my husband. I had given him enough time to figure out what trouble he was in, but now I wanted to tell him about what just happened. I wanted to blame him and cry to him at the same time. I turned my phone on and made the call. He immediately answered and acted as if he knew it was my birthday all along. He explained that it was supposed to be a surprise, and sleeping in was part of the plan. Pretending that he had forgotten about it was also part of the plan and now I had ruined it. I felt a little bit better. He asked me to come home – some friends were already there for a BBQ. 'Oh, and I've also bought you a surprise present,' he continued.

I was impressed when I got home – there was some meat marinating, the house was clean, there were some decorations and some friends already there too. It looked like he did plan a surprise birthday party. He gave me a gold locket and chain that I had always wanted and I forgot that I was even upset with him that morning. I even forgot about that stupid soap.

Well they say that a husband needs only to forget his wife's birthday once and he will remember it for the rest of his life. Tevita never forgot any of my birthdays after that. It was not until we moved to PNG that he finally confessed that he did forget about my birthday that day. A birthday that I will definitely never forget.

There were more incredible rows before we moved to PNG, but making up made it all worthwhile. All those silly tiffs due to jealousies eventually faded into insignificance. It was sometime in 2012 when we were in PNG, that I noticed we had not had any quarrels for a while. It didn't feel normal and I sort of missed them. I even questioned if we were going through a phase in our marriage. I recall one evening, I was still in my gym clothes when we were arguing about something that I can't recall now. I was never very good at vocalising in arguments and would often freeze up with no words to say. I always preferred to walk my anger off. That night I stormed downstairs for a breath of fresh air, but it was still not enough. I needed my own space so I continued and walked out the gate in the middle of the night. Mind you, we were in Port Moresby. Safety-wise, driving alone at night for a female was never advisable, let alone walking by yourself. I was consumed with so much anger that I did not care. I headed for a friend's house about forty minutes' walk away. There was hardly anyone on the street. The few lights were barely lighting up the street. About a hundred metres ahead I could see the road bending to the right where it started to get dark. Suddenly, each step closer to that dark bend I felt terror crawling up from my feet. I was no longer angry but now terrified and yet still did not want to go home. I looked back expecting to see Tevita storming out the gate but saw no sign of him at all. Oh crap, what do I do now? I took the first road on the left that would circle back to my home. I saw a few boys on the street ahead of me but I refused to turn back. I was still in my gym clothes and was ready to run for my life if they tried anything. I walked past them looking very brave but terrified on the inside.

Our house girl and security guard came looking for me a few minutes later, and told me that Tevita had driven out to look for me. I rushed home feeling silly and sorry for my husband.

The kids knew that we had argued. I waited for about five minutes in our room before I heard the car pulling up. I didn't know whether to run to him or wait. I was still contemplating this, when I heard his footsteps running up. That's it, I couldn't wait any longer so I ran and met him halfway up the stairs. We were both very sorry, and the kids were there too. We hugged and both apologised to each other. It was important for us to apologise in front of our kids. We had always encouraged them to apologise whenever they got into an argument and it felt right to set them an example. I asked him why he hadn't run after me, that I was expecting to see him coming after me. Well, he explained that he thought that I had only gone downstairs.

We had a good long talk after that, and he made me promise never to walk out like that ever again. He encouraged me not to be afraid to voice my feelings especially when I was mad, but to stay and talk things over. This is something that I was never good at; I would normally just shut down, give him the silent treatment and let him do all the talking. And it always annoyed the hell out of him. But I managed to tell him that I not only wanted him to listen, but to hear me and understand why I felt the way I did. Over time we managed to improve on that. He learnt to listen and understand, and I learnt to speak up like he did.

It was a few months after the renewal in 2016. I had flown out on an overnight flight schedule while Tevita stayed back in Port Moresby. I spoke to him before going to bed that night and he told me that he was at a friend's house having a few beers. I instantly had this strange, weird feeling that something bad was going to happen, but I brushed it aside thinking that I was just being paranoid. I begged him to spend the night there if he was going to have too much to drink. Then I went off to sleep.

The next day he waited for me in the pilot's crew room, then walked me to our car. He carried my flight bag and walked ahead of me. He tossed my bag in, turned and was just staring back at me. I knew the look. He was waiting for a reaction from me. At first, I thought he was just being funny, but the guilty, sorry look he had on was telling me something else.

'What is it?' I asked.

'I'm so sorry babe, I had an accident,' he replied, pointing to a dent in the car.

Oh, my Lord! I was both thankful that he was not hurt and mad at the same time. He told me how he would have tumbled down a very steep hill, if it wasn't for a tree that saved him. That was exactly what I was afraid was going to happen. I knew the house he went to the previous night was up on a hill. And the road up to that place was dangerously steep. I could have lost him that night. Alarmed and afraid, I held his hand and told him how much I was afraid to lose him. And how I was also very disappointed in him for being so careless.

To make up for it, he texted me the following day while I was at work to tell me that he had made some special reservations. He wrote, *It's a surprise so you will have to wear something nice.* I chose to wear my favourite black dress, while he wore the same purple shirt that he wore at our renewal of vows. It was exciting getting ready together. I remember closing my eyes the entire drive until we came to a complete stop. He then insisted that I wait in the car for him to open the door. I stepped out, and in front of us was one of the best fine dining restaurants in Port Moresby. I was impressed.

We were warmly greeted and ushered to our table where Tevita pulled out the chair for me to sit down. The lighting and the cosy set-up was just perfect for a romantic night out. They even had a gentleman playing some very soothing music on the piano. There were only two other couples in the restaurant and it almost felt like he had hired the whole restaurant just for the two of us. We ordered steak, salmon, and indulged ourselves with a bottle of red wine. It was the most romantic candlelit dinner I ever had with him. (On his funeral day, I realised that we were both wearing the same things that we were wearing on that date night, except for the vest and the tie he had on.)

One afternoon that I will never forget: we were in our room getting ready to go grocery shopping and I struck up a very interesting conversation with Tevita. We were sharing our dreams and goals, our passions, places we had been and places we would like to see together in the future. It was exciting and it continued on our drive to the supermarket parking lot. Then the topic suddenly changed to talking about when we were little; then growing up; our high school days; secret crushes; and his first girlfriend, proceeding to the first time we met to our first kiss and even our silly dramas and quarrels. We occasionally reminisced about those days but something was different this time. I noticed that he was telling me stories about his experience of growing up as a boy, and I thoroughly enjoyed listening to them. He shared how much he adored and missed his mother and wondered what life would be like if she was still with us. He went on and told me about his tricks of missing school on most Mondays when he was still in primary school. His parents never found out, and he loved telling me this story. He would wait for them to leave for work, remove his uniform, and sit and watch cartoons all day. Then he would wrinkle his uniform and put it back on just before they got back home. Despite missing out on those school days, he still did well and managed to get into one of the well-known, prestigious high schools in Fiji.

He loved reading English and had very neat, immaculate handwriting. His all-boys boarding school experience at Queen Victoria School was another of his favourite stories to tell. Some boys would come and ask him to write their love letters for them in exchange for storybooks. He proudly shared how he took part in a four-hundred-metre relay race and high jump representing his school. That was one of the highlights of his school days; representing his school in one of the major high school sports events in Fiji. Then we both laughed when he told me about how he and a few other boys stole a boat they found near the school for a short joy-ride. Well, they got a good whacking from one of the prefects the following day. I always found it delightful listening to his life story and getting to know who he was growing up, before he met me. It made me feel like I'd known him all his life.

With the engine still running, we continued reminiscing about all our favourite sweet memories together. Beginning with the night we first danced in the club, to the night we were dancing under the stars at our renewal night. We were like two best friends who hadn't seen each other in a long time now catching up, joking, and laughing. Looking back now, it feels like he was telling me his whole life story for the last time. But the magical thing was, we somehow reignited a spark in the process, without realising it. By merely talking, sharing, and reminiscing about all our sweet, beautiful memories, we were falling in love all over again. It felt almost the same as when we first fell in love, only this time it felt, incredibly, much deeper and more mature. All this time we were still in our vehicle and had totally lost track of time. The sun was slowly setting, and we had not realised that we had been talking for almost an hour. It felt only like a minute, and we still had so much that we wanted to talk about. So I turned to him and said, 'We better go and get what we came here for.'

Something was happening with us. I remember getting out of the car feeling like hundreds of butterflies were warming up my stomach with that wonderful feeling of being in love again. We had always loved each other, but to fall in love all over again was surprisingly enchanting. I slid my hand into his, and we walked into the shopping centre side by side, hand in hand. There had never been a happier moment. As usual, he was pushing the trolley around for me while I was picking out our groceries. I even caught myself checking him out, admiring his good looks, muscles, and the trademark goatee beard that I loved. Whatever was happening, I was loving it.

He was a good gentleman who had a lot of respect not only for me, but others as well – a quality that I greatly admired in him.

We got back home, and unpacked our shopping. I then excused ourselves to the kids and the house girl saying, 'You guys cook whatever you want for dinner tonight, Na and Ta will be going out on a date.' That was nothing new to the kids. Every now and then we would tell them that we were going out on a date – they understood and would even get excited for us.

Tevita was the first to be ready, while I was still standing in front of the mirror perfecting my makeup. His patience was another quality in him that I greatly admired. I recall him sitting on our bed watching me while I was putting on my makeup. As for me, I never really had much patience for waiting around like he would, but his loving, gentle character taught me to be patient as well.

We left the house and drove straight to one of his favourite hangout places – Jackson's Bar, a short twelve-minute drive from home. There we continued to indulge ourselves in reminiscing about our sweet early days of being in love – but now with a few tequila shots that he bought me and a few glasses of gin and tonic. We had a lot of fun and laughed a lot that night, just the two of us. He had always believed that those butterflies were only part of the first phase of being in love.

After a few years of being married, life slowly changes and some things fade away when bills, work, stress and kids come along. I refused to believe it, but that was the reality, he would remind me whenever I would mention how I missed those early days. How many of you married women would agree with me that we do aspire and yearn to keep the passion and intimacy alive in our marriage? I always thought how boring and monotonous married life would be, if none of that was alive in a marriage.

My darling husband finally confessed to me that he also felt something in the car that afternoon and that he was wrong. After ten years of being married, weathering some storms together and three children later, he was falling in love all over again. He had always adored and loved me but he never thought that he would be falling in love with his wife again. So yes, he was surprised and I loved rubbing it in his face that night that he was wrong. We had reignited that spark again. I don't know about him but it only took just one touch of his hand to feel those butterflies again. I was like a teenager in love again for the first time.

I had forgotten this: the way your senses explode and your pulse races, as if you were waking up after a long sleep. I had forgotten the thrill, the desire, the melting sensation. It just wasn't possible after ten years of marriage. That was part of the deal. Everyone knew that. She'd accepted the deal. It had never been a problem, and I hadn't known I'd missed it. If I ever thought about it, I felt childish and silly. Like butterflies and sparks. But I dismissed the thought as there were three children to care for and work to be done. I had completely forgotten the power of it.

Holding hands became our thing from that day, so I decided to create a photo album on Facebook dedicated solely to the journey that had just begun. I wanted our hands to be telling a story in every photo. I then took a photo of our hands just touching each other and uploaded it as the first photo in the album entitled *InstaL0v3*. From that night onwards, I continued to capture our hands up until I was holding his lifeless hand. Till death do us part.

It was only a few days after Tevita's passing that I finally noticed the date on the first photo I had uploaded to the *InstaL0v3* album. Dated September 17th: that was when we had fallen in love again, three months exactly before his date of passing. Not bad for our short-lived love life. After eleven wonderful married years with Tevita, I can confidently say – yes, you can fall in love over and over again with the same person. You can reignite that spark again and keep the fires burning if sufficient effort is put into it. I strongly believe that conflicts are healthy in a relationship. They provide us opportunity to express our emotions, to say what we like and what we don't like. In the process, they deepen our understanding of each other. We get to know one another much better. As a result, our love, patience, and care will grow. We must never give up too easily on our love. It is when we are at our angriest, that we need to dig deeper within to find that love. It will be our umbrella through the rain until the rainbow at the end of it.

12

Singapore Memories

Live for the moments you cannot put into words.

ANON

Jacksons Airport was buzzing with passengers and those who came to see the travellers off. Travellers queued up with an array of luggage and coloured suitcases colouring the bland interior of the airport as they waited their turn to check in for the flight to Changi Airport, Singapore. The date was October 8th and among the crowd my husband stood beside me patiently waiting as I completed the customs forms before proceeding through to the boarding lounge. The day I had dreaded for some time now had arrived, and I was not looking forward to our time apart. Though we had been apart before as work pulled us away from each other from time to time, we had grown strangely closer these past three months than we had ever been before. This time at the airport we both felt it was slightly more difficult saying goodbye. I held my husband a little longer before heading to the departure lounge with a heavy heart that day. Little did I know, that pain was but a hint of the immense ache and agony I would have to endure just ten weeks later, when my husband and love of my life would depart from me for good.

A miserable day in April 2017, upon completing check-in for Singapore again, I stood in the same spot as before, staring down at the customs form. A sudden rush of sad emotion shot through my being as I struggled to bring myself to accept that I would now have to tick the box labelled 'widow'. I recall how so proudly, for the past eleven years, I had ticked the 'married' box. How life can be so unfair is a mystery. We had so much life planned ahead of us. Never in my life had I dreamt that I would be widowed at such a young age. On the contrary, I had only dreamt of growing grey and old with the man I loved, the man who had sacrificed so much for my happiness.

I received my ticket several weeks earlier to travel to Singapore for the proficiency check, also known as base check, which is valid for six months. It is one that every pilot undergoes every six months to demonstrate their competence in carrying out normal, abnormal and emergency procedures. I decided then that I was going to start on this chapter as soon as I got to Singapore. Despite my optimistic plans, I had no idea what kind of emotions I was going to feel when I got there. One thing I did know was that I wanted to write about our time in Singapore while I was there again, as a way of healing. But now seated on the plane with the world thirty-eight feet below me, and six hours of flight time ahead, I made a start on Chapter Twelve.

It has been a long six months since I last visited beautiful Singapore, and four months since my dear husband left me to be with the Lord. Oh, how I miss him terribly every single day, is indeed an understatement. Life has been extremely lonely and tough since his hands became cold in mine.

For the four years since he was diagnosed, we had lived knowing something we both dreaded – that he could be leaving me and the children behind any day. In a way, I tried to remain positive, thinking of it as a privilege, of having time to prepare and love more. But little did we realise just how impossible it is to prepare oneself to lose your very heartbeat, love, and entire world.

During the six-hour flight from Port Moresby to Singapore, I sat gazing out the window and into the undisturbed, peaceful blue sky outside. Painful reminders emerged of how he had described his flight to Singapore. 'It was a painful six hours,' I recall him saying. 'Six hours of excruciating pain. Yaca was playing around me, having no idea of the amount of pain I was in,' he shared. 'I just shut my eyes and kept telling myself, It won't be long now, this pain will go away soon.'

'Oh, my darling husband,' I cried inside.

'Au na yaco ga qo vei noqu babey au bula – I will be better as soon as I see my baby,' he silently told himself. He strongly believed that all his sudden weakness must have been just from being separated for too long. Four weeks of being apart may not seem long for some couples, but to us, this seemed like four long years.

A week before they left Port Moresby to join me in Singapore, he had messaged me and told me that he had a fever. I insisted that he go and see a doctor but he reassured me that it was nothing and that I shouldn't worry about it. He knew that I was busy studying in Singapore and didn't want to trouble me.

In the first two weeks, I felt as if my head was going to explode from the intense studying I was doing. The cramming, the practising of the normal, abnormal and especially emergency procedures. As a pilot himself, Tevita knew exactly what I was going through, and the last thing he wanted was to have me worrying about him as well. He never mentioned anything further about his fever, so I assumed that he was better. He kept insisting on one thing though; that we should never be apart from each other for too long ever again. He was with our son in PNG and I was in Singapore, while our two daughters were in Fiji. The separation weighed heavily on both our hearts. Four days after he had told me about his fever, I was surprised when he sent me a picture of a glass of water with two aspirin dissolving in it and captioned, *Need to take this before I go to sleep.* All the blood running through my veins at that moment suddenly went cold for some reason. I instantly feared the worst. He should have been better by now, how could he still be sick? I knew he was not telling me something.

'Baby, are you still sick?' I worriedly asked. I already knew the answer to my own question, but I just wanted him to reassure me that all would be well, like he always did. My greatest fear was always there at the back of my mind, taunting me: the cancer. From what I had experienced with my late sister Annie, I feared that it was only a matter of time before there would be a sudden drastic change in his health.

Still, I was determined and had strongly convinced myself that cancer was not going to take him too. I had already lost two sisters and an aunt to cancer, so to lose my husband to it too was unacceptable. It was too painful to even think about it. The thought of losing him would shatter me inside. I chose to stay positive.

He finally went to see a doctor the day before their flight to Singapore. He was given an injection that helped him sleep, after a couple of sleepless nights.

On the third of November 2016, the day of their travel to Singapore, he woke with a sharp pain in both his shins. Our son Yaca had no clue that he would also be travelling with his father to see me that day, as we had kept it as a surprise for him. Tevita was constantly sending me videos and photos to update me, but I never had a clue from any of those videos and photos that he was silently in pain.

Meanwhile, in Singapore, I was excitedly anticipating their arrival and went to Changi Airport two hours early. I watched as a few Papua New Guineans came through the arrival gates pushing their trollies right past me, but there was not a sign of Tevita and our son. I quickly ran to check the screen hanging from the airport ceiling to confirm that their flight had landed. Did they miss their flight? No, he sent me a picture of them on the plane. But what could possibly be taking them this long to come out? I could not think of a single reason why, until I saw one of our co-workers who was on the same flight. At first, it was a relief to see him, knowing that he would have seen them on the plane. Before I even opened my mouth to ask him, as if he had read my mind, he said, 'Oh they're on their way but very slow. Tevita is sick.'

'What?' I asked in shock.

'He said his legs were in pain; he's coming, but very slowly.'

'But he never mentioned anything about that to me,' I said, worried.

My heart was now racing madly. I was extremely worried and confused. How bad can this be, for them to be this slow? I wondered. I turned back towards the arrival gate, watching every single person coming out, like a hen eagerly searching for her young, too afraid to blink for fear that I might miss them. Finally, after what seemed an eternity, my husband slowly emerged, dressed in a red round-neck sweater and blue jeans, with his black backpack on his back. Little innocent Yaca was beaming with a smile as he walked beside his father. My eyes suddenly lit up, happy to see them, only to be downcast a split second later, when I saw that he looked unwell and was limping. It felt as if a heavy rock had been hurled at my heart, crushing it. As he got closer I noticed that he was not only limping, he had also lost an amount of weight that was too obvious not to notice. All this while they had not seen me watching them through the thick glass separating the arrival and waiting areas.

Tevita was the kind of man who would sacrifice and take any amount of pain for his family. So, I was not surprised when he suddenly put on a brave face, and pretended not to limp as soon as he saw me. Our eyes met, like first lovers again, but my smile was with a heavy heart and through that thick glass wall I could see that there was a tremendous amount of pain behind his sweet smile.

My worst fear was now shooting from the back of my mind, like a sleepy volcano awakening and it was burning inside me. At the same time, I was yearning for and craving his reassurance that everything would be okay, but my thoughts were racing, and he was still on the other side of the glass. Finally, the glass doors slid open, and I quickly ran to greet them. I first threw my arms around my son and planted a kiss on his cheek, then I slowly looked up to kiss my husband on the lips. Almost as quickly and apologetically, with a worried look on his face, he said, 'I'm sorry babe, I'm still sick.' With the amount of weight I noticed he had lost, the limping, and what I just heard, I looked into his eyes and my spirits sank. It felt like my blood went cold all of a sudden, as I saw our future together begin to slowly fade away before me.

Having kissed him on the lips, I reassured him, 'It's okay Ta, you're here now.'

I guided them to the taxi, feeling both happy and terrified at the same time. His look reminded me of my late sister when she was in her last stages of breast cancer.

That night did not go as I'd imagined. I sat in the backseat of the taxi clinging to him, shaking like a leaf. I saw a look in him that did not guarantee my future with him. I held his hand tight and poured out my fears to him.

'I'm scared, I'm scared of losing you Ta,' I said, sniffling, with tears flowing down my cheeks. 'I want to grow old with you Ta,' I whispered.

'I'll be okay, I'll be okay,' he gently reassured me with a tired look that was not convincing. I was not used to seeing my husband weak and frail like this. I knew he was just saying that, to stop me from sobbing like a baby, knowing how emotional I could get. We noticed the taxi driver was getting concerned and kept looking in his rear-view mirror.

Our only son even asked, 'Are you two fighting?'

We both answered curtly with a no. I tried to explain to him that I was just thinking about a sad story. For half of the drive from Changi Airport to the Ibis Hotel I was crying, but just before we arrived at the hotel, I managed to get my mind off my worst fears of losing him.

We got to our room at about 9 o'clock that night. It was obvious that he was way too exhausted to go out for the dinner I had planned. Trying not to worry too much, I left the room with our son to find something for dinner. We walked out, and Yaca was quite excited to be able to walk around a street at night, as it was something he was not accustomed to back in Port Moresby. The smile on his face lightened the load of fear and pain on my heart that night. We got back to our room with a few takeaway packs of hot soup and stirfries.

Tevita had had a quick nap but I couldn't help but notice how tired he was. He later mentioned that he was running low on his pain-killers and would need some more the following day. The pain in his shins would only go away when he took the painkillers. So, the next morning, November 4th, a Friday, I walked to the closest shopping mall to look for painkillers to ease his pain. I had already made plans, and bookings for places for us to visit together. Fortunately, that particular day was my day off so it was a perfect day to take my husband to the most spectacular hotel in Singapore, which had been on our bucket list for a while, just waiting to be ticked off.

With all the unfortunate events that had happened, I tried to comfort myself with the thought that at least we would get to create some beautiful memories at the Marina Bay Sands hotel (MBS). It is a bittersweet memory for me, reminding me that at the end of it all, we would have to part ways at some point in life, leaving behind only these memories.

It was another beautiful day in Singapore as we excitedly got in a taxi and headed for MBS. I had just bought a small camera, a Canon G7X to document our time in Singapore and to start a vlogging channel on YouTube. I had discussed my plans and excitement with him about the channel. It was mainly to be a keepsake for our family memories. We both loved the idea as we imagined watching all these videos of the kids and us, when we got old and grey with wrinkled but happy faces.

It later turned out to be one of the many things that I became grateful for. I captured all our special moments there, even from when he was admitted to Singapore General Hospital, and his last few days back in PNG. Now I don't struggle to recall those beautiful memories, as I get to watch them whenever I want. We managed to capture our last month together.

We arrived at MBS at around 2 o'clock in the afternoon to check in. We could not help as we walked in but be amazed by the exceptional architecture. Our room was on level eight in tower three so we took the lift up and found ourselves stepping out into a nice warmly lit passage with a soft, cosy rug under our feet. Our son was just as excited as us. He opened the door and was surprised to find a curtain inside the room opening by itself. It was obvious that he had never seen a curtain like that before. We unpacked after our little inspection of the room, before heading down to the lobby for a late lunch. The painkillers were doing a pretty good job, as Tevita managed to walk around comfortably without any complaints.

That night we settled our son in our room, content but tired, before heading up to the infinity pool for a dip. Even before we got into the infinity pool, the view from the top deck was just breathtakingly spectacular.

It wasn't long after that we slowly waded into the cold water to the very edge and the deeper end of the pool. From there the view took our breath away, literally, as we looked down from what seemed like thousands of metres high. It was cold and windy at that height of over a thousand feet, so we only spent fifteen minutes in the pool. We made sure we enjoyed every minute of it.

I hate thinking back about that night now; there was something in me that knew that it could be our last special carefree time together, and that I needed to enjoy that beautiful, memorable moment while it lasted. I'm so grateful that I also captured those moments on video. Tevita ordered two mojitos for us, after I told him a funny story about me drinking a mojito. After we got out of the pool and onto our lounge chairs, we gazed at the skies above, both secretly pondering life and what it had in store for us.

Our drinks arrived just in time, and we ended a perfect night, sipping away at glasses of mojito while being entertained by the laser lightshow from the MBS infinity pool.

I told Te my funny story of a few days earlier when I went to meet up with my sim training partner, his wife, and another ex-workmate of ours at one of the malls. It was about twenty minutes' walk from the Ibis Hotel, and since I decided to have a little adventure with the map app on my phone, I walked instead of taking a taxi. They were all there when I arrived and already sipping their drinks. I noticed a glass of clear drink with a slice of lemon, garnished with mint leaves, in front of my sim training partner's wife. It instantly gave me the impression that it must have been a health drink with lemon to detox. As the waiter approached to take my order, I requested a glass of the same thing that she was having. My 'health drink' arrived five minutes later when we were chatting away. I cautiously took a sip and noted it indeed tasted as healthy as it looked, until about twenty minutes later when I noticed I was laughing a little bit louder and talking a bit more than usual. I had a tingling feeling in my feet and was feeling jolly. I wondered why, then the drink in front of me caught my attention. I embarrassingly asked my workmate's wife if the drink contained alcohol. She quickly answered, 'Yes,' with a smile. I just burst out laughing. I could not help but laugh at myself for unintentionally getting myself tipsy that early in the day. I grabbed the menu to check the mojito's ingredients and was surprised to see the word 'rum' in the list. Well, that explained a lot … laughter is the best medicine and my mojito gave me a good healthy dose of it that day.

It's moments like that, that Tevita would tease me for being such a typical village girl, and he even did this while we were sipping our mojitos that night at the MBS.

It was a beautiful and memorable night. From the pool, we went straight for a nice warm shower, dinner, and sweet sleep.

For the next six days, while juggling my training rosters and studies, we managed to visit a few other places including Cloud Forest, the zoo and the well-known Universal Studios.

We also caught up with a few friends from PNG over dinner, then later we all went to watch the Daveta team from Fiji play in a sevens rugby tournament there. He was so excited about watching the game, but I noticed that he was starting to limp again from the pain and exhaustion. I made sure he took his painkillers before we went to watch the game, so he could enjoy it. The nonstop roaring cheers coming from every corner of the pavillion filled up the whole arena with excitement. Children with painted faces were running around and dancing. Women and men buzzed around with red plastic cups of beer in their hands, proving that everyone was having a good time. The exhilarating atmosphere must have helped to keep his pain at bay as he was thoroughly enjoying himself, but I noticed that his body was saying otherwise. He was still limping, and it might have been that he had ignored the pain that day. I had to keep slowing down to walk beside him and he constantly needed to rest. The Daveta team was not due to play until a few hours later in the final, so we headed quickly in a taxi to the hotel for Tevita to get some rest. I couldn't help but notice how much he was pushing himself to walk around with us, without complaint. I had suggested that we just call it a day and for him to get a good long rest, but he insisted that we go and watch the final. We did, and I was as thrilled as he was that the Daveta team won.

Regardless of the pain that he was silently suffering, he managed to have a good time and said, 'It was worth it.'

Our visit to the zoo was also a beautiful, memorable experience with nature and animals. We saw lots of animals. Many were a first for our son, including a polar bear, a white tiger, a lion, a giraffe, a zebra, and monkeys, and we even fed an elephant. The zoo covered a massive area, so you can imagine how long we spent walking around the zoo. I remember checking the time and telling him that we had been walking around for almost three hours. We hadn't noticed the time, and I was impressed at how long we walked around, with hardly any rest for him. We finished our tour with a little family feast in the zoo's KFC before heading back to the hotel.

He seemed to have gotten his appetite and energy back, which was heartwarming to see. He would need more for our visit to Universal Studios the next day. It initially started off as a little fun adventure, when we had to ride a cable car twice to the island of Sentosa where Universal Studios is located. We got there and ended up lost for a while trying to find the entrance to the studios, which added a bit more fun. We finally found it and went straight onto the inverted roller-coaster. We were all excited lining up and watching people getting into the roller-coaster seats, then disappearing with their screams, only to reappear seconds later. Then came our turn. I took the first two seats in front with Yaca, while Tevita took the seat behind us. I thought the two front seats would give us the most thrilling sensation, as there was nothing in front to block our view. It was the longest ninety seconds of my life. I was screaming at the top of my lungs as we blasted off, almost hitting a wall, then we were turning, and twisting, and hanging upside down. Every fibre of my being was screaming as I felt I was going to fall out of my seat – I shut my eyes tightly and could still hear myself screaming, but this time I was swearing too. I was regretting getting on that ride. Surprisingly our eight-year-old son, sitting next to me, hardly screamed at all. I could also hear Tevita screaming behind us, but not our son. It was good to see Tevita having fun and enjoying himself, even if only for a short time.

After our ride, I could see that he was walking more slowly and struggling to keep up with us. We sat down to have lunch, and he said something that startled and terrified me.

'I'm hungry babe, but my body doesn't want to eat.'

I worriedly stared into his exhausted eyes with fear that the cancer was now slowly taking him away. It was frightening to hear, especially when I was yearning to see some good positive signs. I could not hold back the tears flowing down my cheeks, as I sat myself down next to him, grabbing his hands to seek comfort.

We cut our tour short, and made our way back to the hotel. That night I spent hours Googling, searching, and reading up on all the symptoms he was having. What I couldn't understand was that he was taking his leukaemia medication yet was still having all these symptoms. I felt around his abdomen and noticed that his spleen was enlarged. Oh, that scared me. With his night sweats and fever, I was even were more petrified as I discovered these were among the symptoms of leukaemia in its late stages. Terrified, like the world was about to come to an end, I held his hand and squeezed it tight, telling him that I'd be taking him to the hospital the next day.

The following day, Friday November 11th, we went straight to Singapore General Hospital after our breakfast. The facilities of the hospital and the service from the doctors and nurses were quite impressive. We had to leave our son Yaca waiting in one room, while we went into another to wait for the doctor. The hospital was very strict about wearing medical face masks so everyone going in to see a doctor had to wear one.

We waited for about forty-five minutes before they finally called his name. I reassured him that wherever this illness was going to take him, I would be right there with him, supporting him all the way, with all my heart. A young doctor welcomed us with a friendly smile and asked us to take a seat. He asked Tevita numerous questions while typing his notes on a laptop in front of him. He then proceeded to take his temperature, a urine test and a blood test. They informed us that the blood test results would be ready in about two to three hours, so we decided to go back to the hotel and wait there.

We managed to get some rest, as it was obvious that he was exhausted. He remarked on how impatient he was to get better.

I received the call for us to make our way back to the hospital as the blood results were ready. We decided to just go ourselves and let our son wait in the safety of the hotel room with some snacks and cartoons. After brief instructions on what to do if he heard the fire alarm, and not to open the door to any strangers, he excitedly went back to watching his movie. He was thrilled, feeling like a big boy, that we trusted him enough to leave him in the room. 'We'll be back soon son,' Tevita assured him before we left.

Reaching the hospital, we were informed that Tevita's white blood cell count was excessively high and that they would have to admit him for observation to try and bring this count down. I had mixed feelings. Although I was happy that we were in a very good hospital with high standards and exceptional medical service, at the same time I was apprehensive and anxious. I feared that he had reached a serious life-threatening stage of leukaemia.

He was immediately put on a drip and wheeled to a bed to be examined while they organised a room in one of the wards for him. Two female haematologists arrived within minutes to examine him. They asked very specific questions revealing that they were experienced and doing their jobs exceptionally well. It was comforting to know that he was in very good hands. More comforting was that we were answering no to most of their questions, except for a few. No fever, no nausea, no vomiting, no cough, no chest pain, no headaches, and no blood clot spots on his lips. He had almost none of these symptoms, except when asked if he had any blurry vision. He had a tiny blurry spot on his left eye that had been there for about eleven months.

It was not until after we got back to PNG, about two weeks before his passing, that he started to get all the symptoms they had asked about. Fever, blurry vision and, worst of all, vomiting in his last few hours.

The staff at Singapore General Hospital were incredibly kind and professional in taking care of us. About an hour later I was walking beside a Malaysian lady who was pushing Tevita in a wheelchair. Then through a passage, and after a few left and right turns, we came to a building labelled Block Eight. From there we took an elevator ride up to level eight where he was then wheeled into a room with four beds. It was a good spacious room with a few comfortable chairs and a coffee table on the left as I walked in. The two beds on the left and the first one on the right were all occupied. He was wheeled to the second one on the right, which was empty. It was quite a good-sized hospital bed that could fit two people comfortably cuddling. I turned and joked to Tevita that I would be squeezing myself in next to him in the middle of the night. One of the nurses gave him a nice clean, sky-blue hospital shirt and pants to wear.

After settling in and taking some chemo medicine, the doctors took more blood samples to test, and advised us that they would be monitoring his blood by taking samples every four hours. It was difficult to leave him there at the hospital alone, but I needed to go and check on our son.

I took a taxi back to the hotel, quietly opened the room and found our son sleeping snugly under the warm white sheets. Not wanting to wake him up, I tiptoed across the room and slowly sat down next to him. My mind despondently pondered how I had excitedly planned so many activities for us to do, yet here we were being admitted to hospital. We had only just started creating beautiful memories together in Singapore. I never imagined that Tevita would be admitted to a hospital here. I felt so alone, downhearted and depressed. The other person apart from my husband that I would vent to and completely pour my heart out to was my Twinny – Mrs Tali Piokole. We have this weird twin bond, which I will share later. Aside from Tevita, she was my other half. We had constantly been keeping in touch on WhatsApp throughout my time in Singapore, and more so that night.

I sent her a sobbing voice message at 9:19 p.m. 'Twinny, I just got back to the room, and Yaca is sleeping. They have admitted Tevita to the hospital … I wish you were close by to talk to. Oh, Yaca is awake now.'

I quickly wiped off my tears so Yaca would not see them. I saw his little wondering eyes searching around the room for his father, then he slowly asked in a tone that felt like a sword piercing through my heart. 'Na, where's Ta?'

That sweet little innocent voice of his was asking for his father. I froze, absolutely terrified at the thought of losing the father of my children. I could barely contain my tears, but managed to quickly explain that his father needed to stay in the hospital, so the doctors could take care of him. I hastily headed for the bathroom, locked the door behind me, and burst out crying. What if our son had asked me that question, and I couldn't answer it, because Tevita was gone? Lost forever to cancer. It's the most terrifying thing one can ever imagine, to lose your husband, and then having to break that heart-wrenching news to your children. It felt as if a part of me already knew that shortly I would be doing exactly that. At that particular moment, I needed my husband to hold my hand and comfort me, to tell me everything would be fine. But he was not there.

I tried to pray, but I couldn't – I must admit that I had not been on the right track with the Lord for some time, and at that point I felt unworthy even to pray. With no one else to turn to, I confided in the only person who was there in the room with me - my son.

'Son, Ta is very sick, and I am scared that something might happen to him. I'm scared son,' I cried. 'Please pray for your father to get better.'

Without wasting another second, he grabbed my hand and squeezed it, bowed his little head, and started to earnestly pray, begging God to heal his father. I must say it was one of my proudest moments with my son. I witnessed his father's strength in him; instead of breaking down with me, he put on a brave face.

9:29 p.m.: *I've been researching leukaemia online. There are three stages: chronic, accelerated and acute. He is at the second stage now, the accelerated phase. My late sister managed to live on for another five years, after being diagnosed with breast cancer.*

9:31 p.m., her reply: *Aww, Twinny, my sister. I know how you're feeling, please be strong.*

I read more of my messages as I poured my heart out to her.

9:33 p.m.: *I can see it in his eyes, Twinny. He tries very hard to show me he is strong … but I can see right through him. I am strong sometimes, but most times I just can't hold back my tears. Just the thought of losing Te is breaking my heart already. Whenever I need strength, it is usually him that I go to, but now it's heartbreaking when I want to turn to him, he isn't the usual strong Te. He can't walk for long and wants to sleep most of the time. How can I be strong now, on my own, without Te? Loving each other more every day now. I know I need to be strong, but I need someone to tell me that … I'm trying to stay positive, but I'm scared Twinny. I want to grow old with him, and watch our kids grow up together.*

9:35 p.m., she replied: *I will tell you that every day Twinny, BE STRONG. I really wish I was next to you right now. Please be strong my sister. Be strong for your kids and most importantly for Te. I know so well how you feel Twinny, please be strong in love. Whatever it takes, however long it takes and however far it goes, remain positive. I can't explain the hurt I feel for you right now. It would be harsh and wrong to say, don't cry, or don't worry, or be negative. There is nothing wrong in crying. You have to let yourself cry it out. Don't bottle it up. All I can tell you is to throw your burdens on God alone. He will see you through. He will give you the peace you need right now. Te needs to see you positive, so he can stay positive.*

I replied: *I would have shared stuff like this with my sister Annie, if I hadn't lost her to cancer. I'm so glad and thankful for your life, my Twinny.*

I remember that all I wanted to do that night was to weep, sob, and cry some more. Memories playing in my mind kept me thinking more about my two late sisters, how I never thought that I was going to lose them, but eventually did. I recall tears flowing uncontrollably down my cheeks, releasing the frustration, hurt, and pain that was welling up inside. I was mourning part of the life that I was not going to live out with my dear husband.

I quickly packed a few of his clothes and toiletries and headed back to the hospital with Yaca. By 10:30 p.m., I was back beside Tevita, holding his hand, taking a selfie and sending it to my Twinny. I felt so much better after chatting with her.

10:45 p.m., I sent her another message: *Thank you for lifting up my spirits, Twinny. I just wanted to send you that pic … I feel much better now, and Te was happy to see us. Thank you for your encouraging words … just what I needed to hear. Love you, my Twinny … thank you so much. Chat again later, I'll let you have your beauty sleep now. Xo.*

I got back to the hotel with Yaca just after midnight and tried to study but could not; he was all that was on my mind. It was a lonely, sleepless night and I missed him terribly. My ATR flight test was coming up that Monday, but I was glad that I had that weekend off to juggle hospital and studying time.

12th of November was a warm Saturday morning. We both slept in and woke up around 10:30 a.m. only to find a text message from Tevita sent at 6:00 a.m. *Wake up sleepy heads. It's morning – woke up and can't go back to sleep. Missing you Na.* We were so looking forward to going and spending the rest of the day with him and even more excited to learn that we could actually sleep with him in the hospital. To keep Yaca occupied at the hospital, I brought some of his favourite toys, and to keep myself occupied I packed all my notes to study.

It was there that Yaca befriended a Singaporean girl name Chloe, who was about the same age as him. They became very good friends, after spending hours and hours playing together and sharing toys in the hospital. I was glad to see that they were happily keeping each other busy at this difficult time for them both.

At one point Yaca came to me blushing – I wanted to laugh but held off in front of him. I always like to be open with my children and make them feel like they can be upfront and authentic with me and tell me anything and everything. From his reaction, I did not want to make him feel uncomfortable. It was obvious that he liked Chloe a bit.

Her grandfather had already been admitted to the hospital when we arrived and Tevita was given the bed next to him. Every day, Chloe and her mum were there by his side. They would leave around 9 o'clock at night when Chloe's uncle (her mum's brother) would come and stay until the next morning. I later learnt that her grandfather was also suffering from leukaemia. They had spent more than a hundred-thousand dollars on treatment and were told by the doctor that he was clear. However, one day, he collapsed suddenly and later it was found that he still had the cancer. Sadly and tragically he passed away, a day after we arrived back in PNG.

Although Tevita spent only five days in the hospital, that was enough time for a friendship to blossom between these little ones. I learnt about Chloe's grandfather passing away when she messaged Yaca and told him about the sad news. Yaca was deeply saddened for his friend.

That night we found ourselves excitedly making our way past corridors to Tevita's room. Despite the fact he was unwell, we had been granted permission to sleep with him in the hospital. We were excited, as if we were going on an adventure, and this helped lift our dampened spirits. As soon as we reached his room, we quickly looked around to decide where and how we were going to organise ourselves to sleep that night.

During the day, the patient in the bed opposite Tevita's was kind enough to point out the cupboard where a towel and other changes of bedclothes were kept for each patient. 'You can also have your shower there,' he called from across the room, pointing at the cupboard and the toilet. I looked at Tevita, confused, and he stared back at me, wondering what the man was talking about. All we could see on the other side of the room were four cupboards, one for each patient. A sink was next to the cupboards as well as a door that was almost always left half-open – this apparently was the toilet door.

It was almost midnight and Tevita was desperate to have a shower. Most of the lights in the room had been switched off, and the other patients were already asleep. We quietly made our way across the room, passing Chloe's grandfather's bed on the left and a small-sized door that had been shut ever since we first arrived there. Next to that closed door was the toilet; the door was a little bit bigger, with a sink just in front of the toilet and the four cupboards.

'Where is the bathroom?' Tevita whispered.

'Well that guy pointed this way, so it should be somewhere here,' I replied. But the only door we could see open was the toilet door. I checked inside and saw a small shower-like head hanging on the side of the toilet seat and noticed a pool of water on the floor slowly draining away. Judging from the wet floor, it looked like someone had just finished having a shower, so we assumed this must be where they had their shower too. We thought maybe it was the Singaporean way, to have the shower and the toilet in the same room.

I recall how I was puzzled at first when I walked into a toilet in one of the shopping malls there and saw that I needed to squat to use the toilet. I also noticed a tap on the side, but it did not have a showerhead like the one in the hospital. The one in the hospital had about a one-metre-long pipe hooked on the side, and I noticed it was long enough to bathe with. We both concluded that we had found the shower. Tevita hung his towel inside and was about to undress when we heard Yaca yell from behind me, 'I found the bathroom!' It was the other closed door in the room. If it weren't for Yaca, Tevita would have showered using what they use to clean their bottoms.

We blamed our ignorance on the fact that there was no bathroom sign on the door and it was always closed. We both thought that it must have been a storeroom for bedsheets or other medical equipment. That could have been a hilarious story for our grandchildren, which Yaca and I will now have to tell.

After his refreshing shower, Tevita was snug in his bed and as comfortable as possible and I managed to catch up on some reading. Optimistically, I already saw myself passing this test and flying next to my husband, once he recovered, someday soon. I felt much better studying next to him.

By midnight, Yaca was comfortably sleeping on a bed we made for him using two chairs pushed together. We took two seats, almost as long as beach chairs, that perfectly fitted his eight-year-old body, and placed them facing each other next to his father's bed. The nurses were kind enough to give us an extra blanket for him.

Getting ready for my flight test that Monday, I managed to complete reviewing things while Tevita was watching a movie on the screen hanging just above the foot of his bed. Each patient was privileged enough to have their own little flat-screen TV for entertainment. I kept on studying, seated next to him, before dozing off to sleep. It was not particularly comfortable as I kept twisting and turning, trying to find a better position, but it was still far better than my comfortable hotel bed. There was nowhere else in the world I would rather be than right there close to him. Surprisingly, under the circumstances, we all managed to get a good night's sleep.

The next morning bright and early at six, the nurses came to collect more blood for tests. His white blood count was slowly decreasing and stable, but still high. It was a beautiful Sunday morning with the sunlight bursting through gaps between the hospital's thick curtains. Tevita went back to sleep and I finally managed to get a few minutes of sleep on Yaca's two chairs while he played with his toys. We spent most of that day with Tevita, keeping him company, but could not stay that night. I needed to go back to the hotel to get ready for my ATR flight test the following morning. All the hard work and study I had been doing with my sim partner, Captain Alistair Dissanayake, was in preparation for a four-hour flight test the next morning from 10 a.m. to 2 p.m.

I recall how we would sit in the hotel restaurant bar during our many study sessions, our training books spread out in front of us, our hands reaching out here and there, switching invisible buttons in our imaginary cockpit. The bartender would keep running back and forth, thinking we were waving for him, and only refrained after we repeatedly told him we were studying. I'm sure there must have been some people there who thought we were crazy.

I could hardly wait to get the test over and done with, to get it off my mind and concentrate on my husband. Again, Yaca had to stay by himself in the room and wait for my return. I made sure though to leave more than enough food for him, knowing that he could be a big eater. We got a ten-minute break after our first two hours, and I managed to make a quick call to Yaca. First thing he mentioned was that his father had also called to check up on him. Two hours later the test was over and I felt relief and a load lift off my shoulders.

I sent Tevita a picture of me shaking the hand of the testing officer with the caption, *Done babe.* He replied with a congratulatory text and informed me that he was waiting to go and have his bone marrow biopsy. He really wanted me to be by his side when they did the procedure, but unfortunately, I could not make it in time. We were hoping that he was going to be discharged that day, but the doctors needed to keep him in for a blood transfusion. I asked if he wanted me to change our return tickets to a later day so he could get as much treatment from the hospital as possible. He simply replied, 'No Na, I just want to go back home.'

That was to be his fourth night in the hospital, and our second night sleeping over with him. We were a bit more excited than on our first night. Yaca knew what to do and arranged his bed himself this time. As for me, I tried sleeping while seated beside my husband, but it wasn't long before my body was aching all over. Tevita saw that I was uncomfortable, and as if reading my mind, shifted himself to the other side of the bed, leaving enough space for me. We both knew that the nurses would eventually chase me away, but for now it didn't matter. I felt safe and loved in his warm, gentle arms, and did not realise that I fell asleep. Recalling this now is such a sweet moment, and it is among my most treasured memories.

I remember waking up to the nurse checking the drip on his arm. She obviously saw me, but only smiled back and waved that it was okay. Later there was another nurse who came to wake me up and told me that the bed was for patients only. I know she was just doing her job but I didn't care. I crawled right back next to Tevita as soon as she disappeared, and refused to let that nurse ruin my moments in my husband's arms.

We woke up to another beautiful morning in the hospital on Tuesday the 15th of November, and as planned, I later took Yaca to a children's amusement centre in Singapore called KidZania (an indoor kid-sized city where children get to play in a miniature city, and for once feel like an adult). There was special money they could withdraw from a bank in KidZania, and he even got himself a driver's licence that he proudly displayed in a pocket of his wallet. It was wonderful to watch him lose his shyness and mingle with the other kids. But I was missing his father enormously, and even more, I missed watching our son with him. I felt incomplete and could not wait to get back to the hospital. We made plans that we were going to bring the two girls, Mela and Ipa, to KidZania. I kept updating Tevita with photos and messages to let him know how his son was doing and I knew he was really happy to see Yaca having fun.

We got back to the hospital in time to be there for his first ever blood transfusion. He was feeling much better, and I saw his face light up when he was told that they would be discharging him that night. Hours later, we were back in our own little hotel room feeling somewhat complete.

With Yaca already snoring, I caught myself staring and taking in every detail of Tevita's face from his eyelashes to his nose and cheeks, then tracing my hand along his jawline. Living and loving that very moment, I found myself appreciating all of him and being thankful that I got to spend another night in his arms.

The next morning, we headed down to have breakfast in the hotel restaurant, and it was so good to see Tevita with his appetite back. He loaded about eight mini pancakes onto his plate and it made me smile, thinking, Now, that is my husband. We planned to go and check out the Merlion, do some shopping, then head back to the hotel and pack for our flight back to PNG that night. Yaca was very concerned about flying at night and he kept rattling on about his worries that the pilot might fall asleep and that we would crash. I had to explain, as best I could, that flying at night was OK, reassuring him that we would reach home safely.

It was a beautiful, attractive sight at the Merlion and a lot of tourists from all over the world were posing next to it. I tried to make my husband enjoy as much as he could, but it was difficult with him being drained from exhaustion. I also saw how hard he was trying to enjoy this with us but the effort was showing on his face. He was walking much slower and had to sit down to catch his breath. It was not long before we headed back to the hotel. With all that he was feeling, he still insisted on accompanying me to the market for some last-minute shopping.

It was there that I finally managed to make him laugh, when I decided to try a snack called Dragon's Breath. It was like sweet music to my ears to hear him laugh out loud from the heart like that again. I had been missing his lively personality, and laughed along with him. The Dragon's Breath was served in cups, and included meringue and puffed cereal doused in liquid nitrogen. Once I poured some in my mouth, I was breathing out cold air, which looked like smoke, through my mouth and nostrils as I munched on the snack. I must obviously have looked like some funny smoker and this got him laughing hard. It was very heartwarming to see and hear him laugh so heartily like that again.

We departed Singapore on the 16th at 8:15 p.m. and arrived back into PNG just before 5 a.m. the next morning, November 17th 2016. That day is firmly embedded now in my mind, as it was exactly one month before he was to part from us, and rest with the Lord.

I strongly urge everyone to cherish every moment with your loved ones, whether they're sick or in good health, and to go on creating memories. Even if one is going through hard times, we can always see the beautiful little intricate parts that make those memories all the sweeter, and be grateful always for the fact that the gift of life has been granted to us. Make time to create those beautiful memories with your loved ones and try to capture them. Nowadays we are so blessed to have the technology to do just that.

I documented almost all our activities in Singapore, just as we did in PNG and Fiji, and I am so glad I did. My children are now able to watch their father on video, especially when we find ourselves missing him deeply and dearly. I know that, years from now, their children will get to watch the grandfather they never got to meet, and somehow feel like they know a lot about him.

To say the least, it has helped immensely with our healing process. We not only get to see and hear Tevita talk, but also, better still, see and hear him laugh. That makes us smile a little, amidst our pain and sorrow, and reminds us that he lived a happy, full life.

Singapore will always hold a special place in my heart, as we created so many beautiful memories during some of our very last moments together.

13

Letting Go

To fall in love is easy, staying in love is a challenge and letting go is the hardest part but the end of life is not the end of love.

ANON

I moved a little closer and softly whispered into his ear, 'I'm here *wajïqu*. I'm here, loving you.'

December 17th 2016 and it was just past midnight and I had just wished him a happy wedding anniversary. But, now there were no responses to my frantic calls to Tevita, my darling.

My heart was racing as I stood there watching the nurses and doctors running around, in and out of that hospital room. They had just changed the oxygen supply from to his nose through a tube, to via a transparent mask now covering both his mouth and nose. Through it life was flowing from the concentrated oxygen bag attached to it. I stood next to him, with my left hand around his head, leaning over, trying to get closer to him than ever before. I wanted desperately for him to feel my presence and to know that I was still there. I could hear the heavy, rough breathing through his mouth, like a soft snore filling up the room. His eyes were closed with his hands across his chest. I stared into his loving and tired face while running my fingers through his dark hair. Slowly I whispered again, 'Loving you, loving you, Ta,' knowing that I wouldn't be getting any response, but I knew that somewhere in him, he heard me. Suddenly I noticed his tight fist loosen on his chest, as if preparing to wave goodbye. My eyes lit up when I saw his hand moving, happy to get a response, and to know that he could still hear me. Little did I know, that was the last response I would ever be getting from him.

I slowly took a step back and watched the nurses as they pushed in a metal cart full of more medical supplies. I saw metal bowls filled with cotton wool, swabs, syringes, needles, tongs, and scissors. I saw a small TV, like a screen monitor with little cords hanging on the side, being wheeled in. They placed it next to the IV drip stand just beside his bed. I took a few more steps back towards the bed opposite his to allow more room for the nurses. I felt as if I was split in three. Firstly, in my heart, I had this fear that I had never felt before. Secondly, my soul – I felt as if my soul had left me and was floating in the air, refusing to accept what was happening, and thirdly, I felt so alone and lost, as though I was reaching out to the Lord for comfort of any sort.

Lord, I'm scared! I'm scared. What do I do Lord? What do I do? I cried from within.

I turned away from the nurses working on Te, with the monitor beeping in the background. I quickly grabbed the Bible from my bag and hugged it as tight as I could – and with that I just let myself collapse on the bed in tears.

With my head down, I cried, 'Lord, my God, I'm scared.'

Immediately, for some reason, my mind drifted back to how we had magically fallen so deeply in love again, just three months earlier. As if the Lord was telling me that my dear husband Tevita would be leaving me soon. I refused to believe it, just refused.

I cried out my questions. 'Lord, were you preparing me for this? Is this why you let us fall in love all over again? Because he was going to go?' Oh, how I felt the answer pierce right through my heart. I refused and fought it. 'No! No! No! Please Lord, not now,' I pleaded with God. 'I still need him – my children, who is going to be their father?'

Just then, I recalled the last Bible scripture I had read to Tevita about an hour earlier. It was Psalm 27:14. 'Wait on the Lord, be strong and let your heart take courage, wait on the Lord.' That verse gave me a bit of strength and hope that my Tevita was going to recover from what only seemed a coma to me. I quickly wiped the tears I had been crying and turned back to see my husband Tevita surrounded by nurses and doctors. Everything was a blurry scene, but I could still hear the beeping sound from the monitor showing wavy coloured lines and some numbers. I moved closer towards him and stopped as the doctor standing next to him pulled out a small torch from her pocket. With both of my hands clasped on my chest, as if I was still begging God, I hoped for a miracle to happen. The doctor carefully opened his left eyelid and flashed the light across his eye a few times while I watched, too afraid to blink.

What did I miss? Had his eye moved, and I missed it?

I refused to believe and accept what was unfolding before my eyes.

About an hour later, I was told that we would be transferred downstairs to the ICU. The look the doctor and nurse gave each other slowly sunk into my heart and shattered what little hope I had.

No! I told myself. I have to wait on the Lord, I have to be strong. I kept reminding myself of the last Bible verse I had read.

Without delay, I started packing our belongings – his small basket of fruit that was on his bedside cabinet, and toiletries from inside the drawer. A quick glance at the wall clock hanging above the nurse's station opposite our room said it was just after 1:30 a.m. I followed behind the two nurses and the doctor as they wheeled Tevita out from the room, along the quiet and well-lit passage, then out of Ward 8. I stood and watched them slowly disappear into the elevator as the door slid shut, separating us. My heart felt a stab at the possibility of that feeling becoming a reality, but I fought it. The elevator wouldn't fit all of us so I had agreed to take the one flight of stairs down. I lost count of the number of times I had been going up and down those stairs.

A lot had happened in the last couple of weeks. My husband had just returned from a flight test in Melbourne, then he and our son Tevita Jnr or Yaca as we called him had joined me in Singapore, where I had gone to do my ATR 72 aircraft type rating. It was there that we created more sweet memories. We visited the zoo, Universal Studios, and the Merlion. And to tick it off our bucket list, we'd spent one night at the Marina Bay Sands. I had passed my flight test while Tevita was in Singapore General Hospital. Almost two weeks later we were on our flight back to PNG, after he was discharged from the hospital, and one week before we would reunite with our two daughters. He had gained a bit of strength, but not as much as we would have liked or expected. It had been six months since our daughters last visited and we hadn't seen each other since then. We had both decided to send them off to spend one year in the village with my parents so they could learn about our Fijian culture, traditions, and mostly to appreciate life.

Before we knew it, the most eagerly anticipated date – Friday November 25th 2016 – had arrived and our family was complete again. I had been busy that morning preparing a small lunch for them and after glancing at the time, I quickly ran upstairs. Their flight was to arrive at 12 midday. Up in our room I turned to Tevita to see if he was going to change his mind and join me in going to the airport. I saw that he just wanted to rest, so he told me to go pick up the girls and my parents from the airport, while he would go and have his shower. It was a beautiful sunny day as I excitedly waited with Yaca for the girls and my parents.

After a few minutes in the waiting area, my thoughts rushed back home to my darling husband who was all alone upstairs in our room, so I made a quick call to our house girl to be on alert in case he called for her. A few minutes later my phone rang, and I found myself standing there trembling, as I listened to him telling me how he had almost collapsed in our bathroom. The only response I could get out of my mouth was a cry of fear and regret for leaving him all alone.

'Ta!' My echo faded slowly over the line. I imagined the worst that could happen – our two daughters running excitedly up the flight of stairs to our room to hug their father, only to be greeted by his pale body on the bathroom floor. He must have heard the agonising worry in my voice, and like always, he reassured me again that he was feeling better now and for me not to worry.

The girls finally arrived with my parents, and my son was the happiest – he was over the moon to have his sisters back. We loaded everything up quickly, wasting no time, and started our drive home. It was my father's first time in PNG, and my mother's second trip, so I asked my father to take the front passenger seat. I was happy to have them there but also saddened, knowing that Tevita was very sick. Dad asked me how Tevita was, and I just replied that he was okay.

We got home, and just outside our front door there was another joyful greeting between the girls and our house girl Auntie Benny, who had been with us for three years. Olimaipa, our nine-year-old daughter, or Ipa as we normally call her, was the closest to their father. She wasted no time and ran in a flash upstairs to see him. I tried to follow behind her with my camera, hoping to capture their moment of reunion and wanting that raw reaction. She was so fast, all I captured in the first few seconds of video was her little feet running up the stairs. She swung the door open and found her father sitting at the edge of the bed wearing a striped white-and-green vest and shorts.

Looking a little bit pale and weak, Tevita managed as always to pull out a smile for Ipa. She ran straight into his open arms and hugged him tightly. He held her a little bit longer and gave her a kiss on her forehead before releasing her to have a good look again at her tanned skin. Melaia, our eleven-year-old firstborn, is the more reserved and mature one. She entered the room with Yaca following behind, and shyly gave her father a hug, then sat down next to him. He briefly joked about their tanned look and how they had lost a bit of baby fat.

Tevita then looked at himself, and with a frown said, 'I've gone skinny too because I'm sick.' Oh, how my heart was saddened hearing his comments and concern about the reality of his weight loss. We had been working out a lot in the gym, and he had been working very hard on building up his chest muscles. Our little family reunion was a mixture of joy and sadness.

We were both happy that our family was now finally complete again, and very proud of the girls for all that they learnt in the village. We knew that it had been a little bit of a struggle for them, but it was for their own good. Yaca had stayed back with us, so he was very excited and couldn't wait to update the girls with all the stories he had gathered to tell them.

I had informed the kids back in 2012 after Tevita's diagnosis of leukaemia, that their father had a blood disease that was very serious. That was four years ago, and it didn't really dawn on them that they could be losing their father to this disease. Since their arrival, the girls now noticed how serious the disease had gotten with their father and would regularly come into our room to check on how he was doing. We all slept in our room from that night onwards – the kids would spread mattresses at the foot of our king-size bed to be closer to us. Ipa, out of our three children, is the outspoken, outgoing and more determined one. She is not afraid to try out things and loves to dress up. Tevita had always joked about how she was going to be the reason that he would buy a gun, to keep the boys away.

They shared a special father-daughter bond. Often I would find her sleeping on the floor beside the bed just to be closer to her dad, and sometimes she'd even jump up on the bed with us in the middle of the night.

On their second night back from Fiji, I took her shopping with me to a supermarket not far from where we lived. On the drive back, while stopped at a traffic light, she innocently asked me, 'Na, if Ta dies are you going to marry another man?' I was caught off guard with that question, not because I didn't know the answer, but because I realised that she was worried about losing her father and what the future would hold for us. I felt for her tender little heart that was already concerned about what would happen if her father died.

She didn't give me a chance to reply but reassured herself, and me, with, 'But Ta is not going to die, right? Because you've been praying for him.'

'Yes Ipa, Ta is not going to die,' I managed to say, trying to stay positive. 'You're not going to grow up without your father.' In my curiosity, I asked, 'Why did you ask that?'

She turned to face me with a tiny frown. 'Because I don't want you to marry another man,' was Ipa's honest reply. As a young mother, I always practised being open with my kids about everything and encouraged them to do the same with me.

Saturday ended, then Sunday went by, and Tevita's energy levels kept deteriorating. Walking up the stairs was too exhausting for him – he would have to sit down as soon as he reached our bedroom for three to five minutes to catch his breath. I would sit and watch him while he showered, just to be close by in case of another collapse.

Monday November 28th came and I spoke with his doctor. He advised me to bring him in for a blood transfusion. By 11 a.m., a nurse was wheeling him up to Ward 8, a private wing at the Port Moresby General Hospital.

The ward was not busy, but there were a few nurses walking around in deep-blue uniforms attending to patients, and most other rooms were empty as we walked past. The blue-painted passage walls and tiles created a calm and strangely inviting atmosphere, and we felt that we would be well-looked after there, however brief our stay would be. The passage was lined with hand sanitiser sprays mounted on the walls, with room fans whizzing away in the distance. We finally reached a room on our right just across from the nurse's station. It was fairly spacious, with tall louvred windows from top to bottom ventilating the well-lit room. Four beds were in the room we entered; two on the left, and two on the right. One of the beds on the left was already occupied, as well as one on the right. We were assigned the empty bed on the right just beside the door. The bed was separated from the rest of the ward by a cream-coloured curtain and a wooden bedside cabinet. We settled in, and before long, a doctor walked in with a syringe and some gauze. I looked on as she drew some blood from my Tevita's frail hand, and sent this sample to the lab.

By now my husband had been sick for over a month, and I could tell he was tired and drained from the experience. He was worn out from feeling tired, helpless and weak. Through his frailty though, I could see a slight glimmer of hope, as I knew he was looking forward to regaining his strength after the blood transfusion. It was at that moment that I felt an overwhelming sadness engulf me. I realised I was missing my husband – I missed him, even though he was right beside me. I missed us. Everything about us. I missed doing grocery shopping, cooking, going to the gym, watching movies, singing, and laughing with him. Night came and with darkness outside, we waited for the blood transfusion.

The chirping of birds woke me with the sun's rays flooding our cubicle. I had managed very little sleep the night before. Tuesday November 29th, I made a few more calls to his doctor. By then, I was told that his registrar was on his way. At that point, we both felt we were desperately running out of time. I had cried myself to sleep that night, wanting so badly to see my husband get better. I was missing him immensely. That morning he was complaining a bit about his breathing and a headache. The nurses came and did their ward rounds at 8 a.m. and I stood behind them, watching the numbers displayed on the small screen of the monitor they'd been pushing around. I pointed at the bottom left number and asked, 'What's this number for?'

'Oh, that one is a bit low, but I think the monitor is not working properly,' the nurse replied. 'Don't worry, we'll only get worried if the patient is having trouble breathing,' the nurse added.

At that point, Tevita was struggling with his breathing, although with his tough personality he tried to remain calm and collected about it. In shock, I was frantic; they had not noticed his shortness of breath.

'It's not broken,' I cried. 'He's having trouble breathing!'

The nurse didn't seem to believe me, so she turned to Tevita, who appeared to be lying in bed comfortably with no shortness of breath at all and asked, 'Are you having short breath?'

'No. Only when I get up to walk to the toilet,' he casually replied. I immediately gave Tevita the 'what do you mean' look.

'You are having trouble breathing, Tevita. You have to tell them,' I said.

Knowing him, he always wanted to show that he was alright, even when he was not, just so he would not feel like a burden to others.

They quickly put him on an oxygen mask and he felt much better afterwards, his headache vanishing in an instant.

The registrar finally turned up at 11 a.m., but with the news that Tevita's blood type, O+, was out of stock in the blood bank. The blood from our faces drained, and with it, what little hope we previously had. He went on to tell us that we would now need to call our relatives to come and donate blood.

'But all our relatives are in Fiji,' Tevita quietly replied.

In his remark, I sensed his anguish and despair and it bruised my heart to see him like that. I immediately turned to the doctor and insisted on donating blood. 'I'm O+ type too and I am ready to give all my blood for Tevita.' I turned back to my husband. 'I am willing to give you all my blood, *wajiqu*. I want you well so badly.' I had seen enough of him being weak, exhausted and struggling to walk. I wanted to restore that hope and give that face a smile again. The warm smile he wore so comfortably as a symbol of life, of love, of promise.

I went and waited my turn at the blood bank.

'What's the patient's name?' the young woman asked.

I wanted to reply, 'My husband, the father of our three beautiful children, the love of my life. It is for him I want to give all the blood I can, that his body needs more than me.'

'Tevita Secivo,' I replied.

They checked my haemoglobin level, and it was well above the minimum requirement, so I was given the thumbs up. My blood started flowing excitedly within me, and I was thrilled that within a few hours my blood would be running through my husband's veins, giving him all the energy, life, and love that he needed to fight back to good health and to us. Just then the lady helping me asked, 'Have you already had your monthly?' I happily informed her that yes, it just ended two days ago. Oh! The frown she gave me threw my hopes right against the wall.

'I'm sorry, you need a few more days to stabilise and then return,' she informed me. 'You can't give blood now.'

I knew I had to find some people willing and able enough to donate blood for my husband. My thoughts went straight to our close friends at work. I knew though that we needed even more help, as they were all flying and had restrictions on donating blood. The next group on my mind was my fitness group, the Commit To Be Fit group.

We had formed this group over a year earlier. We created a Facebook group page where mothers and working ladies had a private place to share their challenges, successes, and tips to help others facing the same situations. We did our own training, took pictures, and posted them on our page to motivate us. The group went beyond fitness and organised fun days with our families when we met and bonded with the men and children in our lives. We even had dinners, and karaoke or movie nights once a month, in celebration of our progress over the past thirty days. What I loved about our group was the love, trust, and respect we had for each other. We had all forged a bond and grown to be more than just friends, more like sisters. This was where it all started between me and my Twinny. She was in Fiji at the time Tevita was being admitted, and I updated her daily.

Now back to the dilemma at hand – I still had to find people to donate blood. I hated that she was so far away, as she would have been the first person I would call if she was in Port Moresby. I scrolled through the contact list on my phone. The first name from my group I saw, was Nicole Lopa.

Nikki, Tali, and a few more ladies in our group are married to pilots, like me. It was no surprise that our husbands got along pretty well, and we were one big happy family. I immediately dialled her number.

'Hey B, how are you?' she greeted me on the other end.

'Hi Nikki.' I was relieved. 'Oh Nikki,' I blurted out, 'we've been waiting for a blood transfusion and they've just told us that there is no type O+ in the blood bank.' I was speechless after that.

I was so relieved to hear a sister's voice when I needed one so badly, and I just couldn't help myself, I cried. I tried to conceal my sobbing, but it was obvious that she could tell from her side of the line.

'Bogi.' … No reply. 'Bogi?' … Still no reply. I was afraid to let her hear my vulnerability through my trembling voice as I spoke. Her firm voice came again, 'Bogi, where are you? I'm coming now.'

'At Pom Gen, Ward 8,' was all I managed to mumble.

'I will be there soon,' was her reply.

In half-an-hour, Nicole was lying in one of the beds at the blood bank. Next to her was her cousin who she had brought along. Needles were inserted into their forearms with rich dark blood slowly flowing out to fill the bags hanging down the sides of the beds.

About half-an-hour later, I was standing at the head of Tevita's bed watching the doctor carefully insert a needle into his right hand. She pushed an IV stand closer to his side and hung up the bag of blood. I looked down, expecting to see a smile on Tevita's face, but instead, I saw tears slowly welling up in his eyes. I almost never saw him cry and could hardly remember the last time I had seen this – I was worried.

'Te, what's wrong?' I quietly asked.

He tiredly shook his head from side to side, as if he was trying to shake the tears off, when he whispered in a slow, soft voice, 'I am moved by your friends.'

In three hours, my sisters from the CTBF group had managed to donate five bags of blood for Tevita. I told him how they had posted messages on social media and WhatsApp to find relatives and friends with the same blood type.

Even my Twinny, Tali, was hunting for more friends in PNG to donate blood, although she was miles away in Fiji. One of the ladies' husbands was sending emails to all his co-workers, asking for anyone with blood type O+ to donate. He himself ended up on a bed in the blood bank donating blood for Tevita. I told my husband how I had met strangers that day who had turned up to donate blood, just for him. He was very touched by the enormous love we both felt from the group and from all those beautiful people.

That day I also called my fifty-eight-year-old mother and our house girl to come and donate blood. However, my mother's haemoglobin level was below what was required, and she was told that she only had enough blood for herself. Our house girl, on the other hand, managed to happily donate blood. A few hours later, I was posting pictures of Tevita getting Nikki's blood to my CTBF group page. I was eager to let them know how he had shed a few tears of joy after such a long time.

By Friday December 2nd, I had spent the night sleeping on the floor next to Tevita's bed since he was admitted the previous Monday. At night, when all the visitors had gone, I would pull out my Fijian mat from underneath the bed and spread it on the floor between the bed and the window facing the passage. The cream-coloured curtain pulled around the bed provided a bit of privacy for us. I loved it; just the two of us alone together once more. It was nice and cosy, and made us forget all that was going on around us. There was not much space on the floor to allow half a single-bed mattress to fit perfectly. I would watch the nurses' feet pass by as I rested on the floor. Regrettably, that was the second place in the world I wanted to be – the first being in Tevita's arms.

That Friday, there were only two patients in the room. The night was chilly, with a cool wind blowing through the ward. There were showers outside, and at that hour, there was silence all around. One patient had been discharged the day before. The other remaining patient next to Tevita's bed was a PNG national. I remember him to be in his early sixties, of average height and slim build. I never saw his wife spend a night there, however, his two boys would rotate nights to watch him. From my sleeping spot under the bed, many nights I would see his feet descend from his bed, put on his flip-flops, and then, accompanied by two other feet, disappear into the passage. I had assumed that it was all his trips to the men's room. Sometimes we would be awoken early in the morning to the smell of some yummy food and I would always wonder who would be eating that early – it was him.

That morning at around 3 a.m., my eyes were heavy, so I didn't bother to turn and look, but I could hear footsteps and his voice chatting to a younger male voice, then it slowly echoed and disappeared into the hall. They were gone for a while and I never saw or heard their return. It dawned on me that he might have been sneaking out.

Tevita received a few more bags of blood during the next couple of days. After breakfast he was sitting up and more energised than when he was first admitted, smiling and cracking jokes, as he was accustomed to doing with his new friend, the patient in the bed across from us. He had become friends with the local patient and they got along quite well. Later he shared with me why they had been laughing.

'The old man snuck home this morning,' Tevita said.

'What? We can do that here? How did he do it?' I hastily asked.

'He tricked his son, and told him he was hot and needed to sit in the car for the air-conditioning.'

'And then what?' I excitedly and impatiently asked.

I was so eager to hear how they had snuck out of the hospital, hoping to pick up a hint or two. The day before, I had been jokingly telling Tevita how I thought I was ovulating, and I felt like abducting him to a hotel room just across the street. 'So what happened next?' I asked eagerly.

Tevita continued, 'As soon as they got in the car, he ordered his son to drive. So the son had no choice and ended up driving all the way to their house.'

I flashed Tevita my widest grin, and with a wink, said, 'We're going to sneak you home too after this,' then finished it off with my left eyebrow slightly raised, for more effect.

We were planning to have baby number four the following year, but when Tevita got sick we were not sure if we wanted to wait any longer. We tidied up his bed and innocently took a slow, relaxed walk along the passage. We went past the nurse's station, and out towards the main door. We were wary that one of the nurses might call us back and question where we were going, but they only smiled at us, probably sensing the chemistry in the air. Phew! That was a big relief. Without a minute to lose we quickly got into our car and made our five-minute drive home in just two.

It felt like we were escaping a prison sentence, like a little adventure, and we were both laughing about it on the drive home. There was a big improvement in him compared to when he first was admitted.

We were both happy that we were going to try our luck for our baby number four. So as soon as we reached home we rushed upstairs and quickly got busy and down to business.

We later headed back to the hospital, this time worried that the nurses might have been looking for him. We ended up laughing again about our little escapade.

The following morning, we got the thumbs up from the doctor that we were okay to be discharged. From the day before, the nurses might have added in a good word for us. At long last, the news we had been waiting for; one week in the hospital was more than enough, and we missed our home. We missed our family and our familiar comforts that we often took for granted.

In the days that followed we were back home and effortlessly enjoyed our time together with our children. Tevita would occasionally join us downstairs for dinner, but most days I served his meal in bed, to let him rest, in the hope of him recovering better. We didn't mind as long as Dad was home. I remember one time he was sitting on the couch and I went and lay beside him, resting my head on his lap. I had been missing all those little things that we did at home. Now it was different. It wouldn't be long before he'd tell me that he needed to lie down and rest.

I also remember how I was excitedly trying on a grey half-laced dress that I had bought in advance for my maternity photo shoot. How I was pushing my tummy out and showing him all kinds of poses that I was going to do. I saw a very tired, smiley face, in his effort to conjure a smile for me. Now, looking back, I wonder what was going on in his mind. I wonder if he had felt that he was not going to win this battle with cancer. I wonder if he felt pain within, that he might easily shatter my hopes and dreams.

Maybe that was why, just out of the blue, he muttered, 'At least I am going to be with my mother.' His mother, who he was very close to, had passed away seven years earlier. To hear his remark was as if he was slowly letting go of us, and that day I died a little inside.

'What about us?' I pleaded.

I could feel what he was feeling. I felt that he was feeling down, and needed some uplifting words to reassure him.

'You're strong and brave,' I reminded him. 'You're a conqueror, and you will fight this.'

One week after being discharged, I was to join the rest of the ladies for our CTBF group Christmas dinner. He seemed fine as I was getting ready that night, but suddenly started to have a fever again. I decided to cancel my attendance. He still insisted that I go and got very apologetic about being sick, and being the reason why I wasn't able to go out with my friends. Being the considerate, kind, and caring person he was, he kept insisting I go. With his puppy-dog eyes and lips in a pout, he begged me to go.

I turned around and asked, 'What's the point of me going, if my mind will be back here worrying about you? Besides, there's no other place I'd rather be, than right here with you. I won't enjoy the dinner so I might as well stay.' He finally agreed.

I'll never forget his prayer as he lay in bed that night, with me sitting by his side. Without any warning he started praying, 'Lord, I thank you for Galuoko's life and for blessing her with a patient care-giving heart.'

I sat there, deeply touched and humbled, hearing his earnest prayer for me. I had never heard him pray like that before, and for the first time, I refused to close my eyes and miss witnessing a sacred communion unfolding before me. I sat and continued to watch my husband with full admiration of his humility before God, and his concerns for me, his wife.

He was sorry for something I didn't expect him to be sorry for, but he continued his prayer. 'Lord, please forgive me for marrying Galuoko when she was still too young. Forgive me, Father, for robbing her of her early years of womanhood. I pray you bless her with a stronger loving and forgiving heart.'

With that, he ended his prayer. In that instant, I held my husband close, reassuring him with love that I was forever grateful to God that we had met early in life and I wouldn't have had it any other way. It was a Friday evening, and he had led our opening Sabbath that afternoon. Little did we know, that was to be our last Sabbath together as a family.

My dad would send the kids upstairs to our room daily at 6 o'clock in the morning and evening to hold hands and pray for their father since he had been admitted to the hospital.

With the passing days, I started to watch his health slowly deteriorate. He again had a high fever, and I would stay up to sponge-bathe him. He had trouble sleeping, his energy levels dropped and the shortness of breath returned. He dreaded returning to hospital. His heart would beat so loudly that he could hear it. Occasionally he would call me to come over and listen to it. I remember one morning, I was making the bed while he sat on one of the kids' mattresses on the floor, waiting for me. When finished I told him that he could get back on the bed. My heart instantly sank when I turned around and saw him struggling to lift himself off the floor. I quickly ran to him, grabbed hold of him under his arms and lifted his now lean body up to the bed. Oh, how it hurt so bad, seeing him in that state. Of the two of us, he was always the stronger one, the one I would turn to for strength, the one who was supposed to be lifting me up, and not the other way around. I couldn't hold it in any longer, and burst out crying behind him as he lay in bed. I didn't want him to see me crying so I ran to the kids' room to let it all out.

Every day my Twinny and I would keep in touch. She had gone to Fiji with her daughters and they were staying in her mother's village. The house where they stayed had only one spot with a good network connection. It was under a lemon tree next to their house, with a bench under it, where she would sit while we chatted. A few nights later she messaged me that the CTBF group had started fundraising to send Tevita to get medical treatment in the Philippines. She updated me and informed me that they had raised K 4,000 in the first forty-five minutes. I was speechless at how these amazing ladies were pouring their hearts out for us again. We were so moved by all their heartfelt effort, love, and care. I informed Tevita of how the ladies were on the move again, fundraising for him, and he again broke down in tears.

Looking back now, I am simply amazed at how God had gathered these beautiful souls together a year or so earlier. He foresaw that I would need sisters by my side, especially in a foreign country. They would cook and bring food to the hospital and home without me asking. They would even do my grocery shopping for me, and drop it off at home, just so I could stay and look after my husband without worry. We were both overwhelmed with love despite the painful process we were going through.

Meanwhile, in Fiji, my Twinny had been braving the rain under that lemon tree while organising the fundraising. I didn't know this until, just before midnight Fiji time, she texted me that she was getting wet, and needed to go inside.

I remember how I helped Tevita shower one final time at home. I can vividly recall, without much effort, and see, and feel, my soapy hand holding his favourite Protex soap, running it up and down his hairy legs. With that distinct, sharp Protex scent, I felt every soapy hair on his chest brushing against my hand. Then, slowly rinsing it off, I revealed his Fijian masi tattoo covering his left chest up to his left shoulder and a quarter of his arm. Just like the well-known actor Dwayne Johnson's tattoo (aka 'The Rock'). Tevita knew I was a big fan, but I told him that he was my Rock and a better-looking one too. Without much thought or fear of regret, I recorded every detail of that scene in my mind just in case it was going to be our last shower together.

I helped him out of the shower and softly said, 'Now we're even. You bathed me once like a baby when I couldn't bathe myself and now I have contently returned the favour with all my love.'

When I was heavily pregnant at eight months with our firstborn I had suffered an unexplained and excruciating pain in both my arms, and for two days I could not do anything. Tevita had fed me, bathed me, dressed me, and had even combed and tied my hair.

Eleven days after being discharged, we were back in Ward 8, in the room right opposite the nurse's station. It was Wednesday December 14th. I remember walking along the passageway again, counting only four patients in the ward at that time, all of whom were men. A man from the previous visit was still there, and he came over the following day to say hello. Despite his being back in hospital, he was quite happy to see Tevita again. Since all four beds in the room were empty I made use of the one next to Tevita. It was more comfortable and I could watch him from there.

Strangely, I still preferred the floor because I could be much closer to him. I got to know the nurses well and they let me sleep on the bed, like one of the patients. I remember how in the other room he would put his hand down for me to hold while I slept on the floor. I would stare up from the floor at his hand with plaster and a needle inserted in it.

He received a blood transfusion that day, and the next morning, I remember telling myself that this time I should not have any problem donating blood for him. I excitedly headed down to the blood bank and went through the same drill again. I was understandably shocked when they told me I still could not donate that day. My haemoglobin level was way below the minimum requirement, due to my irregular meals since being back at the hospital. I felt physically sick. I made my way slowly back up the stairs to Ward 8. It actually explained why I had been feeling a little bit weak and exhausted in the last couple of days. I admit, I hadn't been sleeping or eating well at all.

I got back to Tevita, who was happy to see me, and conveyed the sad news that yet again I could not donate blood. He quickly sent me off to find something to eat. I hurriedly returned with some food and fruit an hour later. Perched on the side of his bed, I ate an early lunch, while he had some fruit. I remember slicing some oranges and feeding him – it felt so good to return my love, and care for the man who had showered me with his love whenever I got sick. I was impressed, seeing that he was slowly getting his appetite and energy back.

We sat there for a while chatting and it was good to see him smiling and laughing again. The room we were in previously had had a view of the hospital staff car park. This time we were on the other side of the hospital facing towards the children's ward. It was a quiet, sunny day, and from inside the room, we could feel a light breeze softly coming through the window. Along with the breeze came a distant, sweet little voice carrying the melodious tune of a famous church chorus. The voice was so pure, innocent, and angelic. I closed my eyes and tried to picture the little girl singing in my head. She went on singing for a while, so I turned to Tevita who was now lying in bed with his eyes closed. I thought he was asleep and wasn't sure whether or not to wake him up. I wanted to share this special singing treat with him.

'Do you hear that?' I whispered, and with a smile, he nodded yes. I couldn't sit there any longer just listening. Something was drawing me to this sweet voice outside. It felt as if it was right outside our window.

I said to Tevita, 'I need to meet this little girl.' I left the room, went out of the ward along the passage, and followed the little voice. Finally, I saw this middle-aged lady, with a face that had been deprived of sleep, sitting on a bench just outside the operating theatre. She managed to flash me a smile from her tired face as I approached her.Next to her was the little girl, about four years old, lying on her back with her right leg resting on her bent left knee. She didn't notice me until I got closer, then she shyly jumped up, ending her singing abruptly. She nervously grabbed hold of the lady's arm sitting next to her, who I assumed was her mother. I held out my hand and shook theirs before introducing myself. In the following few minutes, my spirits slowly sank as I sat quietly listening to this lady relaying the little girl's story.

She was not the mother of the little girl, but her aunt, who had come all the way from her village to take over what the little girl's mother had left behind. I recalled reading the story from one of the dailies about a horrific car crash. I found out that they were waiting outside the operating theatre for the little girl's older brother who was having surgery to amputate his leg. She continued, sharing how the pregnant mother had died in a bus accident, leaving two of her children seriously traumatised and injured, with very little hope that they would ever walk again. Not only that, but there was another child in a coma fighting for her life in the ICU. This little girl was the only one that had escaped serious injury when her mother had thrown her out of the bus window just before it collided with an oncoming truck.

Sadly, they were on their way from their village to visit their father in Port Moresby.

I could not imagine the devastating impact it must have had on the little girl's father, let alone his children. I wondered if he had even had a chance to grieve for his wife and unborn child, and give them a proper burial, and if he would have the time or strength to do it, with three of his children in the hospital.

I remember introducing the little girl and her father a few minutes later to Tevita as he lay on his hospital bed. The meeting, strangely, put things into perspective for us. I recall the words of my dear husband, that whatever hardships we go through in life, there is someone out there going through much worse than you. We were reminded of the importance of cultivating a spirit of gratitude in all things and to give thanks continually through all circumstances.

That Thursday evening as the hospital staff pushed in a trolley of food for his dinner, he politely declined. He was waiting patiently for the Chinese food he craved, which our friends Fotu and Ben Latu were bringing. Tevita had grown very fond of and close to five other pilots at work. They were our other family in PNG who lived only two minutes' drive away from us. These friends were all from different countries: Fotu To'foe and Ben Latu from Tonga, Fred Puni from Samoa, Oliver Aquino from the Philippines, and Esira Donu also from Fiji.

They were almost inseparable, on and off work. If Tevita was not at home, I knew he would be at his other house – the boys' house. If he wasn't with me he would be with the boys, and I must confess, I did get jealous sometimes. Not that I disliked the boys, but I noticed he laughed a different laugh with them, and I knew this drew him to them.

They seemed to have a hypnotic charm that would light-up a different light on his face as soon as he'd enter their home. They would always be cracking jokes, spoiling each other, and laughing when they were together – typical Pacific Islanders. He loved them like he would his own brother, and they loved him back. Fotu had called that evening asking Tevita what he'd like to eat, and he immediately replied 'Chinese' without a second thought. We had a big feast that evening when Fotu and Ben arrived with eight large takeaway containers. They sat and watched us devour the food before us. I was eating in hope of increasing my haemoglobin level so that I could try and donate blood again. It was a big relief to see Tevita that night eating like he normally did. Judging from how he was eating, joking, and laughing at the same time, we all took comfort in that Tevita was coming back and would fully recover in no time.

Little did we know, that was going to be his last supper.

We also had a visit from one of our other close friends that night. Naibuka Tunabuna and I started in flying school in 2003. We again ended up working with Airlines of PNG together in 2011. By 2016 he was with another company, Helifix. During Tevita's illness, Buks, as we called him, would come almost every day, and sit for hours and hours chatting with Tevita. He was the last one to leave that night, at around 10:30 p.m.

Often Tevita would insist on walking to the bathroom instead of being pushed in a wheelchair. That night he asked me to push him around for a bit before he had his shower, so I did. Up and down the passage, in and out of the other empty rooms the wheelchair went. He enjoyed it very much and as I pushed him, it reminded me of my childhood playing and pushing wheelbarrows around the village.

I helped him shower for the last time, helped him get dressed and helped him back into the wheelchair.

The next day was Friday December 16th 2016. He had mentioned how much he missed the kids and wanted to see them. By 12:30 p.m., we reached the hospital car park and I watched the excitement of our three children as they ran ahead of me to see their father. I would have cried tears of sorrow, had I known then that this was going to be their last time seeing their father alive.

He was very pleased to see them – he sat up and greeted each of them with a warm hug and a kiss on the cheek, and he held on to them a little tighter and a little longer. I also remember their last goodbyes being very similar. He gave them his fatherly hug and a kiss each, before he offered his cheek to get their last little tender kisses. In a chorus they waved him goodbye. 'Bye Ta … Love you, see you later.' I cannot recall how many more times they yelled their goodbyes to their father as they made their way out of the room. That last look at their father alive, their last hugs, and the kisses they had just received, without a clue of what was just about to happen.

Tevita could tell how fatigued and tired I was, so he suggested I get some sleep at home when I dropped the kids off. I managed to get about an hour of sleep before returning to the hospital. I told the kids I would be picking them up again around 6 p.m., so we could all go and start Sabbath with him in the hospital.

I got back to the hospital around 4 p.m., and he had just returned from the washroom. He looked okay, but then he said, 'Baby, I've been feeling a bit weak and I did not want to call you.'

'You should have, you know I would have come straightaway,' I replied. 'What if something happened to you and I'm not here?'

A few minutes later he started complaining that he was feeling shortness of breath again. I wondered, How could this be happening again? He asked me to check the oxygen supply level, which I did, and it was still the same as when the nurse had set it. He was still having difficulty breathing, so I called one of the nurses. He came to check it and saw that Tevita was still getting 100% supply into his body. I became worried and opened all the louvres. I cleaned the fan next to him and was even fanning him with a traditional Fijian fan, but all that only improved his discomfort slightly. He later started complaining about a headache. He said it didn't seem like the headache he had before, and I immediately worried that he might already be bleeding in the brain. I made a call to his doctor who quickly arranged for a platelet transfusion.

The female doctor turned up a few minutes later with a bag of concentrated platelets. His platelet count was quite low, and he was at risk of bleeding internally and in the brain. He was good at masking his pain, but this time I could tell that the headache was extremely severe. I had been sitting next to him, and watched as he tried to fight the excruciating pain in his head. I listened as he uttered, 'Jesus! Jesus! I'm not giving up, I'm not going to give up.' How I wished I had supernatural powers to hug him and take all the pain away.

I watched from the side of his bed helplessly, not knowing what to do. It was then that I opened the drawer next to his bed and pulled out our Bible. I found myself opening the book of Psalms and started reading.

I remember telling him, 'I'm just going to read you your book, David's Psalms.' By the time the other male doctor finally arrived, Tevita was lying sideways and seemed to be sleeping.

'Is my husband bleeding in his head?' I asked, worried.

He took another good look at Tevita and said, 'No, if he was bleeding in the head, he wouldn't be sleeping like this.' I knew Tevita was in a lot of pain and did not want to show it.

I rested my hand on his side and asked, 'Ta, does your head still hurt?'

He slowly turned his head around halfway and mumbled a long, slow, 'Yes,' with both eyebrows raised in confirmation, just in case I had not heard his voice.

Knowing Tevita and how he liked to keep his pain to himself to be strong, I quietly begged him, 'Please, you have to show the doctor that it still hurts.'

He then slowly nodded his head, and I could see his eyes struggling to stay open for the doctor. I remember the doctor ordering him an immediate morphine shot for the pain. The thought that I could be losing my love suddenly choked some air out of me. It made me shudder, and it felt as if something cold rippled in and out of my heart, causing it to pound with panic.

I wanted to gather all the help in the world for my husband so I slipped away into the passage and found myself in a quiet, still moment. Standing in one of the dimly lit empty patient rooms, I stared up into the stars through the window. I quickly dialled a number on the phone that I had been clutching against my chest. Ruth Pisi, a very well-spoken lady working with UNFPA (United Nations Population Fund) with an open and warm personality, whom I had met back at the Singapore Hospital, answered the other end of the line. Her sister Melisande was also part of our CTBF family. I had met her when she was at the hospital for her husband's brain operation, and I remember she had mentioned a highly experienced PNG national neurosurgeon that was looking after her husband. They had been a tower of support during that rough time.

In an urgent voice, I relayed my fears about Tevita's condition and asked if she could check whether her husband's doctor was around the ward that night. I was yearning for someone to tell me that everything was going to be okay, like my Tevita always would. Now that he could not be there, I felt lost and afraid.

I returned to be next to Tevita again, while the medical aid attended to him. He had been given two bags of platelets and was now getting a blood transfusion. The morphine must have worked its charm, I thought. He seemed a bit more at ease, now lying down with his eyes closed, and his hand resting across his chest. Then I watched as he slowly raised himself up to a sitting position.

'I want to throw up,' he said softly.

'Hang on, I will run and get a bowl quickly,' I exclaimed.

I had just one foot out the door when I heard the splattering sound of his vomit behind me. I turned around in shock, to see that he could no longer wait. I saw the dark maroonish colour of vomit staining his bedsheets as I came around the bed, then saw more of it on the floor. I quickly tore out some paper towels that were next to the sink on the other side of the room. I remember mopping his vomit on the floor with a paper towel, hoping to see his last meal or any signs of food, to reassure me that this was just related to food like every other time.

What I saw was what I thought to be some thick, old blood clots, with a few spots of fresh blood. It instantly reminded me of how my late and dear older sister Luseane Annie used to vomit, before she finally lost her battle with breast cancer three years earlier. The sheer terror of losing him too like this suddenly overwhelmed me and my tears burst forth like water from a dam, flooding down my cheeks. I picked myself up from the floor, wiped away those tears and cleaned up the stains on the bedsheets.

There were a few more episodes of throwing up after that first one, and each time he vomited I would hold him, rub his back, and helplessly watch as more energy drained from him. I remember sitting right next to him as he turned and slowly uttered in his deep soft voice, 'Move closer and hold me.' As I moved closer, he immediately let himself collapse on me.

I held him up with my left arm around him tight and my right hand holding up his tired and heavy forehead that seemed to have had enough by then. I felt my heart slowly shatter into a million tiny pieces as I watched him painfully vomit yet again. I tried with all my might to fight back the tears, but by this stage it was simply impossible. I knew he needed me by his side, I knew it was my turn to be strong for the both of us, even though I knew I was fragile and breaking up inside.

'How long will this go on for?' he cried. 'I want to be at peace,' he muttered slowly under his breath.

It was at that moment that I realised I needed to let go. I would normally reply with a 'You're strong and you're a fighter Ta, you will recover from this' line. But this time I replied with silence to signify that I was slowly letting go, not physically, but in a tender, emotional and sentimental sense. I had seen him fight with all his might, trying to stay strong for the kids and me. I had seen enough of him suffering in the last few hours. I mentally prepared myself to embrace whatever was going to happen – slowly letting go.

It must have been around 10:30 p.m. when they gave him another shot of something they told me would help stop the vomiting. Just when I thought he was resting, I noticed him talking and saying things that were not making sense. I asked a few questions that he could not answer correctly, and it tore me up inside. How can anyone ever be prepared to see their loved one like this?

'Loving you Ta,' I whispered into his ear.

'Loving you Na,' he replied softly. That reply renewed my strength that I believe held me till his last breath. At least, I comforted myself, he still replied correctly to my words of 'loving you'.

Those were his last words to me. Our final conversation, before he went silent, with only his breathing echoing in the room. I remember turning around to see Ruth and her husband making their way into the room. I was both surprised and happy to see them. They told me how they had prayed, after she hung up the phone. 'Lord, if it is your will for us to go, then you will provide transport.' They stepped out of their house in faith and were met by the Pom General Hospital bus, right outside their house. They knew straightaway that they needed to make their way to the hospital as God had provided them with the transport. While on the bus, the driver revealed that he normally dropped off the staff at 10 p.m., but that night it was at 11 p.m. They could only smile, as they knew why.

We surrounded Tevita and held hands as Ruth's husband, Henry Kave, said a prayer. His voice was deep and clear as I listened to his earnest, thankful words of praise to God. We said our amen. I opened my eyes, looked behind me through the louvres to the clock on the wall and saw both hands at 12 o'clock. I smiled down at Tevita, looked up to Ruth and her husband through my teary eyes and said, 'Today is our anniversary! This time last year we were getting ready to get married again, on our 10th wedding anniversary.'

Not long after, we parted, though I was now strengthened in faith, as they left to go back to their young children still asleep back home.

I was now making my way down the stairs to the ICU in Ward 7, a floor below Ward 8. I stood silently and watched over the shoulder of one of the nurses as they lifted him on to the ICU bed. I glanced around the room and saw three other beds, one occupied by an old man in his sixties. He had a couple in their forties sitting on each side of his bed – I thought, Maybe he is the father of one of the couples. I looked back at the nurses in their white uniforms busy working on Tevita. Their facial expressions were extremely serious, unlike the friendly faces I saw in Ward 8.

I grabbed the chance to be much closer to him, when I noticed the little gap between the head of his bed and the wall, and I managed to squeeze myself in between. Away from the nurses and doctors, but much closer to Tevita. My hand felt the warmth of his face as I lightly and gently rubbed his forehead with my thumb.

I leaned forward with my lips, almost kissing his ear, and whispered, 'Baby I'm here, I'm here loving you,' in the hope that he could still hear me. I remember going to ask the nurse behind the nurse's counter if he was in a coma or just sleeping. I wanted to hear a yes, and that he would wake up again. The nurse looked at Tevita, then looked back at me with a reluctant nod. How I wanted to believe her, but judging from her facial expression it was obvious that she was trying to hide Tevita's real condition from me.

I went and sat down next to him. I looked down at the floor, wondering how long I was going to be sleeping there while he was in a coma. Maybe he will wake up after a month or two, I thought to myself. He was still breathing through his mouth and the sound was gradually becoming louder and louder. It must have been only five minutes later when I noticed his breathing getting a bit slower and deeper, with his chest ascending and descending with his slow breathing rhythm. I thought I saw what looked like someone taking his last breath.

I stood up and made my way out to ask the nurse, but they had been watching the monitor from their desk, and were already rushing to check on Tevita.

Across the hallway from me I saw an empty wheelchair. I quickly pushed it out and sank into it, so I was facing the wall. I buried my face in my hands so no one could see it flooding with tears. There was no one there with me, only God, so I cried to Him in prayer. 'Lord,

I need you now. I am not strong, I am not strong. I need you,' I cried out in my heart.

I held myself together and walked back to the nurse's station. From there I could see the nurses and doctors surrounding him. I knew it was serious. I had tried to accept and let go, then our children's faces flashed before me and it hit me in the heart; what about them? Were they ready to let go too?

I immediately dialled my mother's number. 'Na, where are the kids?' I slowly asked while trying to calm every fibre in me that wanted to just drop down and release the loud wail that I had been concealing inside.

'They are asleep,' Mum replied.

'Please wake them up, tell them to pray and beg God to save their father,' I asked steadily.

'Okay, I will wake them up now,' she said.

In the stillness of the early morning, I stood back, watching the nurses and doctors through the louvres and the door, working on Tevita. I could hear the light, sharp beeping sound of the monitor following the distinctly loud breathing echoing down the hallway. Tevita was slowly leaving us. I made another call to Mum.

'Please ask them to beg and beg God to spare their father's life, he doesn't look good Na,' I cried. From there I gathered myself together and briskly walked back into the room and stood just at the foot of his bed. My eyes fixated steadily only on Tevita. Then the beeping sound drew my attention towards the monitor and then the numbers as they gradually decreased.

Ninety-three, then it disappeared ... eighty-six … seventy-five … sixty-seven … No! It's not going to go any lower than that, I thought to myself. Then fifty … thirty-two … and 20, followed by a long straight line and a steady beep.

I had seen this so many times in movies. I must have tricked my mind into believing that I was only watching a screen monitor from a movie, and not my husband's. I hardened my heart not to believe what my eyes were seeing, and not to let him die in my heart. I watched as they tried to resuscitate him a number of times. All I could see was a straight line on the monitor.

No, he is going to come back, I told myself.

Slowly, as if everything was in slow motion, they looked at each other and all agreed with a slight nod.

A quick glance at the clock showed 3:40 a.m. The lady doctor looked at me and asked, 'Are you the wife?'

'Yes,' I replied slowly.

'I am so sorry, we tried everything we could.'

I clearly heard her, but my heart did not want to accept or believe what I just heard. To me, Tevita was still alive in my heart.

It can't be! It can't be, I thought to myself.

'I'm so sorry,' she quietly uttered.

Gritting my teeth, refusing to acknowledge what I just heard, I only replied with a slight nod. I knew it was true, but my desire for it not to be true was so overpowering. I wanted to beg for it to be made untrue.

Then one by one they left the room quietly and there I was, alone with him. I walked over to the left side of his bed in disbelief, removed everything from his mouth, and kissed him on the lips. He wasn't kissing me back. Then I felt both sides of my mouth slowly dipping into a sad frown. I pulled up his grey t-shirt to expose his chest and lowered my right ear to search for his heartbeat. I had hoped that the monitor was wrong, that the doctors and nurses were wrong. But complete silence was all I heard. Nothing. It felt as if the utter silence from his chest went right through my ear, into my heart, and settled in as total emptiness. He was gone.

I slowly ran my left hand softly from his forehead down his left cheek, my thumb lightly rubbing his lips. I knew he could no longer hear me. 'You will always be alive in my heart. You will always be alive in my heart, Ta. You will always be alive in my heart.'

I knew I had to let go, though he was still very much alive in my heart.

14

The Funeral

I did not give you the gift of life, life gave me the gift of you.

ANON

The festive season approached with a jolly atmosphere and just a week away from Christmas, I was left planning my husband's funeral. Despite the colourful lights that decorated shops, enticing potential customers during the holiday season, my day hung gloomy and indifferent. My son repeatedly remarked, 'Na, I wish this was only a bad dream,' as we prepared to go through our first Christmas without their father.

Each morning after December 17th, I'd wake up with a heavy heart, knowing that the instant I was fully awake, my eyes would reveal an incomplete world without my better half in it. I hoped in vain that someone would wake me up from it all. Deep down, reality weighed heavily on my heart, and I knew I had to gather myself together and do this for my husband.

I thank God that I had my parents there with me in PNG as the events unfolded. With their support and guidance, I was able to get through the traditional formalities of a typical Fijian funeral. I would have been clueless otherwise, as to how to start planning a funeral, while going through the heartache of it all. The closest thing I had ever done to planning a funeral was for my dear mother-in-law, Tevita's mum, six years earlier. I knew that funeral traditions for Pacific Islanders could be particularly stressful. Although it was different now, because back then, I had Tevita and other relatives who helped. Now in a foreign country and at a time when I really needed him the most, I was overcome with emotion and just wanted to break down.

Unexpectedly, apart from my parents, I was moved by the love and overwhelming support I received from our friends here in PNG, which gave me that extra push that I needed at the time. My father made the first call to my father-in-law to relay the message. From the other end, overcome with grief, my father-in-law decided that every decision made for my late husband would be totally up to me. I was moved that he respected me as his son's wife, allowing me to decide where he would be laid to rest.

Knowing how Tevita was close to his mum, I knew that he would have wanted to be resting close to her. Picking the place was easy, as we had laid her to rest in Nadi. After a few calls, however, I was told that there was hardly any space left at the cemetery there. My heart could not have sunk any lower as I realised that we might very well not fulfil his wish. It was a relief when his cousin Seru Saukuru later suggested that they make a tomb for him next to their family house in Sabeto, Nadi. Having bonded as close as blood brothers, attended the same high school, and even chosen a career path as teachers so they could study at the same college, Seru wanted nothing more than for Tevita to be laid to rest near him. Although my husband was not from Sabeto, Nadi, he was very close to his cousins there. Growing up and having spent holidays with them, he could speak their dialect fluently, making one think that he was in fact from Nadi.

I loved the idea of him resting in a tomb with the famous Sleeping Giant Ranges as a backdrop. I also was comforted knowing that Seru's family would be looking after him when I returned to PNG, thousands of miles away. They adored him, just as he adored them, so it was not difficult agreeing to Seru's suggestion.

My mind took me back to the many good memories my husband and I shared at his cousin's home in Sabeto, and it was also not far away from his late mother's resting place. This was where he lived for a few months when he first started at the flying school. I was content that I had made the right decision.

The next few hurdles in decision-making were yet to come. I was expected to choose his date of burial, the venue for his function, the church for the service, a photo for the newspapers and, the most testing of all, his coffin. Iyata, our good friend, had to do a lot of driving around sorting out all the required paperwork for me. Having tragically experienced intense loss himself, he was the person I relied on to accompany me and help me pick out Tevita's coffin. It was hard, and something I did not want to do, but I knew it needed to be done.

With no criteria or plan, I picked the only coffin that stood out to me. It was beautifully painted in pure white with gold handles along the sides. It instantly spoke to my heart, as I felt it was the only coffin in that room that best represented his pure loving, caring character and his heart of gold.

Many of these difficult decisions caught me off balance, but what eventually overwhelmed me was holding his death certificate in my hand for the first time. I hated that single piece of paper I was staring at. It seemed to be screaming confirmation of all that I had been fighting not to accept. Part of me was still refusing to believe that he was really dead and gone. All this finally reached its peak during that trying week, leaving me depleted and exhausted with a constant flow of tears down my cheeks.

About midweek as we prepared the funeral arrangements, I recall driving out to the bank one morning with my Twinny's younger sister, Michelle Mefeae. Intelligently soft-spoken, she is fondly known to us by the name of Shelly. She worked with UNICEF, a UN agency for children and her schedule was busy with work and travel. However, she was homesick without her sister or nieces and nephews whom she was fond of. During the course of the year after my Twinny had left for Fiji with her young family, we became close for a couple of months, giving solace and support to each other. Our bond grew as she would join me and Tevita at the gym occasionally, and at home almost every other weekend. I look back now and can say with confidence that she was my God-sent counsellor. She happened to know just exactly what to say each time I was feeling emotional and on the verge of a breakdown, almost giving up.

The drive to the bank that morning took about fifteen minutes. However, three minutes into the drive I unconsciously reached out, as I would normally do, to hold Tevita's hand on the gear while driving. I missed him and especially holding his hand. I needed to hold a hand desperately that morning, so before taking her hand, I asked Shelly, 'How are your driving skills with one hand *lewa*?'

She knew exactly why I wanted to hold her hand and replied, 'Don't worry, I only need one hand, and we'll let the car and my feet do the driving.'

I held on tight and shut my eyes, pouring the pain from my heart through the tears flowing freely. I was missing my Te unbearably more and more with each new day. I had to grab Shelly's hand on several different occasions just to hold it and thank God for giving me all the supportive friends I needed. I imagined that I was holding onto my husband's hand, reassuring and strengthening me when the pain got too much to bear, and that small act was of immense help.

Shelly and I reached the bank a little early that morning and decided to have a cup of coffee at the cafe next door. It was there, as I sat down, that I received the company email to all the staff of PNG Air formally notifying them of Tevita's passing. It was another blunt and painful reminder that he was truly gone. I could barely hold my tears in. Shelly, being a very understanding and supportive friend, just encouraged me to cry it out. With little thought that I was in a public place, I did just that. I cried out my pain right there and then, and oh how it helped. We were able to continue to the bank and managed to send money ahead to Fiji for Tevita's funeral function.

For the following few days, I found that all food had lost its taste. I was not even hungry and hardly ate at all, despite the colourful array of delicious food that decorated our table each night. Friends started to arrive to show their support, dropping by with food and spending time at the house.

Our close friends from work, Fred Puni and Ben Latu, went out of their way supplying food packs that came in huge boxes night after night for the visitors. Neighbours I had never met before also arrived with trays of food and cash contributions. Many members of the Fijian community arrived with refreshments, mats, condolence cards, and contributions. My sisters from my CTBF group, oh my Lord, they just astounded me, I did not even have to ask for anything, they just volunteered. I recall seeing a few of them arriving with a burner, gas cylinder and pots. They brought food, went straight into the kitchen and started cooking. They sat outside, getting their hands dirty peeling bananas and kaukau (sweet potatoes). I was humbled by their humanity – they were sweating and getting itchy eyes from the smoke but I saw what genuine friends they were.

I walked down the stairs to the living room one morning and saw a huge banner with a photo of Tevita spread across the floor. They had even gone out of their way to put that together for me. I was lost for words and cried, and they cried with me. Good friends full of so much love.

A female pilot friend from work also offered to frame a photo of Tevita for me. Another friend, a female singer, well-known in PNG, whose mother was from Fiji called and offered to sing two of our favourite songs at the funeral service, as her tribute to him. I was just amazed at the overwhelming support, even from people I'd never met before.

I will never forget the first time I met Lanna Assaigo Kami, a lawyer by profession, whose mother is also from Fiji. Her mother was a very kind-spoken lady who always reminded me of Tevita's mum. I recall how I was worrying about the black clothes for me and the kids to wear to Fiji and the funeral. I was not prepared and had no time to even go to the shop to buy them. Lanna arrived on one of those nights – we shook hands as she introduced herself and she told me she had a parcel for me. Oh, how kind of her. I opened it and everything was exactly what I wanted to buy for me and the kids. Black dresses for me and the girls, and a black shirt for Yaca. They all fitted us perfectly. I said a little prayer that night, thanking God for all that he was providing for us, sending people with exactly what we needed.

I did not spend a single penny in PNG on anything at all for the preparations for Tevita's funeral service. All was taken care of by our friends, who became like family; workmates; the Fijian community; and our employer PNG Air, from the required documents, police escort, food, and refreshments, to the coffin and our airfares to Fiji. The support was overwhelming and I was extremely moved.

I had often been told and heard of how Papua New Guineans, especially the highlanders, showed their love and support when it came to losing a loved one. As my Twinny described it, highlanders didn't want to come and be an extra burden to you, they wanted to come and carry the burden for you. I thought I had seen it all, in the few days leading up to the day before we travelled down to Fiji. But that was only the tip of the iceberg.

The full force of support came during the day Tevita came home for the last time. We had discussed having a church funeral service where everyone who wanted to pay their last respects could come and do so.

But I wanted him to come home one last time before he left for Fiji, so he came home instead. I felt that he deserved to come home to us. We wanted him at home, as we were expecting that he would return home from the hospital. I can still vividly recall the day he stepped out of our front door alive for the last time. I was right behind him; he walked around our vehicle to the passenger door while I took the driver's side and drove him to the hospital. It never crossed my mind that this could be his last time leaving home.

His last trip home was sadly from a funeral home – he was to spend three hours at home with us. We put the word out and friends started pouring in. I loved that he was coming home but not that he was coming home in a coffin. My CTBF sisters went into action again – one organised the police escort while two others were with Tevita in the vehicle that brought him home. I didn't know all this until they showed me some pictures. The rest of my sisters from the group waited with me at home.

I had explained to my children that their father was coming home, so we all suited up in our black clothes and went downstairs. I sat with my children on some beautiful colourful Fijian mats to await the arrival of our daddy, our Ta. Mats were spread by my mother, Lanna and her mum. They were mainly for the coffin to rest on as a sign of love and respect. I noticed one thing – my son was getting a little bit anxious and edgy. He wasn't sitting still. Slow, soothing music was being played in the background by our singer friend. And by the time his father arrived, he wasn't seated next to me but with my mother across from me.

When the coffin arrived, the scene was heartbreaking to me. I had always seen him walk through that door, smiling, but this time he wasn't even walking in but being carried in. They lowered his coffin in front of me, removing the white cover that concealed his loving, caring and familiar face, which our girls and I couldn't wait to see. With one of our favourite songs being sung, I stared down and saw how handsome he still looked.

Of course, he was now quiet and not responding, as I leaned closer to call him *wajiqu* (my husband). The song became louder and louder, tears flowed down my cheeks, and my girls moved closer to their father. The song was the same one that I watched him singing to me on my phone. The lyrics and the melody were so soothing, yet piercing right through my heart. Then she sang the part in the video where he turned and sang to me, 'Don't you cry for me, it's just an illusion.' That's when I could not contain it anymore – I burst into tears anew, crying for my husband who was right there in front of me, but could no longer hear me. I cried and cried for his life that had abruptly come to an end. For the life and love that we were not going to continue living together – I cried until I could not cry any more tears.

My son eventually moved closer to his father. He looked at him but was reluctant to touch or even kiss him. We had about an hour to ourselves, and two hours for friends, who lined up to pay their last respects to Tevita. I did not leave his side until they had to return him to the funeral home.

It was difficult and sad to watch him come in and out of the house like that. I stood outside and watched until the vehicle disappeared from our driveway.

It was then that I became aware of the number of people who had gathered outside. We were renting a three-bedroom double-story unit within a compound of four units. The first unit was us, the second was our landlady, and the other two were vacant. The open-fronted car park could easily fit two big four-wheel-drive vehicles. A good-sized space, now all filled up with friends and visitors.

Our house is now called 'the hauskrai' as in 'house-cry', where people gather to mourn and cry together. Friends, workmates and Fijians in PNG all brought plates of food for all to share. I got to meet some of Tevita's friends who I didn't already know – a lot were pilots and engineers from other companies. Again, they came to pay their last respects and give their donations to help with his funeral service. It was something I wasn't t used to and had only heard of. Now I was finally witnessing the true PNG way of support in full force. Envelope after envelope – I had been writing down all their names and the amounts they were giving, but on that night, it was just impossible to keep up. The number of envelopes kept flooding in. I could hardly sit down to finish my dinner, as they kept calling me out to receive more. Some people just came straight up to where I was sitting and eating. I met more of them for the first time, chatted a bit and saw how Tevita had made so many friends.

Then my sisters from the CTBF group handed me another thick envelope with their contributions. I thought to myself that these ladies had already done more than enough for me. It was hard for me to accept after all that they had done. I said, 'This is too much.' But they kept insisting that I take it.

After a while, I thought there would be no more people coming to give contributions, so I snuck upstairs to try and start packing. To my surprise, I was again called downstairs as more people were arriving – pilots, flight attendants, engineers, and neighbours. I was utterly speechless – lost for words – at their overflowing love and support. It was as if Tevita was their own flesh and blood.

The next morning, the 23rd of December, we departed Port Moresby on the Air Niugini flight flown by our close friend Ben Baleikanacea. We all sat in business class. Mela was next to me while Ipa and Yaca sat across from us with my mum and dad behind them. We stopped over in Honiara where Yaca and Ipa had a chance to go up to the cockpit with Ben. Their faces lit up with excitement, and they couldn't stop smiling as I was taking photos.

We took off from Honiara, and arrived in Fiji nearly three hours later. We were first to disembark but the last to lose sight of it from the top of the exit walkway looking down at the 'Bird of Paradise' plane. The kids and I wanted to see the coffin being offloaded and be sure that our beloved was being given the best treatment. We stood and watched the last passenger, and the last baggage being offloaded. Tevita's coffin finally appeared from the baggage compartment and it was not what the kids were expecting. It was sealed in a plywood mini-crate resembling the outline of the coffin. They immediately became disgruntled and started to complain and question, 'Why is it in a box?' I had to explain that it was a requirement by the airline company to have an outer box, but that their Ta was sleeping peacefully inside his white coffin with gold handles.

A few minutes later we were finally walking out of the Nadi international airport and being greeted by relatives, friends, and my Twinny. The traditional rituals of handover and receiving of the body by his relatives were completed, and he was taken to the Nadi morgue by his brothers. I wanted to go with them to see him properly off to the morgue, but was told to go straight to where they had prepared our dinner.

It had been a long restless few days, and I was starting to feel tired and exhausted. A good rest and sleep were just what my body needed.

The next morning, I woke up early when everyone else was still asleep, around 4 a.m. I felt that pain again, that feeling of total extreme loneliness and emptiness, that no words can describe. There was only one way I knew to ease that pain, and that was to go and see him myself. For five days straight, up until the morning of his funeral day, I would wake up around the same time every morning, and go and see him at the morgue. Every morning, I would take his favourite cologne that he had saved for special occasions. I'd spray it on his wedding suit, give him a big hug and a kiss, and immediately feel better. I felt as though I was still performing my wifely duties and still taking care of my husband.

Yaca, our son, finally managed to get over his shock and began to accept that his father was gone, and we were going to lay him to rest. On the night before the funeral service and burial, Tevita was brought home overnight. We lay him on a beautiful arrangement of metres of tapa cloth, brightly coloured mats and an array of wreaths and flowers. On this last night, Yaca finally reached over the coffin and gave his father a kiss on his head.

I had to explain to him that they were about to close his coffin for good, and it would be too late if he changed his mind later. He finally gave him not only one, but eight kisses. He later told me that it was because he was eight years old, probably representing a kiss for every year he spent with his father.

His tomb was completed and ready by December 28th, the funeral day. It was neatly painted in white and shaped like a little house. I loved it, especially the fascinating view from the tomb. I had to pick a tapa to be used to decorate the inside of his tomb, and the one that came to mind was gifted to us by our Tongan friend, Fotu To'foe and his beautiful wife, Malia To'foe on the day of our renewal of vows. It was a massive Tongan tapa with exquisite, elegant print on it. It was just beautiful and worthy to be hanging inside the final resting place of my love.

About this time the previous year, I had suggested that we leave the tapa in Fiji, since it was bulky and so it would be ready in case we might need it for a family occasion. Tevita kept on insisting that we take it and use it to decorate the house. I told him that I would have to cut it in order to decorate the house, but we never got to use it until that day – a whole year later, when it was used to decorate his own little resting house.

The funeral service was beautiful, filled with families and friends who shared in our sorrow and the celebration of Tevita's full life. A few songs were beautifully sung by his side of the family – his nieces and nephews, followed by a heartfelt sermon and message from his own cousin, Pastor Epeli Saukuru. The eulogy was shared by Fred Puni and Ben Baleikamacea, colleagues and friends; his cousin Seru Saukuru, who shared many years growing up alongside Te; a former Queen Victoria School Old Boys' colleague; his dear uncle who inspired him to be a teacher like himself; and Melaia, our daughter, who wrote and read a beautiful poem to her father.

At the end of the service, his casket was carried by our friends, who were all pilots in PNG and Fiji, including my Twinny's husband, Clark Piokole. Afterwards we headed to the tomb where our kids saw for the first time the place that would be frequented by them for many years to come. They loved it, as it resembled a special little home, pure white outside and beautifully decorated on the inside with Tongan tapa for their father.

After a few songs and a prayer, his coffin was placed inside and he was laid to rest. There was enough space, so we crept inside to be beside him one last time. We left with him our flowers and the letters that the kids had each written to him. We said our last goodbyes, kissed the coffin and tossed in a piece of hardened earth as the pastor continued with the ceremony, saying, 'From ashes to ashes, and dust to dust.'

I wept as the men proceeded to place blocks to cover the entrance and sunlight that flooded in. Slowly the beautiful tapa-decorated house where my husband was now sleeping was sealed completely. The wet cement was spread soon afterwards and there I stood, separated physically from my husband for the final time. I pictured him lying there in his handsome suit on the other side of the wall, as I stood, not in my white wedding dress, but in a black widow's dress. I still managed to wear my beautiful starfish earrings and necklace that day, and my mind took me back to the happiness we shared the year before, at the renewal of our vows.

Following the burial service, everyone boarded buses and vehicles, and we gathered back at the Hill residence, where we shared some lunch afterwards. There, we got to greet the rest of our friends and relatives.

Now that the funeral was over, something else was bothering me. What would I do when I woke up the next morning with that pain again? I worried about this, now that I could no longer go and hug or kiss him. I went to sleep that night with our firstborn Mela sleeping next to me. Strangely, the next morning, in that split second before I opened my eyes it felt like I was finally going to wake up from this bad dream. I felt his hands on my cheeks; something we would do occasionally to wake each other up. It felt like either a kiss or a hand brushing lightly on my cheeks. In retrospect, I'm sure I was smiling as well, expecting to see Tevita when I opened my eyes. I opened them, but instead of Tevita, I saw a small female version of him. Melaia, our firstborn, who takes after her father, was sleeping peacefully but that morning her left hand was resting on my right cheek. It somehow took away the emptiness that I dreaded I would be waking up to.

The following morning something similar happened, but this time it was more warming to my heart. I woke up to his voice whispering so close to my ear that I thought I felt his warm breath. It was so clear and so heartwarming. 'I will always love you.' I woke up and smiled. I didn't know whether it was just my head playing tricks or a figment of my imagination. Nonetheless it left me feeling much better than waking up in pain, and I like to think it was God's way of slowly easing me forward, to handle each day after the burial.

Driving towards the range on our way to Sabeto the next day, I smiled, gazing at the backdrop of the majestic range of the three sleeping giants. I could make out two familiar figures, probably each a mile long, that lay in the same direction across the range. I could distinctly make out their Fijian male afro hair, and what would have been their eyes, noses, necks, and chests, upon which their hands rested peacefully. Stretched out before them was one giant after another across the range. The third giant, with the same afro, seemed to be resting in the opposite direction with his feet pointing towards the two. I smiled, as a rainbow painted the sky, marking a new day when my Tevita, a giant at heart, who had lived a full and large life, was now rightfully resting among giants.

15

Living the Dream in my Worst Nightmare

It's hard to wake up from a nightmare if you aren't even asleep.

ANON

It was strange but not surprising, that the kids and I wanted to go back to our home in PNG straight after the funeral. My mother came along with us, to assist us in adjusting to our new life without our Ta, our dad. I thought arriving back home to all the memories would be painful, but instead, it made us feel closer to him.

We arrived just after lunchtime and our house girl had prepared a small lunch for us. I didn't go upstairs to our room until later that evening. The first thing I noticed on our little bookshelf next to our bed, was a ripped photo with half of it missing. The remaining half was of me, and had been placed next to the framed photos of Tevita and me. I recognised it as one of the very old photos from flying school, before I met Tevita. The house girl must have found it while cleaning and left it in our room. In the photo, I was standing back-to-back with one of the boys from the flying school. He had been ripped out of the photo, like someone was furious. I laughed when I found the poor lad in the rubbish bin, in pieces. Knowing my children, I knew only one of them would do that – Ipa. She did confess that she was the one who did it.

My employer had been very understanding and supportive. They allowed me to take as much time off as I needed, and to return to work when I was ready. How will I know when I'm ready? I asked myself.

In the first week back, I kept going back to places we used to go together. It just so happened that Shelly was still on leave, so she accompanied me to all our favourite restaurants, coffee shops, and the mall. Nothing was ever the same without Tevita – it was either boring or lonely. The kids continued asking a lot of questions too, and we spent the first week sleeping in the living room.

Yaca asked me one day, 'Na, how come you still have your father and I don't?'

Mela asked, 'Na, will our surname and village change if we have a stepfather?'

Now and then, I had to do a lot of explaining.

I was itching to get my hands on an aircraft and fly a plane, but I wanted to be ready first. So, I decided to take a visit to the office, just to see how I would feel. Sometime that afternoon, I walked into the office and greeted everyone. I met them with a smile, putting on a brave face. It felt alright, as if Tevita had only gone for an overnight somewhere, like he always did. So I thought I was doing okay until I walked downstairs to the HR department. That was when it hit me. A photo of his handsome face from the newspaper obituary was pinned on their notice board with memos and other notices.

It felt like a splash of icy-cold water being thrown at my face, waking me up to the reality that Tevita had gone forever. I felt cold inside all of a sudden, and I must have stopped breathing for what seemed like minutes, but must have been only seconds. I turned and walked out, close to tears, but daring myself not to cry. Our close Filipino friend Oliver Aquino ended up driving me home, and I cried all the way.

My next stop was our pilots' crew room at Jacksons Airport. A place where we would normally wait for each other after work, so we could go home together. I first made sure that there was no obituary on our notice board, and I chose to ask Iyata to go with me. I needed someone who would understand me, someone who had been through what I was going through, and Iyata was the perfect person for it.

The day I returned to work, memories flooded back. I was back in a dark day in September 2014. It had started off as a cloudy Saturday morning – at around 10:30 a.m. Tevita received a call from the company that he was working with at the time, Hevilift Ltd., where he was a training captain on a DHC-6 Twin Otter.

From the tone of his voice on the phone I knew something was seriously wrong. He hung up, turned to me and slowly said, 'One of our planes just went down.'

In shock, I quickly asked, 'Who were the crew?'

'Liam Rossiter and Kristi Baru, Shanty,' he replied.

'Oh my God, did they survive?'

'They don't know yet, but they've confirmed that there are some survivors.'

'Oh good, I pray they made it.'

I had flown with Captain L. Rossiter a few times, in my first two years of flying in PNG. A soft-spoken gentleman with a lot of flying experience, I had a lot of respect for him. Sadly, I never got a chance to get to know Kristi Baru well, but had met her and rubbed shoulders a few times. She seemed like a very sweet girl when I briefly met her, and wore a kind smile that I will never forget.

Tevita, however, did a bit of her line training and had last flown with her two days before that fateful day. She was Iyata's sweetheart of six years. Unfortunately, we found out later that day that none of the crew made it. It was a very sad, heartbreaking day for us all.

Within less than a month of losing his long-time girlfriend, Iyata lost his father too. His father was a respectable hardworking pilot with the national carrier, Air Niugini. Two weeks later he got a call to start with us at PNG Air. After all that, with not enough time to properly grieve losing two of the most important people in his life, he still managed to get back to flying.

That's exactly why I thought he was the best person to go with me to our pilots' crew room. I also made sure that we picked a time when the crew room would be empty. Just before 8 p.m., I sat down and remembered all the sweet times I had with Tevita in that room. Iyata was patient with me, and he waited until I finished crying and was ready to leave.

Three weeks later I sent an email to the company informing my boss that I was ready to get back to flying. The first step for me, since I was to start on a new aircraft I had never flown before, was to do a couple of supernumerary flights. It was company policy and it was just perfect for me. I sat on the jump seat located in the middle just behind the captain and the first officer. February 13th 2017, one day before Valentine's Day, and it was my first day back at work. It was a delightful day to fly. The weather was just perfect, and I enjoyed the view from the jump seat and loved every minute of it. My first flight and it felt as if Tevita never left. I thought I did alright for my first day.

The following day was to be my first Valentine's Day without my darling husband. We always planned to do something special on that day and I wanted to continue that. So my son was taking me out for dinner. It was our first mother/son dinner date and it was quite memorable. Just like his father, he made me laugh and kept me entertained. However, my daughters didn't take this well, and they wanted to have a special dinner date with their mother too, so we did this on a different night.

The next step in my returning to flying was doing some circuit training, three take-offs and three landings – readjusting and refocusing my mind back on flying. At first, I did not know where to start with my studying. Our dining table became my study table. I began by reading the same book I had been studying while sitting next to Tevita in the hospital in Singapore. The first few seconds after opening the book, I was bombarded with flashbacks of me next to him in that hospital – how I had strong hopes that he would get better. How we used to study, and practise some emergency drills together. It got too much to handle, so I shut the book and ran upstairs to our room. On our bed, I grabbed a pillow and buried my head in it, screaming and crying. It was just too bloody painful.

I was rostered on three times, before I finally got to fly. The first two were both cancelled. I was actually glad about that because I didn't feel ready on either of those days. The second time I woke crazily emotional – I saw his uniform shirt hanging in the cupboard and just burst out crying. So I was happy when they called to cancel my flight that day. The third time, a few days later, I woke up feeling ready to conquer the world. I knew that I was finally ready. A few hours later I was staring at the end of the runway with both my hands on the aircraft controls, lifting off slowly. I was finally living the dream again, but now flying with a bruised, battered, and broken heart; nonetheless, slowly healing.

On several occasions, I encountered some emotions I was not expecting nor ready for. On my second supernumerary flight, from the jump seat looking outside to the walkway, I saw a man in a pilot's uniform from his shirt down. My full view of him was partially obstructed, but he was dragging his flight bag just like Tevita used to do. This immediately caught my attention and for a few seconds, I thought I saw Tevita. He finally came into view, and it was our other Fijian friend Esira Donu. From my seat, I quietly watched as he walked around the aircraft he was going to fly.

Something I used to enjoy doing, was watching Tevita from another aircraft, doing his walk around in his uniform. Thoughts of how life was so unfair started shooting through my head. My heart was heavy and in pain. I did not want to break down and cry. Behind my dark sunglasses, I held my tears back and kept screaming to myself in my head, Be professional, don't get too emotional here. It was a trigger I was not expecting but I managed to get through it that morning and enjoy the rest of that day.

A few days later I had to pick up our other close Tongan friend, Fotu To'ofoe, from work. I parked in the same spot I used to park to pick up Tevita. I started having flashbacks but I managed to brush them off, until Fotu emerged from the sliding glass-door exit of the domestic arrival area. In his pilot's uniform, he walked out across the road on the zebra crossing, just like Tevita did. He had a beard and was wearing sunglasses and a yellow reflector vest, and had a flight bag. Again, for a second there I thought I was staring at Tevita. I wanted it so badly to be Tevita, but it was not.

I had to let him drive me home and I cried all the way. I realised then that the triggers now were our close friends from work. They would be the first people he'd call after arriving home from work. He adored them and they were inseparable. Good brothers. There were a few more similar episodes outside of work and I had to just cry it out. It was too painful seeing them without Tevita. They reminded me too much of what I was missing, yearning, and longing for – his company. The pain would always intensify when I saw them, it was like a nightmare. At one point, when it got too painful to handle, I thought of seeking a job elsewhere just to avoid them. But two months after the funeral, I got over this phase in my healing process and so did the kids.

I would hold their hands whenever I was missing holding Tevita's hand – while driving, sleeping, or walking in a mall. They knew why I was doing it as I would openly share how I was feeling with them. It led them to be open with me too. I recalled one night, in the living room while watching TV, my son turned and asked, 'Na, do you know why I never wanted to touch Ta's body?'

'No, why, my son?'

'Because I'm scared of dead bodies.'

'Oh okay, I understand.'

'And do you know why I gave him eight kisses before they closed his coffin?' he continued.

'No,' I answered.

'Because I'm eight years old.'

'Oh, that's so sweet of you, son.'

After two months, my son finally took his father's seat at the dinner table. He was healing and we were also all healing slowly. It was good to be back flying, doing what we'd both loved, but it was never the same. Sometimes I had to snap myself out of staring blankly into the beautiful blue sky, wondering what life would have been like if he was still around.

Six months after his passing, I had learnt to deal with the triggers and the pain. But on this particular day in June I just could not wait to finish work.

I flew to two of the places that reminded me so much of Tevita, and that made me miss him even more. Two places where I would normally run into Tevita. I would either run to his aircraft or he to mine, for a quick chat, hi, and a kiss.

It was a difficult day of flying with the heartache and those memories, then Iyata crossed my mind. I thought, Oh my gosh, this is what Iyata has to go through every day? In his case, I felt it was worse. The crash site was on the side of a small mountain less than ten miles from the runway in Port Moresby. The mountain stood out and you could never miss it when coming in to land. I thought to myself, If he is able to manage, then I can manage this as well. That thought gave me a little bit of comfort and a boost. It just so happened that Iyata was on a day off that day so he had time to meet me at 2:30 p.m., after I finished work.

I was hoping for a good chat with someone who could relate to my pain. We had a glass of lemon, lime and bitters each. I started off sharing my day, and I couldn't contain the tears I had been holding back at work. I lost count of the number of tissues I used, but I felt a whole lot better after sharing. Then he finally opened up and told me the whole story about that fateful day – the day he lost his sweetheart in a plane crash. Then he told me about losing his father, how he dealt with both tragedies, and how now he had to stay strong for his mother, and get back to flying.

As for me, the cancer had given me some time to prepare, but Iyata's was unexpected – he lost two people close to his heart in less than two months. He didn't even have time to grieve properly, and I doubt that I would have survived what he went through. I shed some tears while he shared his story, feeling the pain that he had gone through.

On the positive side, I also felt his courage to carry on flying. That was a great boost for me, especially when I'm flying and memories get in the way. It wasn't easy, but he managed to make it through, and now he is happy with his current supportive, beautiful girlfriend, Valyne. I am so blessed to have some really good friends like Iyata. Friends who have helped me get back into living my dream, and that is flying.

16

Dear Ta

Goodbyes are not forever. Goodbyes are not the end.

They simply mean I'll miss you until we meet again.

ANON

Ta, words cannot describe how much I miss you every single day. Half of me died with you on that day, Ta. I gently laid on your chest, expecting to hear your heartbeat, and I heard nothing but absolute emptiness. How could you leave me here alone, Ta? How am I supposed to live without you? How am I supposed to carry on without you?

I came home to our room and couldn't stop crying. Ta, my heart and my soul were bleeding for you. My pain, my loneliness, and hurt all blended into indescribable emotions. It was too painful. I felt lost, like I didn't belong in a world that didn't have you in it. You took all the sunshine of my world with you and life became meaningless and pointless. I no longer wanted to live, not when it was going to be without you. You're gone Ta, you're gone, and I miss you, it hurts. You told me that I was going to grow old with you and I believed you. I never thought that I was going to lose you, Ta. It hurts knowing that now I will be growing old without you. Oh, the pain. Remember all our talks of retirement? Our farm, and having our grandchildren visit? I never cried, or suffered so much pain in my life until the day I lost you Ta. Your beautiful heart, my love, showed throughout your funeral. Many people gathered to come and pay you their last respects. Ta, that day I drove you to the hospital – you never made it back, and I am so sorry, my love. That Friday you kissed the kids goodbye, it was your last, and I am so sorry. Why did you have to go?

I wonder if you heard my whisper, 'Happy anniversary,' the night you left me. Did you know that you left on our anniversary day? Now I have bittersweet memories of December 17th.

Your funeral went well, my dear. John Hill and Lisa offered their home to accommodate your last funeral function in Fiji. How kind and loving of them. I know you would have been moved and humbled by their kindness. You spent your last night there, and I slept with the kids next to you.

Remember how you and Yaca used to give each other five goodnight kisses for all of us? Yaca gave you eight kisses on his last kiss – he said it was because he was eight years old. I lost count of the number of times I kissed your cold lips my love, it was different but comforting.

You should see the tomb that Seru, Save, Naibuka, Fred and Esira made for you. It's beautiful my love. I told Seru that if I die before him, he'd better make sure that I am buried in the same tomb with you. Otherwise, I will haunt him in his sleep. We laughed, but I was serious, I meant what I said. I'd hate to be miles away from you, when I die. I will want to be resting next to you.

We're back in Moresby now. I am back flying, and yes, still with PNG Air. Our first time here at home was okay. It felt as if you had only gone on an overnight. I was cleaning our room, and I found your hair clippers under the sink in our bathroom. Some of your hairs were still stuck to it – I wish I had never cleaned it. I miss cutting your hair, my love. I still have your cologne and sometimes I spray it on my wrist just so I can smell your scent. I am so thankful for all the videos I used to take of you. They have helped me so much with the pain. I watch them whenever missing you hurts too much.

Remember when you sang me one of Ronan Keating's songs, 'This I Promise You'? I had totally forgotten that I was video-recording you. Just imagine my reaction when I found the video – I couldn't stop crying. Why do you sound so awesomely good? I told the kids that this will definitely be their future wedding song. This way you will still be a part of their big special day. You might not get to walk them down the aisle, but you will be singing on their wedding day. It was beautiful to watch you sing, but at the same time painful knowing that I will never get to hear you sing in person again. I treasure all your videos, Ta, they make me feel like you're still around.

Do you remember our 2014 Valentine's surprise, our Hagen weekend, our Hawaii trip, the necklace gift surprise, and many more videos? I remember your comment back in 2011 after I made a short video of you. You said, 'I bet I'm going to have so many fancy videos when I die.' I remember punching you on the shoulder, and telling you that I didn't want to hear you talking about dying again. Oh, and your phone, I forgot your pin number, but guess who unlocked it for me? Ipa – when did you tell her your pin? The kids are back in school. The morning of their first day wasn't easy for me. You know how I always look forward to their first day. I spent that morning crying in our bathroom for a fair bit of time. Then I gathered myself together, and yelled at my reflection in the mirror to be strong and to do it for you. The kids miss you, Ta.

Ipa shared with me the other day how she watched a father picking up his daughter from school. She felt sad, but was reminded of how you used to pick her up from school too, and she was thankful for that. On one of our evening family devotions, I asked the kids what they would want to tell you now, if they were given just one minute with you. Mela cried, and couldn't answer at first. Then they all said that they would tell you how much they miss and love you.

Mela turned twelve last month and we held a small BBQ at home with Twinny, Shelly and the kids. And guess what happened on her birthday too? She didn't only turn a year older but she got her period on her birthday too, darling.

Aww, the mats that we had prepared for it and set aside for her 4th night after her first menses, as is customary, were the same ones used during your funeral too. We held a small lunch for her the following Sunday, dressed her up, spread some mats to celebrate her reaching the first step to becoming a woman. I missed you so much on that day. It was something we were both looking forward to – our firstborn reaching this phase of life. Mela is doing well in her class, but she wants to go back and attend the school in the village. She is still doing her drawings and is getting better and better at them.

Ipa is so into baking, it is sometimes crazy. She reminds me so much of how you used to love baking, using the Betty Crocker cake ready-mixes. Remember the heart-shaped cookie she baked for you when you were in the hospital? You should have seen the excitement in her eyes when I came home, and she asked me about what you thought of her cookie.

She is also into singing lately. I bought her a guitar for her tenth birthday and she loved it. She asked me not to buy any cake for her, because she wanted to bake her own birthday cake, which she did. It was a small celebration at home, and she invited two boys from her class who live just around the corner. Very well-mannered boys and they each sang her a song, which was very sweet of them.

So far Yaca is doing well being the man of the house. He took me out for dinner on my first Valentine's Day without you. I was laughing at how he was walking funny because of the boil on his thigh. And he warned me that he was not going to take me out for dinner if I laughed at him again. I had, of course, put some money in his wallet so he could pay for our dinner. He did great, and you would have been proud of him. He is looking after us girls well. Though a bit nervous at first, he ended up singing a song for me during our dinner. He said it was his song for you too. I saw so much of you in him that night. He made me laugh just like you used to. We had a good time. And guess what? He is still asking for his brother. He misses you, and is probably sick and tired of being the only boy in the house now. I've explained it to him that it's impossible now with you gone. I've thought about adopting, but I'm not a hundred per cent sure.

Melaia, being named after your mother, is sometimes called Nau out of respect. One Sunday, we were all seated around the table having breakfast, when the subject came up. Nau said that you wouldn't want me to be lonely. I wouldn't want you to be lonely too, if I was the one who died. Ipa totally disagreed that they should have a stepfather, but she did agree, on one condition: if we can find someone who looks exactly like you. They miss you Ta. I said, 'Well good luck with that, guys.'

You would laugh, and maybe be jealous too, about who he thinks should be their stepfather. Yaca immediately yelled out, 'I know someone who looks like Ta, he's got the same beard and tattoo. He is on your phone.' I tried to think of who he could possibly be talking about, and was eager to see. He scrolled through my phone and then shyly handed it to me to show me a picture. It was Dwayne Johnson, 'The Rock'. Love, I couldn't stop laughing.

Well, he does kind of look almost as handsome as you – he's got the tattoo, the goatee beard, the muscles, except for one thing as I said to Yaca, 'He's got no hair!'

And the girls added, 'And he is married.' Yaca felt a bit ambushed and shyly retired to his seat. We all had a good laugh afterwards. Later that night when it was just the two of us in the bedroom, he asked if 'The Rock' could at least be their uncle. I said yes and that I would talk to Uncle Fred about it because his wife was related to 'The Rock'.

Then he asked, 'Will he be a good uncle or a bad uncle?' I told him that he would find out himself when he meets him. Ha!

The kids have been keeping me busy, and they've also asked a lot of questions. 'Na, will our surname and village change, if we have a stepfather?' Nau asked one day. I reassured her that you will always be their father, they will always belong to your village, and they will always be a Secivo. Remember when we used to talk about if anything ever happened to either of us? I told you if something happened to me, you should make sure you find someone who will not only love the kids when you're around to please you, but who will love them like her own – love them like I did. Whereas you told me that getting married again should be up to me. I honestly cannot see myself as someone else's wife. I don't want that, I only want to be your wife. Not only till death do us part but until the day I die and beyond if it's possible.

It's such a lonely world without you, Ta. I miss our family outings, dinners, and your companionship. I miss sleeping in your arms, and waking up next to you. I miss holding your hand. I miss hearing your laughter filling the entire house when you watch *Just for Laughs: Gags* on TV. I miss lying in your lap watching *CSI*. I miss you creeping up behind me while I'm washing the dishes to kiss me. I miss the yummy lamb curry you always cooked when you were drunk because it always tasted better than when you were sober, and I miss going out with you.

You know, getting excited to glam up together in front of the mirror. Then waking up together the next morning with a bad hangover, then going to look for some nice spicy curry or hot soup. I miss all that, Ta. Now it's just me. You always told me that you were going to be the first to go. Why did you say that? Sometimes I wish that it was me instead, but then I wouldn't want you to go through this painful heartbreaking experience. It's just too much pain to bear. I don't know how you would handle it. I comfort myself with the thought that at least I'm saving you the pain of going through this.

I am back at work, and just got cleared to 'line' last week after successfully completing my training and I'm ready to fly with any captain. You would have been so proud of me, Ta. I miss sharing all the excitement with you at the end of each day. I miss seeing that handsome smile of yours. Coming home is never the same, knowing you won't be there to pick me up – you will never be home when I get there. Sometimes I cry on the drive home, Ta. It's hard but I'm learning to live with this pain. I'm learning to push through the pain when it's pushing me to give up. You never gave up on us, Ta, and you never gave up fighting that bloody cancer. Every time when I feel like giving up I try to remind myself of you always being strong. I think half of you replaced the half of me that died with you on that day.

Iyata has been really supportive too, Ta. You know what he went through, and how he got back to flying afterwards. He has given me a lot of wise and encouraging words to help me keep pushing through the pain. It helps talking and sharing with someone who has been though this pain and understands exactly how I feel. Like you always said, he is a good friend. We reminisce about the day you got so drunk in Melbourne, they had to pack your suitcase for you and he had to check you in. How you made them sing John Legends song, 'All of Me', over and over again in your hotel room. I laughed, and I cried, and I laughed again. The guys at work have been extremely supportive too. I had to ask Esira and Fotu to come and remove some bulbs in the house for me because I couldn't reach them. I went to our favourite karaoke bar with Chantilly, Val and Liam the other night. It was their first time there, we had fun, and the whole time I kept thinking of how we used to have so much fun together there.

A lot has happened, Ta. Would you believe that I'm writing a book? Would you believe that there's a song about us, that's already been released? There is another song yet to be released, and it's just as beautiful as the first one. We're planning to launch it on your one-year anniversary and our twelfth wedding anniversary, at the same place where we renewed our vows and celebrated our tenth wedding anniversary, the Sofitel resort. Let me tell you just a bit about the song.

I have been using Facebook as a venting space since you left. And people started messaging to tell me how they had been moved and touched by reading my posts. I was merely letting my emotions out in writing. Many times, I've cried and sometimes felt bad again for making others cry. Then, I was approached by a few people who wanted to write a song for us. That was very nice of them, but my heart instantly picked someone else. I thought, If there's ever going to be a song, it will be a duet. You know how much we loved singing and listening to duets. The first person I thought of was Elena Baravilala. So, I messaged her and told her a bit about us and also asked her to go to our Facebook page to learn more. That was all I did, and she agreed. Three days later she sent me the lyrics, and I cried and cried when I read the first three lines. It was as if you told her what you would have wanted to tell me through the song. She later told me that it felt like the song was given to her, when she was writing it down. She is incredibly talented, and I just knew that I had asked the right person. I couldn't ask for a better singer to sing the duet song for us than the guy we first saw at Intercontinental Hotel in 2014 on our return from Hawaii. Yes, that young bloke that was strumming the guitar singing and you couldn't take your eyes off him. I wanted him to be the guy to sing with Elena but I didn't know how to tell or ask her. So, I thought I should just let her pick and choose because she would be the one singing with the guy, not me. Well, what do you know, she messaged me and mentioned the same exact guy I had in mind. Out of all the male singers in the whole of Fiji, she picked Pauliasi, the guy from the Intercontinental Hotel – the very same person I had in mind. Everything was just falling into place, Ta. She called me and said that they will be launching the song during the Fiji Music Award night. And guess what – it was on your birthday. I flew down to Fiji, dragged Seru to drive me down to attend the launch, and it was beautiful.

I only wish I could meet you again, and tell you all about this in person, my love. I had gone down to Fiji before that for your 100 nights gathering, as is customary, to commemorate the 100th night since your burial. It all went beautifully well, and was held at Milika Evanson's residence – she has such a beautiful heart. Nei Oli did all the cooking, and there was lots of delicious yummy food. You will remember Nei Oli and her big caring heart. She was always there looking out for me, and us. My father also did the *i lakovi* that day. The traditional presenting of the *tabua* (whale tooth) to ask for me, his daughter, back from your family. It felt like my being your wife was coming to an end, and I was to return and be my father's little girl again. I cried Ta. I will always be your wife, my love – forever and always.

Oh, did I tell you that there's also a motivational group on Facebook created as a tribute to you and our fitness journey together? Flex4Tex currently has more than 3,200 members. The majority are in Fiji, some here in PNG, and some are Fijians from around the world. I'm still doing my workouts. The first time I went back to the gym I felt as if you were still around. I like that every time I go there. I feel closer to you.

Anyway, for old times' sake, I decided to invite some of our ex-workmates for dinner the night before I left Fiji – I guess they were all busy because no one turned up. That was a bit disappointing so I called Lilly and Maizle to join me, and we ended up at Ed's bar. I had two margaritas and a few flaming bazooka shots. Or maybe a little more than a few, because I didn't remember going home. I remember clearing my first tab at the bar, but not the second one. Oops! Lilly and Maizle had to pack my suitcase, wake me up, drive me to the airport, and even check me in. Just like how Iyata had to drag you to the airport in Melbourne and check you in too. Luckily Ben was also on that same flight to PNG, and I was told that he ended up clearing my second tab that night. That was a little embarrassing, and I asked him during the flight how much he ended up paying, and he said not much. I hope he wasn't lying because he has done a lot for us already. I slept almost all through the flight to Moresby.

The next morning I woke up and noticed a number of blisters on my hand from the flaming shots. And I must have burned my lips too. I'm thankful that we both have such wonderful friends who are always there when we need them. Who always look after us when we have a little too much to drink. Remember that night when you and Fred were supposed to come and drive me and Shelly home from Cosmo? But then we ended up driving you guys home. I can still see the two of you that night, staggering out of Cosmo and into the car park in fits of laughter. Fred was trying to open his car with his house key, instead of the car key, and you couldn't stop laughing. I regret deleting that video. That would have been a good one to show our grandchildren and tell them what not to do. I love and miss you *wajiqu*.

We had a fundraising dance in Lamana for the book launch a few months back. The CTBF ladies were there in full force again, being amazing and supportive. We thoroughly enjoyed the night. I'm so lucky to have met these ladies. Oh yeah, they will be joining me in Fiji for the book launch – you can just imagine the excitement, we're so looking forward to it. I've spent a lot of my time on it, and the kids know that they mustn't disturb me when I'm writing at home, unless it's something very important. I sometimes feel guilty – I know I owe them. So, I can't wait to take them for a holiday after the launch. There are quite a number of our friends coming to Fiji for the launch Ta, and they will all come to visit your tomb.

Shelly has been helping me a lot with this book, Ta. Yes, she is still with her tall Iraqi (hehe!). He had to come and change a few lightbulbs for me too, since neither of us could reach them. He had also come for your funeral and sat amongst the Fijian men but did not drink yaqona.

Chantilly and Jason escorted me home that night after the book launch fundraising dance. We stopped at one of the traffic lights, I looked over my shoulder, saw the two of them and was reminded of how we used to escort each other home. Only this time, you were missing, and I was driving home alone.

It's not easy seeing couples hanging out, doing what we used to do. It triggers the pain of missing you. But I'm coping and dealing with it Ta. It's been over seven months now Ta, and I am slowly accepting that you will never be coming back – that my tears will never bring you back again. I will continue to live life for the both of us.

My birthday is coming up in two weeks' time, Ta. I am dreading it, because I am reminded of how you sweetly pulled off a surprise birthday dinner for me last year. Who knew that was going to be my last birthday with you? Thank you, Ta, for always loving me regardless of all my imperfections. Thank you for your unconditional love. You have no idea how your love has been the core of what's been strengthening me all this time. Especially all those painful experiences that we went through together as a couple. Looking back now, I see that it was the very thing that brought us closer and stronger together. Thank you for never giving up on us. I will never give up.

Remember the problem that our vehicle had? I finally had it fixed after two months in the garage. It still has the dent from that day I got carjacked. Oh, I will never forget that experience. After five years of living in Moresby, I sometimes wonder why it had to happen on that particular day when you were not in Moresby with us. Why did I have to have a gun pointed at my face when you were miles away. I laugh thinking about how I was wrestling for my bag with the guy who got in to drive. All I was thinking about at that moment was the video on my phone of us dancing on the night of our renewal. Remember? I had it on the phone you gave me when I turned thirty, and I had not saved it to my laptop. You know me, how I am always into capturing and keeping memories. I know it was crazy of me, risking my life to keep the phone, but I'm glad that I did, as I still get to watch us dancing that night. Especially now that you're gone. They say everything happens for a reason. I certainly believe that what I went through that day toughened me and made me strong. You should have seen me screaming at them, 'My son! My son! Where's my son?' I wouldn't know how to tell you if something had happened to our one and only son, Yaca. When the guy in the front passenger seat pointed the gun at my face, yelling for me to get out, I did what any mother would do – make sure her son is okay. Thank God, Auntie Benny had pulled Yaca out with her when they dragged her out. In a way Ta, I think it was good that you were not there. Knowing you, you would have fought back when they dragged us out of the vehicle. You could have easily taken a bullet protecting and defending us. That day, it all happened so fast. There was so much adrenaline rushing through my body that I hadn't felt the machete landing on my hip. It was probably when they were trying to drag me out of the car. I didn't feel or notice it until later when someone pointed to the injury and told me they had cut me too.

Did I tell you about how Vavine Anangs shared her story with me when she visited? I can't remember if I ever did. You know they could have easily shot me, if they were high or panicked. Ta, they shot her mother right in front of her when she was only about twelve or fourteen. I'll never forget what she told me that day. That experience made her the strong, confident woman that she is today.

You know how I was traumatised. Yaca did not want to leave the house for two weeks. You were so patient, supportive, and understanding. You encouraged me to be strong, face my fears, get myself out of the house, and get my life back.

I feel that losing you was another huge carjacking, but this time I lost a close, precious life; yours. Shocked, shattered, broken and battered, I can almost hear you still telling me to face this heartache, stand strong, never give up and continue to live. That is what I am doing, but sometimes I just want to break down, lock myself in the room, do nothing, and cry all day.

Oh Ta, Jimaima Ledua from the UK sent me a medium-sized cushion with a picture of us printed on it. It's sitting right next to the TV in our living room. I give it to the kids to hug every time they're down, missing you. A few nights ago, Yaca told me that he couldn't stop thinking of you. So I gave him the cushion to hug and told him to pretend that he was hugging you. He hugged it, and smiled. Ta, it's not easy. It's not easy to watch the kids hurting and missing you. But I'm doing the best I can. I'm still encouraging them to be open about anything and everything with me. To pour out their feelings, and to talk to me when they're missing you.

Ta, Ipa came running down the stairs one night with a piece of paper in her hand. She had found your love letter to me, Ta, she read it and was crying. I asked her which part made her cry and she told me that it was the part where you said I was your purple butterfly. Oh my darling, the other part was the last thing you wrote: *It's never too late to live happily ever after, my love.*

She said it was like you were telling us that we should be happy. I know that you would want us to be happy Ta, I would have wanted you to be happy too if you were in my position. But it's hard my love, it's hard to be happy without you. It just seems impossible to live life happily without you. However, with acceptance, with time, and with the surplus unconditional love you left behind, I refuse to believe that it's impossible.

Cancer may have taken you, but not your love from me. You will forever and always be alive in my heart.

Galuoko Bogidrau Secivo

Your wife, forever loving you

To my special White Rose,

I still remember the first time I knew your name, Galuoko. Unlike other names, it did not roll without thought off my tongue. I could not look at your name without an abundance of sentiment attached to each letter. Your name, which many have played with so carelessly, so easily, has somehow become sacred to my lips. A name I won't throw around light-heartedly, or repeat without deep thought. And if I ever speak of you, I use the English language to describe who you are to me. You are nameless, because those letters grouped together in that familiar form carry too much meaning for my capricious heart. May I confess that the instant I laid eyes on you, I not only felt Love but also sheer terror … at the thought of losing what I was yet to gain. You may at times deem yourself imperfect, not worthy of such enamour – insane as it may seem to me, because of the beauty you possess – but I am compelled to Love you unconditionally. I have come to Love not by finding the perfect person, but by learning to see the imperfect person, perfectly. Our first conversation left me captivated. It was not into my ears you whispered, but my heart. It was not my lips you kissed, but my soul. I am honoured to say that I have come to know you as myself.

Purple is your favourite colour and butterflies seem to fascinate you. Because of these two facts, I am intrigued. Purple is the colour of good judgement. It is the colour of people seeking spiritual fulfilment. It is said, if you surround yourself with purple, you will have peace of mind. Overwhelmingly, cultural myth and lore honour the butterfly as a symbol of transformation because of its impressive process of metamorphosis.

My Love, please realise that you are my 'purple butterfly'. Loving you has given me such spiritual fulfilment and has completely transformed me into the better man that I am today. Your Love gives me happiness, joy, and delight. You're the sun in my morning, the moon in my night, and you're the one that I cherish, the Love of my life, and I truly will be blessed, if we become husband and wife. I have fallen in Love many times … always with you. It has often been said that life is a journey, and Love is what makes the journey worthwhile. I cannot promise you a good life, but what I can promise, is a life full of Love. It will be hard, and tears may fall, once the dust settles, my Love – it won't be easy, but it will all be worth it. Experience has led me to deduce, that there are four questions of value in life: What is sacred? Of what is the spirit made? What is worth living for? And what is worth dying for? The answer to each is the same – only LOVE. Though pain and constant renunciation may exist, I will remain as the shoulder to cry on and the strength to rely on. I will never let go, even if it means forsaking the whole world.

For as the Lord is my witness, I will remember: 'Love is patient, love is kind. It does not envy, it does not boast, it is not proud. It is not rude, it is not self-seeking, it is not easily angered, it keeps no record of wrongs. Love does not delight in evil but rejoices with the truth. It always protects, always trusts, always hopes, and always perseveres.' (1 Corinthians 3:4-7)

It's never too late to live happily ever after, my Love.

Yours forever
Tevita Secivo

17

Love Like There's No Tomorrow

Love like there's no tomorrow and if tomorrow comes love again.

Anon

As a couple, my husband and I would openly talk about the inevitable, that one day, one of us would leave before the other. We would argue about who would be the first to go. Somehow, he was always adamant that it was going to be him, when we got grey and old of course. I knew it was his way of telling me that he wouldn't be able to live without me. I knew it was going to be painful and I wouldn't want him to be suffering alone and in pain either.

I would often ask myself, How do I prepare for the inevitable despair and emptiness then? How do I prepare for the unknown extent of excruciating pain if I lose him? We can plan ahead for the next fifteen and thirty years, but how do we know that's even guaranteed? I believe that knowing anything can happen gives us more than enough reason to love and cherish each other harder every single day.

Ever since we got married and watched our little family grow, I always believed that I was going to grow old with my husband. Even with knowing the risk of us both being pilots, there was never a tiny doubt about growing old with him – until the day the doctors confirmed that he had leukaemia. I was terrified to my core, my future with him was hanging tenuously in the air. I knew that it was going to be either sooner or later, but I tended to ignore it most of the time. Imagining my life without him was just too painful.

The following year, I watched how cancer took my sister's health, and how she slowly deteriorated until it finally took her. I lost my sister and my heart was torn with knowing that I was probably going to lose my husband too. This was the most confused and low point of my life. I didn't know what to do. I was scared and terrified, I was silently suffering inside, but I never saw any hint of worry from him, and that worried me even more. Sometimes even frustration kicked in, so I ignored the cancer, I got myself lost in doing my own thing, and we both drowned ourselves in work. For a while there, we were spending little quality time together and we were unknowingly starting to drift apart.

Our love was there, but we were slowly losing the passion and romance. Our routine became monotonous, and I became distant. I feared that our marriage was becoming like what I'd been told about many times. You get married, then after a few years the passion dies, and you might even stop missing each other, and that's normal. No, I did not want to believe in that, and I certainly did not want that in my marriage.

I gave him hints that I was missing the passion we used to have before, but he was not seeing it at all. I don't know why we women always think that men can read minds. They can't. Please take note of that ladies: They cannot read minds. Then I decided to tell him how I felt.

Sure, he had heard me, but he didn't understand me at first.

Now men, please take note. We women are fragile, and we don't think the same way you men do. The silent treatment and tears are our ways of screaming our longing, and begging to not only be heard but be understood. So please don't discourage your lady when she is trying to pour out her honest feelings to you. Give her time.

We were just like any other couple, we had problems, and we were not perfect. I sat down with him one day, and I poured out my heart to him. I wanted to feel those butterflies again. This time he heard and understood me.

After eight wonderful years of being married, in 2013, we decided that we were going to revive the passion and the romance in our marriage again. The first step we took was setting aside quality time for each other every day, and we strived to always make sure that the other person felt loved. We became each other's first priority over everything and everyone else.

We took a family holiday together in Rabaul and welcomed the 2014 new year there. Later, just the two of us took a trip to Hawaii, spending a few days in Sydney and a few days in Fiji. It was a year of reviving the passion and romance and strengthening our love. A year of getting to know more of each other and loving each other more, like there was no tomorrow. We were making more beautiful memories and cherishing each other's love.

Then we got married again, renewing our wedding vows in 2015, taking our love and our understanding of each other to another level. We were not only husband and wife – we were best of friends. We told each other everything, his secrets were mine and mine were his – there was no more giving hints, but there were still some occasional quarrels that kept the relationship real and spicy.

We also noticed that after every argument we learnt something new about each other, and it helped to keep our love growing. So, I believe that arguments are healthy in a relationship. It's the art of strengthening the love. All these efforts blossomed and flourished into a beautiful, stronger, deeper love for each other. We eventually fell in love all over again and I felt those butterflies again. His love, our love, is what's kept me going this far.

Loving like there was no tomorrow had prepared me well and I am thankful that even though I have been left with a broken heart, it is still a content and radiant heart.

Messages from Facebook & Friends

(Edited for readability, with names and identities kept anonymous)

Just like moons and like suns with the certainty of tides.
Just like hopes springing high, still I will rise.

MAYA ANGELOU

I just wanted to let you know that I've been following your page since I couldn't send a friend request (you have exceeded your 5,000 friends limit). I'm not a computer person, but I always find myself on your page to see the latest whenever I have a chance to log into Facebook. I am looking forward and definitely can't wait for your book. I don't know where to start as it'll be useless to repeat your story back to you. All I can say is that I'm sincerely sorry from the bottom of my heart for your loss. Please know that I smiled and cried watching the development of your life with Te. From the height of happiness to the darkest days of losing him forever. I cannot thank you enough for your courage and your brave heart for staying so very strong. (Especially for your kids.) Most importantly, thank you for sharing your personal life. I have learnt so much from your life experience and hope all the very best for you and the kids. I hope there will be a part two when you find a new husband. Lol. So please don't stop here, I'd love to read your second book. Strangely I feel like I've known you & Te for a long time. Thank you for taking time to read this.

*

Hi, I just wanted to share how you have been such a blessing to me personally. I've been following your journey and cannot thank God enough for what He has done and continues to do! You were dealt with unimaginable pain when your dearest husband was called home but through your pain emerged such strength and faith that was only possible with God. As we, your Fijian family all over the world watched on and definitely cried with you and for you, our hearts turned to God to seek comfort. You my dear sister taught me that no matter how much pain, hurt and disappointment life will give you, God's grace and love is enough to carry you through. I now understand the depth and the weight of the words 'just enough' because this is what our awesome God gives us. Just enough to continue putting one foot in front of the other. Just enough to be able to pick ourselves up again and say … yes, I can do this. Just one step at a time!

Thank you for being so strong. Thank you for taking each day as it comes. Thank you for trusting God to carry you in your weakest moments and thank you for helping me ignite the fire that once shone so bright for our Heavenly Father! May you and your beautiful babies remain in God's love at all times and may the beautiful memories of your dear husband live on.

*

Thank you for the beautiful posts … I find myself gravitating to your posts for inspiration and hope. This morning I dropped my Soul off at the airport – he goes back to work in the highlands of PNG. He was here briefly because I was sick. The drive back from the airport was extremely lonely because some of the deepest conversations and thoughts are shared in our car - our future, humour, tears, and fears …

great memories. Unfortunately, he is always far away working. Our ultimate sacrifice as a family is having him work far away but then again, in the process he is saving lives serving rural PNG as a doctor by profession, driven by passion to make a difference. Thank you for sharing your posts. It keeps me going and makes me appreciate more the people in my life.

For that, thank you!

*

Bula vinaka Galuoko,

I apologise for the inconvenience. I just wanted to say how touched I am with the few things I've learnt about you. I will be turning twenty-five next month and am currently working as a nurse in a subdivisional hospital in the west. My boyfriend was the one who sent me a link about your story being a student rising up to live her dream, in the hope of encouraging me towards a career that I hope to pursue, apart from nursing. In reading I could not resist the urge to scroll further down the page and find pieces of, what I can gather is a story of faith, hope and love intertwined with a spirit of courage that I feel most women have. I would like to express my sincere condolences for your loss. Thank you for being the brave woman that you are. I may not know you personally, but I can tell that you are a woman full of love, life, and courage.

I trust all will go well with your book and I pray that as God takes you through your journey, you will continue to inspire other people, especially the young, to not give up but to keep going.

*

Bula vinaka Mrs Secivo,

First off, I am married with two kids (a son and a daughter) and live in Suva. I do not know you personally or at any other level. All I know is that the first time I read about you I was moved and inspired. I am so sorry about the loss of your beloved and my prayers will always be that God grants you and your family his peace and serenity to help you cope with your loss. Your love story is so inspiring and has taught me to love harder, live louder and to enjoy every moment of life, especially with my spouse and kids.

I see that you're beginning to capture all your moments through song, and a book, and I can't wait to own copies and to share your story to inspire others. Thank you for being a beautiful inspiration and for allowing us to be part of your journey (though painful it may have been) and for showing us your vulnerability through love.

May God bless you, your family, and all the plans you have in store.

Love and prayers.

*

Bula vinaka from Seattle, USA.

Please forgive me for invading your privacy. Although we are not friends on Facebook, I've been privileged to be one that has been moved by reading your posts about losing your dear husband. It has been very inspirational. I know they say time heals all wounds yet I do not agree. The wound remains. In time, the mind protecting its sanity, covers them with scar tissue and the pain lessens. But it is never gone. Hearing your love story, I know that you will never be alone. Those who live no more, whom we loved, echo still within our thoughts, our words, our hearts. I was ten years old when my mother died. My dad was lost, but their love for each other continued to strengthen him and he carried on with life through his children. He was my hero. Sadly, he passed on five years ago. He had never remarried; though there were a few nice ladies who wanted to own his heart, he knew that he had given his heart away a long time ago to his only true love. By reading through your posts I could tell that God had prepared you well. He loved your husband so much that He took him back so that he could continue to watch over you and your kids from up above. I pray that you will continue to heal, and your kids will grow up and be the source of your everyday happiness.

Again, my sincere condolences.

Thank you for sharing your struggles, testimonies, and being an inspiration to many like me.

*

Hi,

I may not know you but I wanted to thank you. Your posts have inspired me a lot … I am married with three adorable children and our family has just started … I have two girls aged three and two, and my youngest is a baby boy who is ten months … You may not know this but you have inspired me to the core of my heart. I broke down just by reading some of your posts and watching some of your videos. I have learnt that love is not to be taken for granted … My husband and I were on the verge of breaking up as I had given up already but after going through your posts I have come to realise how lucky I am to still have our Dad around … I'm so deeply sorry for your loss. Thank you for being my saving angel … thank you for teaching me how to be strong just as you are.

May the Lord we serve bestow upon you His eternal peace and may you find joy, happiness and love.

*

Bula,

Thanks for accepting my request. You have portrayed an influential quality of pure love, sacrifice, and strength despite the difficult times you have had to encounter recently. I somehow came across your profile and have been going over it all of last night, this morning and whenever I was free today. The moments and memories you have shared with your dear husband are simply mesmerising, beautiful and sweet. My heart has been torn into a thousand pieces as I learnt a lot from it all. I had to call up my husband who was at work last night just to tell him how much I loved him. I cried a lot while going through the videos and photos of you, your beloved husband and your dear family and realised just how precious life is!

Thanks for sharing with us. I look forward to more of your inspirational posts and have no doubt that you are strong and that you will make it through. I may not know you personally but my thoughts and prayers are with you and your beautiful children.

Remain blessed.

*

I can't even imagine myself in your shoes and I don't know how you can be so strong going through this all. Here I am trying to hide my tears from my colleagues. I feel like I've known you for ages … I just kept thinking of you and your family today. Your posts captured a tiny spot in my heart, which made me come to some sense of realisation, that life and love should never be taken for granted. I wish you and your children happiness with God's divine peace always.

*

Bula vinaka!

Your story really touches my heart! May the good Lord richly bless you and your family! Your story saved my marriage!

God bless you!

*

Isa Galuoko – thank you so much for sharing your love story. You saved my marriage … my husband and I had a falling out. I moved back to my family home while he stayed with the kids in our home

… no one ever believed that we would ever get back together. When I began following you on Facebook, your stories gave us a sense of hope, a longing for love and a pain that all would have been thrown away if it wasn't for your lovely stories. We are now back together, loving each other as if it is our last day … and never giving up on each other. We have now strengthened our weaknesses together, and have learnt from our mistakes, most of all giving our children love together.

Thank you for being an inspiration to many like us. We admire you for your courageous self, having an impact in most lives and families like ours.

*

Bula vinaka.

I came across a photo you shared and loved the inspirational story behind you achieving your dreams. I also saw your 'missing your husband' status and started viewing your page. Your story through your page, I believe is one that God has allowed, to be able to minister to hardened hearts here in Fiji and all over the world! You cannot imagine the impact of your story that is actually breaking down barriers through the hearts of everyone reading your posts. Going through your photos I can see you have captured nothing but LOVE. You're such a beautiful young woman with a beautiful heart! It is just so amazing going through your page! Facebook for Fijians tends to be filled with negativity, sarcasm, hatred, and such. It is such a gem to find someone who is using this platform to portray love – and portray God! I want to say thank you. I know God appreciates you so much! I pray that you will cling to God and the promises of His word at such a period as this! Your story is heartbreaking yet I believe God wants to use your story, and your life to penetrate this world with His love. A world that has grown so cold and deprived of love. I used to work as a clerical officer with the Agriculture Department in the 90s. Seeing your beautiful features, I am wondering whether you are related somehow to Ms Yalikanacea. I think her first name is Susana. She was one of our senior agricultural officers then. Thanks for sharing your story.

Keep sharing about your pain as that will be another journey, to see how God brings you from that unbearable stage to finally be at peace with His decision to call your loved one home. I pray that, however painful the sting of pain pierces your heart, you will use that moment to declare your gratitude and trust in God.

*

Thank you for the inspiration (beautiful love story that my partner and I will learn from) and the motivation (#Flex4Tex) to help us live a happy and healthy life. Last night when you accepted my request, I stayed up till 4:30 a.m. just reading and watching your posts and videos … and the photos … oh my heart! I feel that the passing away of your late husband has enabled you to do things that you never dreamed of doing. In a way, I believe that he did not just pass away because of cancer. I believe that he loved you so much that he wanted to see what you were capable of doing alone since you always did everything together before.

Without a doubt, you did this impeccably, to the greatest extent, and you touched the hearts of strangers like me through your very emotional yet strong and affirmative words. Now your dear husband is in heaven with our Father watching you continue this journey of life with your head held high.

I thank the Lord for people like you.

Blessed day and love to your beautiful children.

*

I'm so deeply sorry for your family's loss. I accidentally stumbled across your page and today I am so grateful I did because I am inspired by your commitment and endurance. I tell my friends and family about your stories, as I believe that everyone could learn a thing or two from your inspiring life.

Thank you for doing all that you're doing. The world needs you to help rebuild relationships and restore families and most importantly to learn to appreciate each other while we still can.

*

Malo and bula,

Thank you for your inspiration daily. You made me rekindle that spark with my love again. I thank God for your life and your late Mr Secivo, RIP. Because not only did it touch mine but thousands of hearts all over. I am living with your teachings daily. It may not be easy but it's definitely worthwhile.

*

Isa bula vinaka,

My wife messaged you earlier and now it's my turn. Where do I start … We've been following all your updates and I know it's hard to lose someone that you love so much. I have to hide my tears from my wife and workmates who follow you, when you upload a video or update your status. I can see that you're a strong woman of God and I just want to thank you for inspiring every married couple with your life story. Thank you for reminding us of what love really is.

*

Bula vinaka Mrs Secivo,

Firstly, we trust you are in good health – our sincere condolences to you and your beautiful children. For us as a married couple, we have learnt so much from you and your beloved late husband. As a wife and mother, I have been blessed to be touched by your daily approach to life after going through that difficult time for your loving family. Indeed, we are grateful that you have inspired us never to take life for granted. May you continue to soar to greater heights – please keep inspiring and changing lives – THANK YOU FOR SHARING YOUR STORY. We look forward to reading your book. God bless you, the Secivo family. Much love, prayers, and thoughts.

*

Bula vinaka,

I don't know whether to start off crying or smiling.

I would just like to thank you … thank you for sharing your story with us. I do not know you personally but from the tags on Facebook I somehow always end up on your page. Your stories are beautiful and real … they remind me of how we must treasure all memories and make treasured moments with our loved ones … yours was truly amazing and beautiful and the coincidence of the dates (your wedding renewals, published in papers) is simply amazing! God had set your story in such a way to encourage others. Life is for living and you encourage those of us who have always wanted to give up! Give up on especially marriage. Thank you. Thank you. Thank you. God sent us your story for such a time as this!

*

Dear Galuoko,

I have to say that for a long time you have been my most beautiful inspiration of love. Thank you for showing me how to be patient. God knows that is my weakness with my love. He is just impossible to love on our most rainy day but still I would not have it any other way.

You're such a wonderful soul and I pray to be half the woman you are.

Stay strong in love with God.

Like my best friend and I always tell each other, no matter what, be real, be true, just the way God made you.

*

Malo bula,

Oh, how it always pains my inner being to see your status … your broken heart healing slowly. It's just too sad yet inspirational as I may say again. I have learnt a lot from your stories and now I will try to rekindle my love for my husband. Thank God for using you to be a great example to each of us women.

Praise God for your life!

*

Thank the God we serve for His love endures forever.

I believe we do fall in love over and over again. Now I cannot help myself being so emotional and teary. You just spoke directly to my heart and I know what I will do. I just cannot wait for your book launch darling. I have shared the beautiful story and memories with my work colleagues and family, and they share the same sentiments of how beautiful you were as a couple. You are a strong woman of love. Blessings and blessings.

It's the sweetest blessing in a marriage to be able to discover how to break out of the old boring mentality of how marriage should be, and become deeper in love with your husband.

*

Aww, I can't imagine how hard it must be for you. Just let your heart write the book. Already you are an inspiration to couples, giving hope to those who have lost it. Your story is one of pure love. One that is rare to find in this day and era. Your plans to launch the book on his anniversary is remarkable and I am filled with admiration for you. Launching this on his anniversary will definitely be a celebration of his life, you two, and that of your children's lives with their dad. Most importantly we look forward to reading your story of unconditional true love. You are definitely a strong woman. I don't think I would be back on my feet if I were you. You are absolutely amazing!

*

Sorry to intrude into your life at this gloomy and sad part of your journey … you have inspired me a lot tonight. You have shared a lot of life experience and I am touched by it all. Thank you for continuing to share with us, despite your loss. My prayers are with you and your children.

A niece of mine shared your funeral viewings video and the time the girl sang that song I burst out crying … It has been one of my hubby's favourites too … I just can't imagine what you are going through … It was as if something pierced me right inside and I felt a hint of the pain that you're going through.

I salute you, my sister, for being strong and bold for those posts that you have put up. You are so amazing and it shows who you really are … a lady with a big heart and God blessed you with a loving husband. Stay blessed my sister. We look forward to reading more of your posts.

Love and prayers from Aussie.

*

Just finished saying a prayer for you and the family. Only God knows what is best for you … I can't say be strong when I truly know you're still in pieces. Grieving takes time so take this one day at a time, as it comes. God already knows you and your story so He is no doubt using you to be a blessing to someone else's life, judging by the number of people commenting on and liking your posts.

You're teaching us to enjoy every precious moment we still have and love like there's no more tomorrow … You never know how deeply I have been touched tonight … May God continue to shower you with inner peace … Love loads you with prayers.

Vinaka and God bless.